Towards Disaster

Towards Disaster

The Greek Army in Asia Minor in 1921

HRH Prince Andrew of Greece

with an Introduction by

John Van der Kiste

FONTHILL

Cover image: Portrait of Prince Andrew by Philip de László, 1913.

First published by John Murray 1930
This edition published in Great Britain in 2025 by
Fonthill
An imprint of
Pen & Sword Books Ltd
Yorkshire – Philadelphia

ISBN 978-1-80420-008-7

A CIP catalogue record for this book
is available from the British Library.

FSC www.fsc.org MIX Paper | Supporting responsible forestry FSC® C013604

The Publisher's authorised representative in the EU for product safety is
Authorised Rep Compliance Ltd., Ground Floor, 71 Lower Baggot Street,
Dublin D02 P593, Ireland.
www.arccompliance.com

For a complete list of Pen & Sword titles please contact

PEN & SWORD BOOKS LIMITED
47 Church Street, Barnsley, South Yorkshire, S70 2AS, England
E-mail: enquiries@pen-and-sword.co.uk
Website: www.pen-and-sword.co.uk

Or

PEN AND SWORD BOOKS
1950 Lawrence Rd, Havertown, PA 19083, USA
E-mail: Uspen-and-sword@casematepublishers.com

Introduction to the 2025 Edition

For Greece, the war fought against Turkey between 1919 and 1922 was a humiliation if not an outright disaster. Several of those who were regarded as responsible for defeat were convicted of treason and executed, and Prince Andrew, brother of King Constantine, was fortunate to escape such a fate.

Greece declared war on the Central Powers in July 1917, and took part in the final offensive in September 1918 with British, French, and Italian troops, fighting in Macedonia and advancing into Serbia and Bulgaria. The defeated Bulgars asked for an armistice, thus cutting Turkey off from her allies in Europe. Turkish capitulation was soon followed by the armistice and the end of the war, and Greek troops took part in the Allied entry into Constantinople.

The Greek prime minister, Eleftherios Venizelos, led a nation fixated on Anatolia's heritage as part of Ancient Greece and the Byzantine Empire, before its conquest and absorption by the Turks in medieval times. At the Paris Peace Conference in 1919, Venizelos asked for northern Epirus, Thrace, Smyrna (modern-day Izmir) and the surrounding district, and the Dodecanese to be added to the territory of Greece. This met with guarded reaction from the Allies, who were deeply divided about the future of the defeated Ottoman Empire. Britain, France, and Italy each had divergent claims and interests in the area. Nevertheless, with the support of British prime minister David Lloyd George, Venizelos was authorised to send Greek forces to occupy the city of Smyrna, which took place in May 1919. In establishing a military administration there, the Greeks launched a series of successful offensives over the next few months, expanding the Greek zone of occupation.

In August 1920 the Treaty of Sèvres was signed. Its terms included the transfer of the exercise of Greece's rights of sovereignty to a local parliament while leaving the area within the Ottoman Empire, and a commitment five years later to a plebiscite overseen by the League of Nations by which a local assembly might vote for either Turkish or Greek sovereignty. To protect the Christian population from attacks by Turkish irregulars, the Greek Army expanded its jurisdiction to nearby cities, creating a 'Smyrna Zone'.

Like the majority of his countrymen, Venizelos was confident that within a few years Greece would reign over a greatly enlarged Hellenic kingdom astride the Aegean Sea. Certainly, had the treaty been enacted, the result would have been a much diminished and bitterly resentful Turkey. Mustafa Kemal Pasha (later Atatürk), prime minister and subsequently president of the country, declared that the Greeks were being given land formerly held by the Ottoman Empire to which they had no right, and insisted that the treaty should not be ratified. It was apparent that the issue could only be settled by force of arms, and in October 1920, Venizelos ordered Greek troops at Smyrna to advance against the army of Mustafa Kemal. Advancing inland, they captured several cities but were halted by Turkish forces at the Battle of the Sakarya, which lasted three weeks between August and September 1921. The Greeks were defeated, ending their hopes of imposing a settlement on Turkey. They remained on Turkish soil for several months while support for their cause diminished among their European allies. In August 1922 a counterattack by the Turkish forces led to final victory for Mustafa Kemal, and Greece was forced to sue for peace. The Treaty of Lausanne, signed in July 1923, replaced Sèvres, giving international recognition to the new Republic of Turkey as successor to the Ottoman Empire.

*

Prince Andrew of Greece was born at Tatoi Palace, near Athens, on 2 February 1882, the fourth son of King George I and Queen Olga of the Hellenes. His father, King George, was the third of six children of Prince Christian of Schleswig-Holstein-Sonderburg-Glücksburg and his wife, Princess Louise of Hesse-Cassel. In November 1863 Prince Christian and Princess Louise became rulers of Denmark, and in the same year their seventeen-year-old son William (soon to be known as George), then serving as a cadet in the Danish navy, was chosen as sovereign by the Greeks, who had just deposed their unpopular and childless Bavarian-born king, Otto. William was the prince's second forename and George, his last forename, was chosen as his regnal name.

As part of their education, King George's eight children, who were princes and princesses of both Greece and Denmark, learned Greek, Danish, German, French, English, and Russian. Andrew, the fourth son, was considered the 'most Greek' of them all. As a child, he made a conscious choice to speak only Greek, unlike his other siblings who conversed with each other in German and English. Despite poor eyesight, Andrew joined the Greek Army as a cavalry officer, serving in the 3rd Cavalry Regiment as a lieutenant-colonel during the Balkan War of 1912–13, in which the Greeks fought alongside Bulgaria, Serbia, and Montenegro against the Ottoman Empire. Greece and her allies emerged victorious, but King George did not live to witness their triumph. He was assassinated in March 1913, and his eldest son, Constantine, succeeded him to the Greek throne.

When the First World War broke out in August 1914, the Greek royal family, which had close familial ties with crowned heads on both sides, strove to remain neutral. However, Prime Minister Venizelos supported the Allied powers, presenting an impossible problem for the king, particularly as, on an official visit to Berlin shortly after his accession, Constantine had been made a field marshal in the German army by his brother-in-law, Kaiser Wilhelm II. The European press feasted on the story, driving suspicion that Constantine was a secret ally of Germany. The rumours were false, but his position became untenable, and in 1917 he was forced to abdicate.

Most of the family went into exile in Switzerland—among them Constantine's wife, Queen Sophie, who was a sister of the kaiser (which, although she thoroughly disliked him, was largely the reason for the Allies' distrust of them both), and their eldest son George. The latter was considered to be an unacceptable successor to his father as he had served in the German army before the war. Constantine's second son, Alexander, was therefore chosen to reign in his stead and remained in Athens. Three years later he died of blood poisoning after being bitten by a pet monkey. In a plebiscite to choose his successor, the electorate overwhelmingly demanded Constantine's return to the throne—to the dismay of Venizelos and the Allies.

Constantine and his family came back, and he took personal command of the Asia Minor campaign. The generals who accompanied him included his younger brother Prince Andrew, who had been reinstated in the army as major general and was appointed to the command of Greece's 2nd Army Corps. Meanwhile, Andrew's wife, Princess Alice of Battenberg, a great-granddaughter of Queen Victoria, and their four daughters lived in Mon Repos, on the island of Corfu, where their youngest child, Philip, was born in June 1921.

By now the Turkish nationalist forces under Mustafa Kemal, fighting the Italians in south-west Turkey, the French in the south and east, and the Greeks in the west, had withdrawn into their country's deep interior, settling on the village of Ankara as their revolutionary capital. Constantine's forces followed them there, winning battle after battle but never striking the decisive blow needed for them to maintain international support. Coupled with Constantine's reinstatement, the absence of a decisive victory had wearied the British and French attachment to Greece's cause. In August 1921, however, the opportunity for that victory presented itself at the Sakarya river, outside Ankara.

At a critical juncture in the ensuing battle, Prince Andrew, commander of the Second Army, was ordered by his commanding officer Anastasios Papoulas (spelled Papulas by Andrew) to attack the Turkish positions, but he refused to so on grounds that it would expose his men to unnecessary danger. Instead, he followed his own strategy. After three weeks of bitter fighting along a 60-mile front, Papoulas disengaged his forces and began retreating westward, placing the blame for defeat squarely at Prince Andrew's door.

Andrew asked to be relieved of his command, but his request was refused. After being granted three months' leave, he returned to his family in Corfu, where he saw his baby son Philip for the first time. In March 1922, with the war still ongoing, Andrew was appointed commander of the 5th Army Corps in Epirus and the Ionian Islands. Victory, however, was looking unlikely, and the promises outlined in the Treaty of Sèvres increasingly impracticable. The Allies proposed an armistice between Greece and Turkey, but knowing that Greece was losing support in Europe, Mustafa Kemal, who was receiving military aid from the Soviet Union, refused to discuss any settlement while Greek forces remained in Anatolia. He redoubled his efforts for a final offensive while the war-weary Greeks strengthened their defensive positions, begging Britain for military and financial support at the same time. Among the population there were demands for a complete withdrawal from what looked like a hopeless cause. Demoralisation set in among the troops, yet they stayed in their positions, planning to seize Constantinople as a last-ditch attempt to salvage some form of victory. However, this was abandoned in July 1922 in face of Allied opposition.

At the end of August, Turkey launched a devastating offensive that forced the Greeks back to the Aegean, with the final humiliation occurring at the coastal city of Smyrna, when the majority Greek population was driven out, marking the end of Greece's historic presence in Asia Minor.

Furious at this turn of events, the Greek armed services led an uprising against the government. King Constantine was ordered to abdicate for a second time and was succeeded by his eldest son, now deemed acceptable, who became King George II. The revolutionary government arrested a number of royalist generals and politicians whom they considered most to blame for the defeat. Prince Andrew was regarded as particularly culpable, and troops were sent to Corfu to bring him to Athens to be court-martialled. He was accused of disobeying direct orders, acting on his own initiative, and abandoning his position in the face of the enemy with disastrous results not only for the troops under his command but also for the entire army. Whether or not he was guilty of insubordination, it was an astonishing charge to bring fifteen months after the event, especially as he had not been relieved of his command during the intervening months.

At the trial, a staff officer named Colonel Kalogeras affirmed that the prince had disobeyed an order to attack. Colonel Sariyannis and General Papoulas both insisted that had he obeyed that order, the Greeks would have triumphed at Sakarya. Andrew was found guilty of disobedience and abandoning his post. He was stripped of his rank.

Several defendants in the subsequent treason trials were executed by firing squad, and for a time Andrew feared he would share their fate. The anti-royalist general Theodoros Pangalos, Andrew's contemporary at the Hellenic Military Academy, who would in three years become dictator of Greece, visited him in detention after the trial. He asked him how many children he had, and when told, remarked, 'Poor things, what a pity they will soon be orphans.'

At length, a more moderate Greek revolutionary, General Nicholas Plastiras, a future prime minister of Greece, agreed to spare Andrew. The British government, which had broken off formal diplomatic relations with Greece since the executions, was behind the scenes, applying pressure. Instead of execution, Andrew's punishment was to be banishment from Greece for life. He and his family, including his eighteen-month-old son Philip, went into exile aboard a British warship, HMS *Calypso*. Stripped of their Greek nationality, they travelled under Danish passports and settled in a house at St Cloud, near Paris, lent to them by relatives.

King George II reigned for eighteen months before Greece became a republic, but the monarchy was restored in 1935, and he was called back to the throne which he held until his death twelve years later. Andrew's sentence of banishment was lifted in 1936 and he returned to Greece for occasional visits, though he was never made to feel welcome. By this time, he and Alice were living separate lives. Their four daughters had married German princes, three with close Nazi connections, while Philip was brought up by his mother's relatives and educated in Britain. In 1930 she began a two-year stint in a Swiss sanatorium, having been diagnosed with paranoid schizophrenia.

Andrew refused a commission in the Hellenic Navy for his son Philip, arguing that his rapid expulsion would surely follow: 'That's what they did to me, not once, as you know, or twice, but three times!' After leaving school in 1939, Philip completed a term as a cadet at the Royal Naval College, Dartmouth, and returned briefly to Athens where he lived with his mother, who had returned there the year before. Upon the outbreak of war in September, he resumed his naval training and went on to serve in the Royal Navy. He was awarded the Greek War Cross for his actions at the Battle of Cape Matapan off the coast of Greece in March 1941. After the war, Philip became a naturalised British subject, ceased using his Greek and Danish titles, and adopted the name Mountbatten from his mother's side. In 1947 he married Elizabeth, elder daughter of King George VI of the United Kingdom and subsequently Queen Elizabeth II, and was created Duke of Edinburgh. Despite his nickname 'Phil the Greek', he had no affection for the country of his birth and the uneasy crown it offered its rulers. A grandfather assassinated and a father condemned to death, he once said, 'does not endear me to the perpetrators'.

Prince Andrew spent his final years in France and Monaco. He died in Monte Carlo in December 1944, aged sixty-two, and was buried in the Russian Orthodox Church at Nice. In 1946 his remains were transferred to the royal cemetery at Tatoi. His widow, Princess Alice, later moved to Buckingham Palace upon the invitation of her son and daughter-in-law. She died in December 1969.

During his first years of exile, Andrew wrote *Towards Disaster*, an account of the campaign in Asia Minor in which he strongly defended his decisions and actions, especially during the Battle of the Sakarya (or Sakharia, as he calls it), when he was intent on avoiding needless loss of life in a hopeless battle. It was translated from Greek into English by his wife and published by John Murray in 1930 with a short print run of about 1,000 copies. These are now collector's items. According to Hugo Vickers, Princess Andrew's biographer, the book contains passages that are stylishly written, but 'much of it is an apologia', its interest limited 'to those with a penchant for detailed analysis of battles'. Yet due allowance must be made for the author's circumstances. His father had fallen victim to an assassin and he himself was fortunate to escape a death sentence, despite having served his country to the best of his ability in hopeless conditions.

Prince Andrew was a humane commander who hated wasting lives in battle. He did not feel that his trial was conducted fairly; of the many witnesses he called for his defence, only three were allowed to appear. In the same way, only a small handful of his brother officers were prepared to speak out in support of him. One, Major Tsangarides, bravely risked his career by protesting that Andrew was being made responsible for the decisions of General Papoulas. His letter was read by counsel for the defence but was dismissed by the president of the military court as being only the writer's personal opinion. The commander of the corps engineers, Colonel Botsaris, who had congratulated Andrew on his decision to disobey orders, saying it was the only correct course to take, was forbidden by the military tribunal from appearing in court as a witness.

According to the old cliché, history is all too often written by the victors. It is only right, therefore, that Prince Andrew of Greece was allowed the chance to tell his side of the story.

John Van der Kiste
August 2025

Contents

Preface

The author of these military memoirs was born in Athens on 2 February 1882; he was the fourth son and seventh child of King George I and his consort, Queen Olga. He very soon manifested a desire to embrace a military career, and at the age of fourteen he became a cadet and attended the classes at the military college at Athens, as well as pursuing his studies of Greek, etc., with masters at home. Contrary to general belief, and in spite of their Danish extraction, the author and his brothers have complete mastery of the Greek language and are in the habit of conversing with each other in that tongue.

In May 1902, at the age of twenty, the author entered the Greek Army as a subaltern in the cavalry. He took his duties very seriously, as he loved his profession and wished to earn his promotion like any other officer. He consequently spent a year in the garrison town of Larissa in Thessaly, on the old Turkish frontier, as a squadron-commander from 1905–1906. Until the year 1909, he was constantly with his regiment, working hard at training recruits—for Greece has a conscript army, and every man on reaching his twenty-first year has to do his military service. Most of the recruits were raw peasants from the mountains, who had never left their goats and had never even seen a horse in their lives, or, at the most, a small mountain pony. The task of training them was, consequently, no mean one, and besides his regimental work, the author completed the whole Staff College course at home. This gave him the staff training which was to prove of such value to him in the ill-fated campaign in Asia Minor.

This, combined with his efficient work in the regiment, had won him the approval of his superiors when, in the year 1909, a military league was formed by dissatisfied officers who had not received the promotions or appointments as ADC to the king or princes which they had expected. The ostensible aim of this league was to upset the government, under the pretext that it was weak and not governing the country in a satisfactory manner. Other unsuspecting officers joined the league for this purpose only, with the result that by August 1909, the league was strong enough to organize a military insurrection. The author's regiment took part in this without his knowledge until one of its officers, who was a member of the league, led it out to join the insurgents. The author soon discovered that one of the aims of the league was to prevent the sons of the king from doing any responsible work or holding any high commands in the army. Wishing to lighten the task of his father, King George I, who was trying to come to an understanding with the insurgents and accept Mr Venizelos, whom they had secretly sent for from Crete, as prime minister, he voluntarily sent in his resignation. His brothers, Nicholas and Christopher, also resigned from the army, and his brother George from the navy at the same time. The years 1909–1912 were thus spent in idleness, to the author's great grief, as his work was stopped, just when it was beginning to bear fruit.

In September 1912, the famous Balkan Confederacy declared war on Turkey, and the author asked to be reinstated, without making any stipulations as to promotions to higher commands. He was accepted and appointed with the rank of major to the general staff of the commander-in-chief, Crown Prince Constantine, as he then was.

The two Balkan campaigns of 1912 and 1913 ended victoriously for Greece, and the old feuds of 1909 seemed to be forgotten in the hour of victory, so the author took up his regimental duties again as colonel commanding the 3rd Cavalry. For four years he was strenuously occupied in raising his regiment to the highest degree of efficiency, and in 1915, owing to a general mobilization, he was sent with his regiment to Salonica, which had become a big Greek garrison town, after its conquest in 1912. There he remained for six months, entirely engrossed in his military duties, and nearly losing his life by being often bombed by Taubes while drilling his men. During this time, he kept aloof from all politics.

In the summer of 1916, King Constantine sent the author on a diplomatic mission to Paris and London, but in the winter, 1916–1917, he was again working with his regiment until King Constantine's departure for Switzerland. M. Venizelos, on his return, instantly dismissed Prince Andrew and 3,000 other officers from the army, for being loyal to the king. Although these were the men who had heroically led the Greek soldiers to victory, they were replaced by half-trained officers promoted hurriedly from the military college and from the ranks.

The author thought that, as he now held no office or appointment, he would be allowed to remain in Greece with his nephew, King Alexander. A month after King Constantine left, however, a member of the French mission informed him that M. Venizelos made a point of his leaving the country too, and had asked the British and French Legations as a personal favour to have him removed from Greece. The Legations were very polite and apologetic, as they said they knew that he had always abstained from politics, and was solely occupied with his military duties, but they had no option in the matter, and much to their regret requested him to leave the country.

So, in July 1917, the author found himself constrained to depart with his wife and family for Switzerland, which country he was forbidden to leave on any account until June 1920, when, with great difficulty, he obtained leave from the Italian Government to move to Italy, France and England having refused to grant him permission to enter these respective countries.

When the elections of November 1920, which drove Venizelos from power, took place, the author and his family were in Rome, and he and his brother Christopher left the next day for Greece. They were accorded an enthusiastic reception and were dragged from their car and borne on the shoulders of the populace, frenzied with joy, the whole way from Phalerum Bay to Athens, and he was forced to make a speech from the balcony of the palace to the vast crowds gathered below. A month later, King Constantine returned under conditions known to all, and the author was promoted to the rank of major-general. The first campaign in Asia Minor had already been inaugurated in June 1920 by M. Venizelos before he fell, in spite of King Constantine's repeated warnings that this was far too dangerous an operation for Greece to undertake. The author immediately asked for a command at the front, but no notice was taken for some time, in accordance with the old idea of 1909 that the princes should not hold high commands. Ultimately, however, after six months' waiting, he received the command of a division in June 1921, and thus began his experiences in the Asia Minor campaign, which commenced so well and ended so disastrously.

As long as the campaign lasted the officers, whom Venizelos had put into the army in 1917, were occupied with their military duties, but as soon as the army had fallen back from the Sakharia and established itself in its winter quarters in the trenches, these officers recommenced their political intrigues which the author found he could not check, as he was not allowed to dismiss the ringleaders. Not wishing to bear the responsibility of the serious consequences which would inevitably ensue, he asked to be removed from his command of the 2nd Army Corps, which he had received, together with the rank of lieutenant-general, after his victorious advance to Eski Shehr. He was given the command of the 5th Army Corps of Epirus and the Ionian Islands, with headquarters at Janina. He was holding this command when, as he had foretold, the Greek Army in Asia Minor was overwhelmed by a terrible disaster, caused by treachery in its own ranks, which enabled the Turks to break through and practically precipitate the whole army into the sea.

The instigators of this frightful debacle then hurried back to Athens, forced the government to resign, and the king to abdicate and leave the country in September 1922. They then formed a military government, and informed the author that he could stay on his property in Corfu on condition that he resigned from the army. A month later, however, he was brought to Athens and kept a prisoner for seven weeks, until his trial in the Chamber of Deputies on 2 December 1922, by a jury of officers, who had previously decided that he must be shot as a member of the royal family, and who took the pretext of his so-called disobedience to orders and desertion of his post before the enemy as an excuse in the eyes of the world.

HM King George V, realizing the deadly peril he was in, took the necessary steps which resulted in Lord Curzon, the minister of foreign affairs, sending out Captain Gerald Talbot to try and save the author's life. The way in which Sir Gerald, for he was afterwards knighted by the king for his services, accomplished this miracle is for him one day to relate. Suffice it to say, that he successfully got the author out of the clutches of the military dictators and brought him and his family away from Greece on the day after the trial in a British man-of-war. Both the author and his wife owe a deep debt of gratitude to HM the king for the promptitude and efficacy of his action, which was the means of saving the author's life.

Alice, Princess Andrew of Greece
Saint Cloud, Paris, 1929

The translator would like to thank Miss Virginie Simopoulos, Vice-Admiral Mark Kerr, and Lieutenant-Colonel Richard Crichton for their kind help.

Introduction by Prince Andrew of Greece

Owing to the manner in which, after more than twenty years' service, I was dismissed from the army on 3 December 1922, I consider it necessary to relate the events which took place in Asia Minor in the summer of 1921. My account is based on official documents, personal notes, and recollections. For a while I hesitated, feeling that perhaps the publication of the events of that time would be more harmful than useful, and that it might bring to light occurrences and individual actions prejudicial to national and military interests. After what was said at my trial as to my action in Asia Minor, however, and after the suppression by the revolutionary censorship of the evidence of some of the witnesses for my defence, I consider that I am no longer bound to silence. My doubts also gave way after the verdict, dishonourable to myself, of the revolutionary military court, according to which I appear 'as having abandoned a position without orders when in contact with the enemy, as undisciplined, and as being without the necessary experience for a superior command.'

In Greece and elsewhere there exists in general a complete ignorance of the essential facts of the campaign of the summer of 1921, which must be attributed, firstly, to the indifference of the public as to the events of the war, and, secondly, to the energetic efforts of revolutionary circles to veil and distort those events.

My intention is to give an account of the military events of that summer as regards the XIIth Division and 2nd Army Corps, an account necessarily incomplete by reason of the absence of indispensable documents concerning the other units of the army in Asia Minor. I have avoided all direct reference to politics; but if in some parts I touch on questions of a political nature, I only do so in order to make the whole situation more clear.

The leading political personages of that time no longer exist—King Constantine, Gunaris, Stratos, Protopapadakis, Baltatzis, and Theotoky—I would be happy if words of mine could throw more light on or do greater justice to their work.

Mistakes, many and serious, were certainly made; but who amongst us is without fault? The intentions of those leaders were perfectly honest and patriotic; it was only that they fell victims to their credulity and good faith, victims of the disunion amongst the Greeks of which they were not the cause.

It is impossible for me to acknowledge that my trial was conducted fairly. It is sufficient for me to say that only three witnesses for the defence were called, from the many whom I suggested. It suffices to read the accusations of the revolutionary prosecutor to be convinced of the prejudice of those who tried me.

What made the deepest impression on me was the complete silence of my numerous brother officers, with whom I had served through the whole of my military career.

I should naturally have thought that some of those who were aware of the circumstances, and were with me during the critical part of the campaign, would have come forward. The leader of the outbreak against me, Colonel Plastiras, was under my orders in the 2nd Army Corps, as commanding officer of the 5th Regiment of Evzones. His regiment formed part of the outposts before Kalé-Grotto, and he certainly knew the state of our troops and that of the enemy. The other leader of the trouble, Colonel Gonatas—afterwards premier in the revolutionary government—was also on the spot as chief of the staff of the neighbouring Army Corps. He was aware of my plan—for which I was afterwards tried—for when this was telephoned to him by my chief of staff, Colonel Gavallias, he accepted it and criticized the action of General Headquarters, which he described as useless and destructive.

Only one man came forward, Major Tsangarides, himself a revolutionary, who risked his future career in the army by writing a letter, in which he protested that I was being made responsible for a crime, which he attributed to General Papulas. This letter was read by counsel for the defence at my trial, but the president of the military court, Major-General Nicholas Vlachopolos, gave it as his decision that it was only the personal opinion of the writer. This ruling of the president was no doubt correct in view of the silence of the others.

All these considerations decide me to clear myself, and to relate honestly and fairly the events concerning my commands in Asia Minor in the summer of 1921, indifferent to the result and ignoring the criticisms of those to whom my narrative may be unpalatable. My military career being ended, no attacks or abuse will induce me to reply to any further criticisms. Personally, it was satisfaction enough for me to receive the following words from the late King Constantine, who wrote to me in December 1922, after my departure from Greece, as follows: 'I regret that you considered it necessary to give me your assurance that the accusation against you of abandoning your position before the enemy is not true. You might have known my opinion of you by now, that I consider you … an honourable, conscientious, and able soldier'. The above testimony given by the king, who was the leader in two victorious wars, is more than enough for me, as it would be for any soldier who served under his command.

About the beginning of June, after I had reached Smyrna, the first offer of arbitration in the Greco-Turkish conflict was made by the three Great Powers—Great Britain, France, and Italy.

The government, represented by the premier, M. Gunaris, the minister of war, M. Theotoky, and the minister for foreign affairs, M. Baltazzi, who had just arrived in Smyrna, did not consider it possible to accept that offer. I do not precisely know the reasons for their refusal. I only know that exaggerated optimism, chiefly based on Colonel Saryannis' advice and on secret encouragement from abroad, unduly influenced the decisions of the ministers. To this must be added the idea that any retreat on the part of the Greeks in the Asia Minor question would have an alarming influence on the interior situation, and that this would be a weapon in the hands of political enemies to upset the recently re-established legitimate constitution.

As the responsible opinion of GHQ (Colonel Saryannis) was that not only would the enemy be defeated, but that all his fortified positions would be destroyed, it is not surprising that the government was carried away, especially when one considers that the whole army was in Asia Minor, enthusiastic and ready, and such opportunities do not often occur in the life of a nation. Greece, granted success, would be transformed as if by magic into a large and powerful state, the riches of Asia Minor placed at her disposal, her military and naval prestige increased in the eyes of the other Balkan States. Lastly, Constantinople seemed an easy prey, the crown of the whole achievement, the fulfilment of age-old dreams of the race. Alas! this was the ideal aspect of the question, but there was also the practical one. Who could guarantee that the enemy would remain in his positions to await destruction? and if the enemy should retire intact from his positions—as occurred—carrying away all his material, how far would we be able to pursue him? Could we follow him through the immense expanses of Asia Minor to Kurdistan and the frontiers of Persia? No direct answers were ever given to such questions; it was only generally and vaguely said, that in that case we would occupy the territory, the cultivation of which would pay our expenses. One has only to cast a glance at the map of Asia Minor to see whether it is possible to occupy such a country with our feeble forces, while, as for cultivating and exploiting it, there existed neither roads nor railways. There was no reason for the enemy to remain inactive in the meantime; he could have harassed us continually and seriously with his irregulars, which, as a matter of fact, he eventually did. The result would be that our army, instead of being demobilized soon, as everyone, especially the government, hoped, would have to remain on indefinitely to protect the new frontiers, which would probably follow the line Brussa-Ushak and southwards, either on the Sangarios or the River Alys. In addition, the strength of the existing army would not have sufficed, for it is not possible to guard frontiers 500 to 600 kilometres long in absolutely hostile country with a force of 100,000 men. Sooner or later, we were bound to find ourselves in an *impasse*, for, even if victorious, we should be in the position described above.

What was the real aim? The conquest of Asia Minor and the annihilation of the Turkish State. This enterprise was to be conducted by Greece with her feeble military forces, partially mobilized, without any financial support, and without any assistance from abroad. As I have said, no retreat was possible, and the party in power at that time willingly or not took on their shoulders the burden of an imprudent policy, which ended in the destruction of Hellenism once flourishing in Asia Minor, the dissolution of the Greek Army, and the accumulation of heavy misfortunes for Greece.

To enable one to realize the state of the army at the commencement of the campaign in June 1921, I must turn back a little to the past, and briefly describe its evolution after the end of the Balkan wars of 1912–1913. The territory of Greece was doubled by the Treaty of Bucharest as a consequence of her two victorious wars, and her army had to be increased in proportion to the defences of the new state, and in view of the new political combinations and conditions in the Balkans. The general staff of that time decided on the formation of four army corps of three divisions each, and one army corps (in Epirus) of two divisions, the artillery and the engineers being increased in proportion. This sudden growth created many problems, the most serious of which was undoubtedly the shortage of trained officers. This shortage was made good by placing a number of reserve officers on the active list, and by promoting many non-commissioned officers to the rank of officers. This method was certainly not an ideal one for the formation of a body of capable and trained officers, but it was not possible to do otherwise, because the circumstances were very urgent, and the organization of the new units was imperative. It was then hoped that in time, by the creation of various training schools, the situation would improve, and that the officers who passed out of these schools would gradually complete the army, and consequently the useless elements would be eliminated. I do not wish to underrate the value of the reservists put on the active list, or the value of the non-commissioned officers who became officers; on the contrary, I consider that the greater part of them, through their experience of war, showed themselves equal to the regular officers. At the same time, I do not hesitate to state that, from the beginning, I felt that the use of such methods in forming a body of officers was detrimental to any army, and that such a system should be avoided as much as possible.

The spirit and the morale of the troops during the post-war period was excellent from every point of view, and their training had reached a high state of proficiency. The progress accomplished was evident and very encouraging for the future. Our army reached midway to perfection during the years 1914–1915.

It is from 1915 onwards that one must reckon the fatal malady beginning which finally caused the decomposition of the Greek Army and hastened its destruction in 1922.

As we know, the European War brought confusion to the political life of the country, and, unfortunately, the corps of officers did not remain untouched by the turmoil which ensued. When the Salonica movement commenced in September 1916, many officers joined it, and constituted the so-called 'Amyna' or 'Defence', which became the nucleus of the army, for participation in the 'Great War', organized by the so-called provisional government, against the will of the legal Greek State. I do not deny that the motive of some of these mutineers who went to Salonica was a misunderstanding of their patriotism, but, unfortunately, these were in the minority, whereas the majority consisted of men who merely seized this opportunity to sacrifice the principles on which an army is established. The fatal results of the movement were not slow to show themselves, especially after the bloody events of 18 November 1916, in the forcible recruiting by the mutineers in Chalcidike and elsewhere, in the seizure of the islands in the Aegean, and finally in the collision between the mutineers and the regular troops at Ekaterini.

The greater part of the army remained unshaken and faithful to its duty, following with aversion the action of the relatively few mutineers, whom it was impossible to bring back to a sense of duty, on account of the extraordinary circumstances of that time. This aversion was soon transformed to hatred, because of the methods which the mutineers employed. The separation was complete, and any reconciliation between the divided parties became very difficult, if not impossible, especially after the dethronement of King Constantine in June 1917. After that, the mutineers, now masters of the situation and aspiring to anything but reconciliation, expelled from the army all officers, about 2,000 in number, who did not show obedience to the new order of things. The vacancies were filled at once, the senior ones by promoting a number of trusted men from the lower ranks, and the lower ones by putting more reservists on the active list and promoting non-commissioned officers, the majority of whom were illiterate, to the ranks of officers. This must not be considered an exaggeration, for it is a fact that later on, in Asia Minor, in some of the divisions there were schools for teaching officers to read and write, just as there were for the recruits.

After that, it is not strange that the nature and quality of the army should have altered fundamentally, and that the *esprit de corps* of the officers became different from what it had been. If this were true of the officers, the situation was not the same as regards the men in the ranks. These, as was but natural, continued in the same way of thinking as the great mass of the people, who were averse to seeing foreigners interfering with the internal affairs of the country, and considered the removal of the king from the throne as a threat to their national independence. In this way, an estrangement between officers and men grew up, and though nothing was visible on the surface, owing to the spirit of discipline of the Greek soldier, a mine lay hidden ready for a spark to explode it at the most hurtful moment. A proof of this is the difficulty of the mobilization, which was only overcome by severe measures.

The real troubles of the army, as well as of Greece, began with the armistice, when war-weary Europe returned to the ways of peace. In Greece, the war continued with a costly and aimless expedition to Russia, and afterwards to Asia Minor. The campaign in Russia ended ingloriously, with suffering for the troops and the destruction of Hellenism in Southern Russia, after it had flourished there for centuries.

Then began the drama of Asia Minor, the first act of which will always be notable for the imbecility of its conception and the want of judgment in its execution. As I was not in Greece at that time, I cannot say under what military conditions the first landing in Smyrna took place; but it is known that this was not executed in accordance with the teachings of military science, with the result that the Greek Army was discredited in our eyes and in those of the foreigners in Smyrna.

Gradually the entire Greek Army was absorbed in the long and costly struggle in Asia Minor. In the beginning there was no Turkish Army facing it, but only some corps of irregulars who harassed our troops in a variety of ways, yet every slight and insignificant engagement was represented as a famous victory reflecting glory on first one and then another of the army leaders.

I do not suppose there exists any doubt that, in principle, the aim of every campaign is the defeat of the enemy, and his submission to the will of the conqueror. If this be true, I do not know how to describe the beginnings of the campaign in question. Properly speaking, no enemy army was in front of us, there were only some bands of irregulars, but our army had not been authorized to go beyond a definite line determined on by the Allies. That is to say that the Allies had imposed on the Greek Army the obligation to await, in inaction, the organization of the enemy's army and its attack.

At the time when this was happening, we must not think that harmony reigned amongst the officers and their men. It was just the reverse. On one side were the officers of the 'Amyna'; on the other side were those who had served before the mutiny and had not taken part in it, but who accepted the new conditions and hence inspired no confidence in the leaders, but were generally left to nourish bitterness and complaints against the established order. Opposed to the officers were the men, the majority of whom still maintained the same fidelity and devotion as of old to the legal constitution of the country. This was the situation in the army in 1920 when it was decided to hold elections. The then commander-in-chief, Paraskevopulos, and his chief of the staff, Major-General Pangalos, proceeded to take measures in order to influence the results of the elections, which, as they well knew, would turn against them. When it was decided that the vote should be taken by ballot, all the commanding officers were first made sure of, numbers of them were transferred to different places for the purpose of canvassing the troops, and even candidates were prevented from disembarking. In a word, everything that it was humanly possible to do was done to preserve the *status quo*.

In this work, General Paraskevopulos and his staff found ready supporters in the commanders of the three army corps, Generals Ioannu, P. Pierrakos, and Nider; and in the divisional commanders, Tricupis, Tsimikalis, Manetas, Papathanassiu, and others, as well as in the regimental commanders, Plastiras, Kondylis, and numerous other senior officers. It can easily be imagined what an impression these activities produced on the men, and what an effect this was bound to have on discipline in general.

The commander-in-chief openly threatened that if the elections were to turn against the government in Greece, he would disembark at the Piraeus at the head of thousands of officers and force the then head of the government to remain in power—all this without taking into consideration what the enemy might be doing in the meantime. It is clear what the result of elections conducted under such conditions would be.

In the meantime, the elections, which had taken place on 14 November 1920, brought about the downfall of the government; but, in spite of this, the government remained on, hoping that the falsified election results at the front would alter the other results. The results of the elections at the front were certainly entirely in favour of the fallen government, and the army leaders discussed together how they could profit by the situation, when an unforeseen and significant event occurred to put matters straight. The Cavalry Brigade in Kassaba having been informed of the elections in Greece and the machinations of the GHQ staff in Smyrna, sent an ultimatum to the commander-in-chief, in which they declared that if he did not accept the new situation in Greece, the brigade would march towards Smyrna and force him to do so. This threat was accompanied by the information that the brigade had left Kassaba and was on its way to Smyrna. Lieutenant-General Paraskevopulos well knew that this mutiny of the Cavalry Brigade would inevitably draw most of the other units with it, for no one knew better than he the feeling of the troops and the conditions under which he had organized the elections; consequently, he understood that a refusal to accept the ultimatum would mean a general revolt with incalculable consequences. It is certain that neither the commander-in-chief nor the others who were his tools took into consideration what the enemy might do in these circumstances. They only calculated that a mutiny in the army was dangerous to their own persons, and that the support of their few faithful adherents would be of no avail; therefore, they gave in, and declared their adherence to the new order of things in Athens.

This timely action of the Cavalry Brigade averted many distressing complications at the front, while loosening at the same time the bonds of the other units. Senior and junior officers, panic-stricken with the turn of events, deserted and departed for Constantinople. The commanders of army corps and some of the divisional commanders, trembling before their enraged men, asked to be replaced immediately, and the great Colonel Kondylis was forcibly sent away by the regiment which he commanded.

Thus the situation in the army was pregnant with many dangers when the newly-appointed Commander-in-Chief Papulas disembarked soon afterwards in Smyrna.

The appointment of Lieutenant-General Papulas was made very hurriedly on account of the critical situation, and therefore certain considerations which usually influence the appointment of a commander-in-chief had not been sufficiently weighed. General Papulas had distinguished himself to a certain extent during the Balkan wars, in which he commanded a regiment and reached the rank of major-general, but his general education and especially his military training were not of the standard requisite for the command of an army, more especially in such a difficult and complicated war as that in Asia Minor. The circumstances demanded the presence of an experienced general with an iron hand, alive to the intricacies of the situation and capable of forming his own opinion, regardless of the various and fatal influences engendered by the politicians. In Lieutenant-General Papulas, these qualifications were lacking. Although he had plenty of personal courage and intelligence, he was excessively conceited, and he thoroughly enjoyed the atmosphere of fulsome flattery with which he was surrounded. If I add that he was notably ignorant of military science, we have a complete picture of the man. He was chosen to be commander-in-chief owing to the urgency of the case, but chiefly because he had spent the three years' interval, from 1917 to 1920, in prison for his loyalty to King Constantine. Queen Olga, the then-regent, before signing the decree for his appointment, told him that she would first ask the opinion of the king, who was still in Switzerland. Two days later the king answered, proposing the appointment of Lieutenant-General S. Gennadis in preference to the other, and he only agreed to Lieutenant-General Papulas' appointment if the nomination of the former was impossible. Unfortunately, in the meantime, the new government had ordered Lieutenant-General Papulas' immediate departure to the front, and he left in a few hours.

The new commander-in-chief arrived in Smyrna prepared to forget the past, and to grant a pardon for all the misdeeds that had been committed. He retained on his staff the greater part of, if not all, the officers who had been true to the former commander-in-chief, among whom was Colonel Saryannis, who was considered, curiously enough, to be the only expert on the situation. Not only that, but many of the higher commanders remained unchanged, only those being replaced who had asked to be sent back from the front. I lay special stress on this, because it was said later that the failure of the campaign was due to the fact that the higher commands were in the hands of incapable officers.

This was a unique opportunity to reorganize the army and strengthen discipline, which had become very lax. The reinstatement of the many officers dismissed in 1917 would have been a guarantee that the various commands would be entrusted to firm hands, and the army would thus settle down once more to its purely military duties. On the other hand, it is to the credit of the new government of that time that it was filled with a genuine desire to reconcile the two parties; but, afraid of foreign criticisms, it showed reluctance to investigate certain frankly dishonest actions of the opposite party, and to dispense even elementary justice to the reinstated officers who had endured so much suffering. It was contended at the time that the latter were not experienced in the art of modern warfare, as conducted in the recent European War, and that on the contrary the officers of the 'Amyna', and those who had remained, did possess the necessary experience, and also that one was not morally obliged to dismiss men of such longstanding service who had risked their lives on the field. But also it must be recognized that the majority of the reinstated officers were excellent, having passed through the training schools, that they were forcibly sent away from the army because of their principles—that it was their services during the Balkan wars which gained the victory; yet this side of the question, I repeat, was unfortunately not taken sufficiently into consideration. The government did not dare to readjust the positions of these officers: the members of the 'Amyna' and some of the others had received one or two promotions each during the three years' interval, consequently the reinstated officers found that the others who had formerly served under them were now their superiors.

It must also be remembered that a large proportion of those promotions, during the period 1917 to the end of 1920, was made as a reward for political activities, and not for military ability. There was, at this time, undoubtedly great friction between the various classes of officers, which it was imperatively necessary to allay, the difficulty being to decide whether it was better to promote the reinstated officers so that they regained the seniority they had lost, or to revert the officers of the 'Amyna' to the grades they had previously held.

It was ultimately decided to promote the reinstated officers, so as to avoid offending the susceptibilities of the 'Amynites' and the others.

The result was fatal, for besides the creation of innumerable superfluous posts in the upper ranks, the 'Amynites' and others were dissatisfied, for they lost the advantages acquired during the three years' interregnum. The evil was not rectified. The plethora of generals and colonels was such, that it was found to be impossible to make use of them all at the front, and the action of Lieutenant-General Papulas, who tried by every means in his power to keep all the commanding officers at the front in their posts, created serious friction with the reinstated officers. The statement made that the latter, satisfied with their reinstatement and promotions, preferred the pleasures of Athens to the commands of units at the front, is entirely incorrect. Of course, there were a few who did; but, generally speaking, the majority of them petitioned and agitated in every way to get transferred to Asia Minor, but in vain, because Lieutenant-General Papulas accepted few of them at the front. It was only natural that much dissatisfaction was created among the reinstated officers, who realized full well that public opinion would attribute to them a reluctance to serve at the front. The consciousness of having been sacrificed for an ideal, and of having suffered material hardships as well during the three years after their dismissal, together with the fact that service in the army brought them now only ingratitude and coldness, was a bitter disillusion to them. In general, it may be said that the constitutional government in its desire to appear just and broadminded, and in its attempt to cast a cloak of forgetfulness over the misdeeds of the past, overstepped the mark by deserting its own followers and supporting its opponents, with the result that the latter plucked up courage again, mistaking this liberal attitude of the rulers for weakness, while the former, completely disillusioned, were seized with utter indifference as to the future.

1

From 23 June to 23 July

On my return to Greece with King Constantine, after three years' exile in Switzerland, from 1917–1920, I was promoted to the rank of major-general, and, after many struggles, was at last given the command of a division in Asia Minor, where the campaign against the Turks had already been launched by the previous government. The prejudice against those officers dismissed from the army in 1917, of whom I was one, was deliberately greater in my own case. Many and varied were the discussions that took place at that time; a not insignificant part of the staff at GHQ looking askance at my being given a command in the army, and using every means in their power to prevent it. Before the persistence of the War Office, however, the opposition gave way, but every care was taken that I should be appointed to a command where any influence I could possibly exert should be reduced to a minimum: hence the staff at GHQ proposed to entrust me with the command of the Cavalry Brigade.

I certainly had no objection to accepting this command, as I had always served in the cavalry, but the War Office did not consider it suitable for me, the post being one for a colonel and not for a major-general. GHQ then suggested my being appointed second-in-command of the army, with a special staff of my own, forming part of the suite of the commander-in-chief. I should, however, have been under the continual supervision of the commander-in-chief's staff, and would thus have become a superfluous commander with a high-sounding title, but no responsibility. It was impossible for me to accept such an appointment, and, therefore, I forwarded a request to the War Office asking for an active post at the front. My request had to be considered, and at last I was informed that the command of a division would be given to me as soon as a vacancy occurred.

After the failure of the operation of March 1921, the government was obliged to call up some more classes, and the divisions, thus formed in Greece, were sent to Smyrna.

Towards April, the IVth Division, to which no commander had yet been appointed, was preparing to embark, and I naturally thought that I should have obtained this command; but the commander-in-chief, in a telegram to the War Office, drew attention to the fact that my presence in the army was not desirable until the situation, after the recent failure in Asia Minor, had become clearer.

Finally, towards the beginning of May, I was told that I would receive the command of the XIIth Division then being formed in Thrace, which was to embark for Smyrna toward the end of the month; and, on its arrival there, I took over the command. The commander of the XIIth Division at this time happened to be Colonel-of-Infantry Kurevelis, an all-round capable officer, but not being on good terms with Lieutenant-General Papulas, the commander-in-chief, he was curtly ordered to hand over the command to me and to depart.

I should like to add that the relative seniority between myself and the other major-generals at the front was not apparently taken into consideration, for officers junior to me held senior commands. For instance, Major-General A. Vlachopulos, the commander of the 2nd Army Corps, and Major-General Gidas, the commander of the Southern Group, both junior to me, became my immediate superiors. I did not, however, draw the attention of GHQ to this fact, because I did not consider it would lower my prestige in any way.

The king left Athens for Smyrna on 11 June, after having issued a proclamation placing himself at the head of his troops, and I accompanied him. Certain representatives of the Greek Army Headquarters Staff at Athens—namely, General Dusmanis and Major-General Stratigos—also went with the king.

During the voyage on board the battleship *Lemnos*, I remember a long discussion which took place between the prime minister, Gunaris, and the minister of war, Theotoky, on one side, and the chief of the headquarters staff and General Dusmanis on the other, as to whether the king ought to take over the actual command of the army.

General Dusmanis was insistent on this being done—in accordance with the proclamation just issued—but the ministers expressed their disagreement with the arrangement.

This question gave rise to many varied and bitter arguments, and ended, finally, with the king keeping aloof from all military direction, in spite of assertions to the contrary, which were made after the catastrophe of 1922.

It is not for me to say whether the king's taking an active part in the leadership was in the general interest or not, but perhaps the prestige which he enjoyed with the troops and his great military authority might have prevented some of the rash decisions, and have slightly restrained the boundless ambitions of some of the younger members of the staff at GHQ, ambitions which the commander-in-chief not only did not curb, but which he rather encouraged in his unrestrained egotism and ignorance of the art of war.

Arrival of King Constantine in Smyrna, followed by the commander-in-chief, General Papulas (on right) and the author (on left).

From the first, the discord between the representative of the HQ staff and the staff of the commander-in-chief at Smyrna was apparent. The relations between Generals Papulas and Dusmanis were strained to the utmost. In addition, the sub-chief of the HQ staff, Major-General X. Stratigos, did not find General Dusmanis' views to his liking, and, therefore, inclined towards the views of GHQ. The commander-in-chief's staff studiously avoided all intercourse with the representatives of the HQ staff on account of their dread that the king should assume the direction himself, and that they would thus find themselves excluded from the hoped-for glories of the campaign.

The two ministers, being civilians, did not realize to what a pitch the passions of the military parties could rise and, groping about in the web of intrigue, attempted in vain to bring about an agreement. Such was the situation when the commander-in-chief was ordered to present himself to the king to explain the plan of the next operations. It may be that the king was not actually in command; but all the same, according to the constitution, he was the supreme chief of the forces on land and at sea, and the commander-in-chief was obliged to present himself to him and receive the approval of his plans from the supreme chief. Finally, he came, accompanied by Colonels Pallis and Saryannis, and these two officers submitted to his majesty the plan of General Papulas, who looked on in silence.

Before my departure for the front, I had seen the minister of war, who gave me the impression that he was floating in a cloudless heaven of optimism, and he enquired if I was now satisfied with the command which had been given to me, and assured me that the XIIth Division was a model one, stronger than the usual divisions, and complete from every point of view.

When I recall the quality of the personnel and the organization of the XIIth Division on the eve of the most important operations which the Greek Army has ever undertaken, I shudder, and feel thankful that we did not find ourselves facing strong opposition on the part of the enemy, or in some of the difficult situations which fell to the lot of the other divisions. I recognize the difficulties of GHQ, in face of the varied and repeated demands which came from all sides, but I do not understand their complete and ever arrogant indifference to the well-being of a portion of the army which was shortly to take part in a most difficult movement against the fortified enemy. The mission confided to the XIIth Division was not insignificant, as it formed the mobile right wing of the army. Other divisions possessed mountain artillery, Schneider-Dangli, and field and heavy Skoda guns, wireless, and two heliograph apparatuses, and the quality of their infantry regiments was infinitely superior. What was the reason of this indifference to the XIIth Division? Perhaps at GHQ there were some who felt bitterness at my presence in the army, and the subsequent development of events does not exclude such a suspicion, on the contrary it rather strengthens it. It was evident that they had the dreadful hope that the XIIth Division would suffer disasters, in which case I would have borne the responsibility. They were utterly indifferent to the fate of a Greek division or to the danger of a disaster to it spreading to other divisions.

What I have just said must not be considered as an exaggeration. Friction between officers and political passions had reached a pitch impossible for anyone not in the army to realize. The conduct of Colonel Saryannis during the events of the Sangarios and his deposition as a witness at my trial have confirmed my suspicions of that. If these plots did not succeed during the short time that I was in command of the XIIth Division, this was partly due to the fact that the enemy continually retreated and did not attack, and partly to the officers of my staff. And, in truth, I always had the good fortune to be served by strong, able, and loyal men on my staff, such as the tireless and ever-present Colonel Gavallias, the resolute Captain Skilakakis, Major Karavelas, and others to whom I owe a debt of gratitude. The fact that the plots against me failed during the first part of the operations did not mean that the intrigues had ceased. Later on in the campaign, if there had been any pretext for it, the events at Kalé-Grotto would have been taken advantage of to remove me from the command of the 2nd Army Corps. Luckily for me, the fear of my denouncing the malcontents, which unfortunately I refrained from, owing to my faith in General Papulas' word, prevented this. The hatred, passion, and bitter enmity of those persons burst forth finally after 4 September 1922, when from their own safe positions they let their venom stain all that was

The author with his chief of staff, Inei.

sacred and holy in Greece. The fact that I did not follow the slaughtered innocents into eternity, in November 1922, was certainly not due to their good-will.

When I took over the command of the XIIth Division the army was in a transitional stage, as after a tempest. Calm and discipline were gradually being restored; but the fire was still smouldering, and it must not be imagined that this transition was accomplished without some conflicts. The three years' interregnum had created passions and hatreds which could not easily be smoothed down by ordinary methods. The greatest patience and foresight had to be exercised by the commanders and superior officers in handling their commands, and when I add that some of the officers created by the late government were men who did not even know how to read and write, the difficulties of the situation can well be understood.

The state of training in the army was not bad. The successive campaigns from 1912 onwards had been the means of giving the troops valuable experience and self-reliance, and many parts of the army—as, for example, the IInd Division (Athens)—were practically model fighting units. Besides the infantry, the artillery, except for its material, which was nearly worn out, had reached a wonderful degree of excellence in training, but, unhappily, I cannot say the same of the XIIth Division. This division was composed of the 14th Infantry Regiment and the recently formed 41st and 46th Infantry Regiments, one group of mountain artillery of two batteries, one company of sappers, one half-squadron of cavalry, one sanitary detachment, and their dependent services. Unfortunately, the methods used in Thrace in its formation were not such as to ensure discipline.

For instance, the majority of the men of the 46th Infantry Regiment had been drawn from the punishment-training companies of Macedonia and Thrace, and many of the officers were men whom the above-mentioned garrisons did not wish to keep, on account of their conduct and lack of discipline. The whole division was chiefly composed of Thracians and Cretans—good, strong men, but untrained, and with no war experience. The situation was only saved by the regimental commanders, Colonels G. Ziras of the 14th, Vlachos of the 41st, and Panayotakos of the 46th.

The group of mountain artillery was composed of two batteries of 6.5, and consequently was too weak to be of general use. It was intended more for the immediate support of the infantry and to accompany them, and was used entirely for that purpose. The engineers of the division had no material, not even a heliograph. Later, after a desperate struggle, we received one, but of a very antiquated pattern, which refused to function at night. A wireless outfit naturally did not exist, and, in spite of all my efforts and the promises of the commander-in-chief, I never succeeded in making good this deficiency.

As soon as I had taken over the command of the division, I began a series of inspections, so as to find out how things were, and I confess that I was horrified. But there were still some days left, and these were spent in feverish preparations. Naturally, it was impossible for me to hide from myself that a ten days' intensive instruction of untrained personnel was of very little use, and that these troops would all melt before the enemy like snow in the sun, but it was impossible to do more. If it had not been for the regimental commanders, the commander of the divisional infantry, Colonel Kallidopulos, and the officers of my staff, who one and all strove with almost superhuman zeal to achieve some semblance of training, it would have been impossible for the XIIth Division to take part in the general operations.

The XIIth Division, which, with the IVth Division (Colonel Dimaras), formed part of the Southern Group (Major-General Gidas), was split up as follows: the 41st Infantry Regiment, the 12th Group of Mountain Artillery, the 12th Half-Squadron of Cavalry, and the Sanitary Detachment in the village of Inei; the 46th Infantry Regiment to the south of the village; the 14th Regiment and the company of sappers in the small town of Giubek, about 4 kilometres east of Inei; lastly, my HQ were at the railway station of Inei, where the Greek stationmaster refused to give me the hospitality of the station building, and I was obliged to establish myself in a tent, and the officers of the staff in an adjoining stable.

After the unsuccessful issue of the operations of March 1921—so lightly undertaken by GHQ—the government was at last convinced that the war in Asia Minor could not be brought to an end without enormous sacrifices, and they therefore decided to call under arms some more classes of reserves.

The four months from March to June had been occupied in reorganizing and strengthening the army—a task which was carried out unmolested by the enemy,

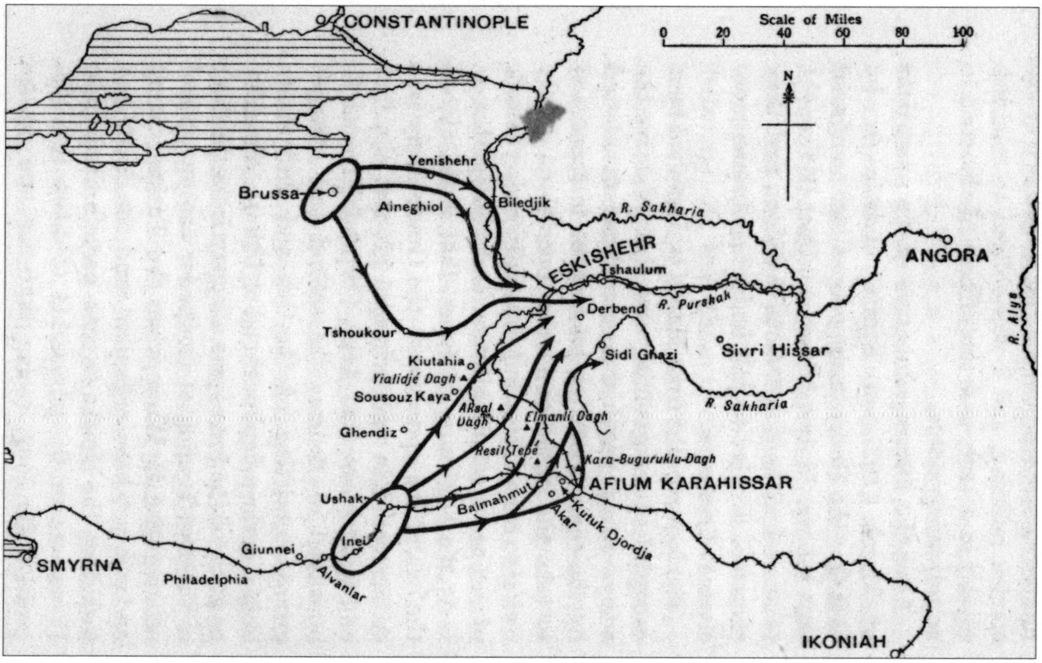

The march of the Greek Army, 23 June to 23 July.

because he was not in a position to take the initiative in new operations, partly owing to exhaustion, but especially owing to lack of means of communication and transport.

At the beginning of June—that is to say, on the eve of the operations—the Greek Army was concentrated in two principal groups: the first and weaker one (3rd Army Corps) in the neighbourhood of Brussa; the second and stronger group, consisting of the 1st and 2nd Army Corps, in the neighbourhood of Ushak. This disposition of the forces was a legacy from the days of the first landing of troops for the purpose of occupying Asia Minor when the Turkish Army had not yet been organized, and the Allies had forbidden the Greeks to cross certain fixed lines. It was naturally impossible to keep this disposition for long, seeing that the two masses were separated from each other by a distance of more than 100 kilometres, and vigorous action on the part of the enemy might produce an irreparable catastrophe.

It is true that the country between the two portions of the Greek Army was of a mountainous, impassable nature, and that the Turks were not in a position to undertake such an operation, owing to their lack of the requisite material for mountain warfare. On the other hand, this disadvantageous situation permitted a manoeuvre to be carried out which might almost have caused the destruction of the Turkish Army, if it had not been commanded by leaders of great military capacity as Mustapha Kemal Pasha and Ismet Pasha.

Facing this disposition of the Greek troops, the Turks, in general, held the line from Eski-Shehr south to Afium-Karahissar—i.e., the fortified positions west and south of Eski-Shehr; further, the positions west and south of Kiutahia: Yialidjé-dagh—Kires- dagh—Aksal-dagh—Elmanli-dagh; and the positions west of Afium-Karahissar: Resil Tepé, Bal Mahmut, Kutuk Djordja. This line was a naturally strong one, but the Turks rendered it practically impregnable by the addition of strong fortified works.

It is evident that in a direct frontal offensive on this line our losses would be enormous, and the consequent weakening of the Greek forces would not only render the success of the present operations doubtful, but would expose the whole campaign to ultimate failure. The only way to avoid these losses was to outflank one of the enemy wings, and for this purpose their left was considered the more suitable, partly by reason of our numerical superiority on that side, but chiefly because the nature of the ground here lent itself to this manoeuvre.

The problem which had to be solved was twofold—firstly, the union of the two separate groups of the army, and, secondly, the assault. In view of the enemy's inaction, it was possible to consider a concentrated attack, and the consequent union of the two groups on the battlefield—somewhat like what occurred during the campaign of 1866 when the two groups of the Prussian Army were united on the battlefield of Sadowa. The general plan having been thus decided upon, the details were settled in the following manner:

Northern Force

The Northern Group (IIIrd division, Major-General Tricupis; XIth Division, Colonel Kladas), under Major-General Tricupis, to march from Timbu and the Lake of Askania towards Eski-Shehr.

3rd Army Corps (Xth Division, Colonel Sumilas; VIIth Division, Colonel Platis), under Major-General Polymenakos, to march from Brussa towards Kiutahia.

Southern Force

The mixed detachment (Colonel Tsiroyannis) to march from Ushak towards Kiutahia. 1st Army Corps (1st Division, Colonel Frangu; IInd Division, Colonel Valettas), under Major-General Kondulis, as well as 2nd Army Corps (Vth Division, Colonel Trilivas; XIIIth Division, Colonel Digenis), under Major-General Aristoteles Vlachopulos, from Ushak towards Aksal-dagh and Elmanli-dagh.

The Southern Group (IVth Division, Colonel Dimaras; XIIth Division, Major-General Prince Andrew), under Major-General Gidas, from Inei towards Afium-Karahissar via Akar and afterwards towards the north.

The general impression which the enemy would receive from this manoeuvre would be a frontal attack on his fortified lines, and a threatening movement against his right by the northern group. It was hoped and expected that the enemy would be induced to reinforce that part of his front, and at the same time it was hoped that he would be slow in perceiving the movement of the southern group, and would in consequence be pinned down to the positions already taken up, and our outflanking movement rendered possible and easy.

The greater part of the southern force, as I have said, was concentrated in the region of Ushak and Inei. This concentration had been effected quite openly, the enemy being perfectly well able to perceive what was in progress, because his aeroplanes were continually circling above our positions and observing the movements of our troops.

It was quite permissible to hope that the enemy would be deceived as to our real intentions, even when he had obtained exact information as to our concentrations. Knowing the country as he did, it was difficult for him to imagine that we intended an encircling movement on such a scale, for the immense distances and the condition of the tracks—for there were no roads—would make transport excessively difficult.

Rarely were conditions so favourable for the operations of the Greek Army, including as they did the inability of the Turkish Army to take the initiative. It was hoped that by following the plan just mentioned, our wide encircling movement would either result in his complete annihilation or his surrender. In addition, the seizure of the two railway centres of Eski-Shehr and Afium-Karahissar would prevent Angora and Ikoniah from having any communications with each other or with the outside world, and it was calculated that by exerting such strong pressure, the enemy would be obliged to accept our conditions of peace.

But before I enter into the account of the execution of the above plan, it is necessary for me to make mention of certain events which took place about the middle and end of June.

Our concentrations near Ushak-Inei were served by only one railway line from Smyrna, more than 270 kilometres long; the country through which this line passed was unfriendly, and had to be strongly guarded; consequently the importance of keeping this railway line intact, in order to avoid a disaster, can easily be understood. To do so, large detachments of troops were posted all along the line to guard the bridges and tunnels, and these duties employed a number of men, who were extremely necessary at the front, but nothing else could be done.

The country north of Philadelphia was, for the most part, empty of troops, and Angora agents could almost, without molestation, continue to recruit and organize bands of irregulars (Tchets), who, under the leadership of officers of the Turkish Army, made constant raids to destroy the bridges and engineering works along the railway line.

On 27 June, when I was in Inei, I was informed that irregulars had destroyed the railway station at Giunnei—about halfway between Philadelphia and Inei—and that a violent battle was raging, which would end in inevitable disaster for our small garrison if reinforcements were not immediately sent. For this purpose, I ordered two companies to be prepared, but luckily, before their departure, I received news that this information was due to the exaggeration of the military stationmaster, who imagined, on being fired at, that it was a serious attack. For anyone knowing the conditions, it was hard to accuse of panic an unfortunate stationmaster, alone with four or five men, at a station in the middle of a vast hostile country.

A similar case occurred on 6 July, but this time at the station of Alvanlar, where there is a large bridge. At first I thought the news was an exaggeration on the part of another stationmaster, but I was soon convinced that this time the attack was serious, the Turks having two mountain guns.* Two companies were sent who assisted to repulse the attack, but not without losses on our side which amounted to the respectable figure of sixty, amongst them being three officers killed and two wounded.

I now return to the operations. It is evident that it was impossible for all the divisions to start on the same day, as it was necessary for those coming from the north, and those destined to execute the flanking movement, to make an earlier start, so as to reach the alignment of the central force, and to make a combined assault on the day fixed by GHQ.

The first division to start was the XIth, which left Nicomedia on 24 June, but encountering enemy opposition it was delayed, and arrived at Brussa on 3 July. On 3 July, the Northern Group, under Major-General Tricupis, set out from Timbou along the shore of the lake of Askania in two columns, towards Eski-Shehr, and after some lively skirmishes occupied Yeni-Shehr and Aïneghiol. The aim of this operation was to draw northwards as many enemy forces as possible.

The 3rd Army Corps started from Brussa on the 8th towards Kiutahia. This movement far from the enemy could be carried out in complete safety, as the enemy, lacking means of transport, was unable to insert himself between our columns. This march contributed to make the Turks believe that the main objective of our offensive was the fortified front of Kiutahia.

On the 10th, the Mixed Detachment (Tsiroyannis) set out from Ushak in the direction of Kiutahia, with the intention of increasing the enemy's impression that the offensive would be made against the Kiutahia front. At the same time, the 1st and 2nd Army Corps moved towards Aksal and Elmanli-dagh.

* According to the Turkish general Faker Eddin, it was the 1st Cavalry Division.

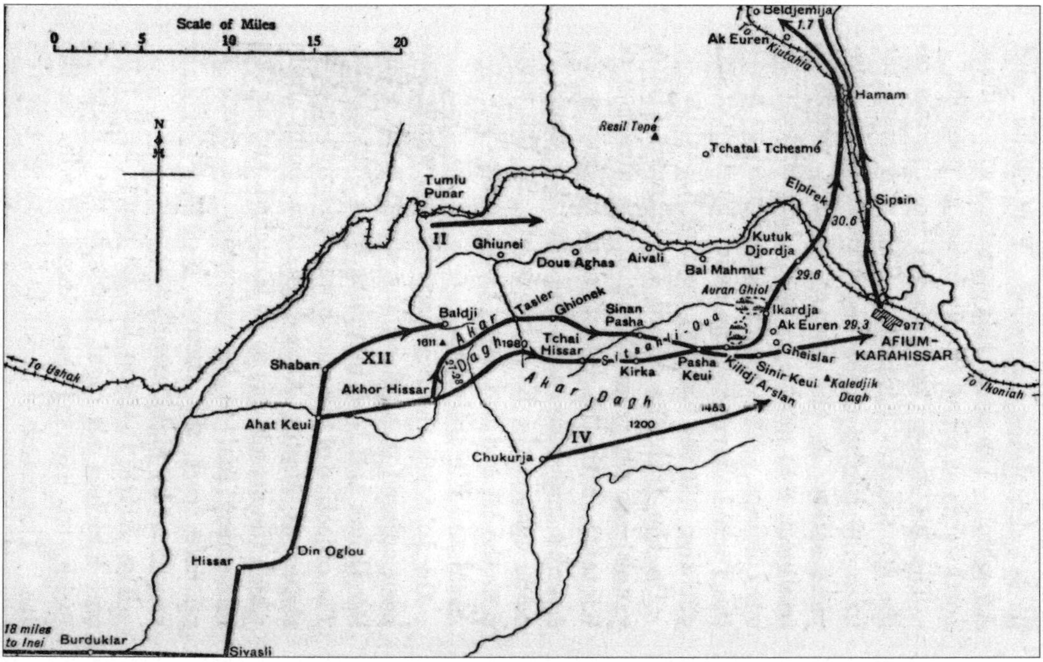

The march of the XIIth Division, 7 July to 14 July.

On 6 July the Southern Group, which had been ordered to outflank the enemy's left wing, left Ushak and Inei, marching from west to east. The objective of this march was the north-eastern slopes of Mount Akar-dagh, the point from which the attack was to be launched, and as this movement had to be concealed as much as possible from the enemy, it was decided to execute it by night marches.

The XIIth Division left its camp at 9 p.m. and marched all night towards the village of Burduklar, arriving there about 10 a.m. on the 7th. This march of about 40 kilometres was well executed, considering that it was night, and that the troops had not had the necessary training; but happily, we were far from the enemy, and, consequently, only the indispensable measures for the immediate safety of the column were taken. In the meantime, GHQ, realizing the laborious fatigue of these night marches for the troops, and convinced that the enemy's whole attention was concentrated on Ushak and Tumlu Punar, decided that in future the approach marches were to be carried out by day. For that reason, the division remained the whole of the 7th at Burduklar, and left the following day, the 8th, at 6 a.m., for Hissar via Sivasli.

At 11 a.m., after a trying march in the terrible heat, we arrived at the village of Sivasli, where I ordered a two-hours' halt for the men to rest. Here I had occasion to deplore the absence of a spirit of discipline in my division. It is certainly not surprising that this should chiefly be conspicuous by its absence, if one takes into consideration under what conditions the division had been formed, but the conduct of the men in entering this village and the indifference of the majority of the officers unfortunately surpass belief. I prefer to cast a veil over what took place, but once I have touched on this question I cannot but deplore and disapprove of the mentality of those who tried to justify such excesses by asserting that the centuries-long slavery of the Greek race under the heel of the Turk permitted, and even demanded, such cruel reprisals against a peaceable and unarmed population, who had always received us with every demonstration of respect and submission. In my own personal experiences, not only during the advance but also during the later retreat from the Sangarios, I never found it necessary, either by reason of hostile demonstrations or any other cause, to terrorize the inhabitants of the country through which we passed. It is, of course, possible that other units may have found themselves obliged to make use of reprisals, but, in general, the conduct of the inhabitants towards us was quite irreproachable, no matter whether the reason was fear or any other.

I always tried, by all the means permitted by the king's regulations, to check these excesses, which I considered as clear evidence of the want of discipline in the army, for the private soldier never lets himself be drawn into such practices if he is held in hand by his officers, and if the latter exercise the necessary influence and supervision. I do not know how to excuse the conduct of those officers who, by their indifference and their occasional open support and participation, tolerated this state of affairs. Unhappily, it was only too evident that the army had contracted habits that were foreign to its nature before 1917.

That same evening, about 8 p.m., the division encamped near the locality of Hissar. At this point we were joined by a brigade of field batteries sent from Ushak by GHQ.

At 7 a.m. on the 9th the march continued via Din-Oglou towards Ahatkeui, over a very difficult road, rocky and so steep that to this day I wonder how the field batteries were able to follow. The division went into camp on the outskirts of the village about 3 p.m. At 5 p.m., I received from GHQ all the directions and scheme as well as the order for the attack which was to take place on the 11th.

One more march had to be accomplished to enable us to reach the assembly position, which was on the north-eastern slopes of Mount Akar-dagh. Thence the division was to advance via Sitsanli-Ova against the fortified positions of Bal Mahmut and Kutuk Djordja, and after that to proceed without fresh orders, in a northerly direction, to prolong our extreme right wing. The right wing of the division was protected by the IVth as far as Afium-Karahissar (the objective of the latter), while on its left was the IInd Division marching in the direction of Tchatal Tchesmé. It is regrettable that the troops could not be given a day's rest after the trying marches of the last days, but this was not possible if the enemy was to be taken by surprise.

In the evening, I sent for the infantry and artillery commanders, and the officers commanding the three regiments, and I read to them the orders of GHQ, after which I explained my intentions. The march on the following day, which was the last of the approach marches, would bring us into territory occupied by hostile troops. It was, therefore, necessary to take measures for the occupation of the heights of Akar-dagh. No serious opposition on the part of the enemy was expected, because, according to our information, there were only inferior forces of cavalry in front of us, but, nevertheless, it was expedient to take measures for the occupation of these heights without loss of time and before opposition could be organized.

For this purpose I decided to divide the division into three columns—(*a*) the 14th Infantry Regiment and the brigade of mountain artillery (less one half-battery), under Colonel Ziras, to march, via Akhor Hissar, towards height 1980; (*b*) the 41st Infantry Regiment and one half-battery, under Colonel Vlachos, to march via Akhor Hissar towards height 1611; and lastly (*c*), the 46th Infantry Regiment, the brigade of field artillery, and a company of engineers, under Colonel Panayotakos, to march, via Shaban, towards Baldji. In this manner the progress over the mountainous ground would be made easier, the deployment more rapid in case of necessity, and assistance could easily be rendered by one column to another. I marched with the 2nd Column.

The movement started at 6:30 a.m. on the following morning, the 10th. The march was carried out without molestation by Vlachos' and Panayotakos' columns, but not by Ziras' column, which met with slight opposition at height 1980; but it was not serious, for only two men were slightly wounded. The march of Vlachos' column was carried out undisturbed, except for one episode. As we were passing through Akhor Hissar and climbing the first slopes of the Akar, heavy rifle fire was heard in the east; but the resistance of the enemy in front of Ziras' column was of short duration, and the column soon resumed its march. A little further on we arrived at a point whence one could clearly distinguish crest 1611, and it was observed through field-glasses that on this crest there were fortifications and that the trenches were occupied. At the same time, in the west, Panayotakos' column appeared, and likewise was approaching 1611. We could not understand why the enemy did not fire, seeing that we were already within range, when the mystery was solved by the appearance on the scene at that moment of the liaison officer, Colonel of Cavalry M. Metaxas, of the IInd Division, who informed us that this sector was already in the possession of his division. Our ignorance might have had fatal results, and undoubtedly GHQ ought to have informed us of the lines of advance of the neighbouring divisions, as it was evident that the march of the XIIth Division would bring it close to them.

The march, in general, had been extremely fatiguing on account of the mountainous ground and the heat, and the men were completely done up by the time the columns reached their objectives at about 7 p.m.

After orders had been given out for the assault to take place on the following day, I received at midnight an order in cipher from GHQ, not even marked urgent, that the general assault was put off till the 12th on account of the delay to the 3rd Army Corps, and leaving it to me to inform the IVth Division. It was already midnight; the assault had been ordered for the following morning at 4:30 a.m., and the IVth Division was about 30 kilometres south-east of my position. There was no wireless; the heliograph, even if it could be worked at night, could not, as it happened, have found the division. There was nothing else to be done but to send an officer with a message, in spite of the unknown country, the thick forests, and the presence of the enemy. For this reason, I sent Captain Presetakos of my staff. Happily, the IVth Division had been informed in the meantime by GHQ itself, as the officer who had been sent naturally arrived long after the hour fixed for the start. I think that if the supreme command had seen to it in time, that the divisions were properly equipped with wireless or heliograph apparatus worthy of the name, they would have avoided such incidents, which lowered its prestige in the eyes of the troops. There would also have been no reason to risk the life of an officer, not to mention the danger to an entire division of finding itself alone in front of the enemy.

The 11th was passed in absolute quiet, and the men were at last able to enjoy a much-needed rest.

No new information was forthcoming about the enemy, and we had consequently to prepare to capture the line Bal Mahmut-Kutuk Djordja-Ak Euren. This line was very strong, for, besides its unlimited field of fire, it included an enormous swamp, which began at the foot of the hills occupied by the enemy and spread over the greater part of the plain of Sitsanli-Ova. Bal Mahmut was an isolated hill-top, extremely steep and rocky, with a flattened summit, which the Turks had transformed into a regular fortress, with heavy guns in position on the top. It was followed towards the east by the Kutuk Djordja, likewise fortified and provided with field-guns. The rest of the line up to Ak Euren was occupied by infantry in trenches. The ground to the south, south-west, and west of Bal Mahmut presented an ideal field of fire, as the northern slopes of the Akardagh descended gradually and evenly, and were bare of cover. Any movement of our troops here would immediately be perceived from a very great distance. Consequently, the task of the XIIth Division was anything but easy, for, after passing Tasler, it would immediately be observed by the enemy, and a little later it would become a target for their heavy artillery, to which we could only reply with one brigade of field artillery. The advance would then become still more difficult on account of the swamp of Avran-Ghiol, which, though it had dried up in several areas owing to the time of year, could only be crossed at certain places. The IVth Division was on our right, but it was too far off to have any local influence on the fighting, and only an advance on its part towards Afium-Karahissar could bring any relief to the situation, and then only on condition that this division did not encounter serious opposition at Kaledjik-dagh. Only the advance of the IInd Division on our left, towards the line Aivali-Resil Tepé, could effectively assist our advance, because this division possessed a brigade of heavy artillery (Skoda), with which it could to some extent distract the enemy's attention from us.

After a local reconnaissance it was seen that the condition of the ground did not permit of any other way of advance, except via Tasler-Ghionek-Sinan Pasha-Pashakeui towards Kutuk Djordja. As our left wing would be immediately protected by the IInd Division, it would not be necessary to take measures of safety on that flank, but this would not be the case on our right, for between the XIIth and the IVth Division lay the entire bulk of the Akar-dagh. I decided, therefore, in order to protect my right, to direct Ziras' column via Tchai Hissar-Kirka- Kilidj Arslan-Sinirkeui towards Ak Euren, with orders to advance parallel to, and a little in front of, the main body of the division, which was composed of the two remaining regiments. The operation order was framed on the above-mentioned basis.

The next day, the 12th, the movement started at 4:30 a.m. After passing the village of Ghionek, I expected that the enemy's fire from Bal Mahmut, to which it would be impossible for me to reply on account of the great range, would open at any moment.

This, if it happened, would be the baptism of fire for the XIIth Division, and I did not know what effect it would have on the men under such unpleasant conditions, for it is well known that the morale of troops may be seriously affected when they come under artillery fire, and especially heavy artillery fire, without being able to return it. On our left towards Ghiunei and Dous Aghas the other columns of the IInd Division appeared, marching parallel with ours; and this had a good effect on the morale of the division in general.

In the meantime, we continued our progress, passing through one village after the other, and still Bal Mahmut was silent. Finally, at Pashakeui, some peasants assured us that the enemy had abandoned their positions two days before, retreating to the north, and in this district, there was left only a small force at Sinirkeui. Relying on this information, which was confirmed in the meantime by the half-squadron of cavalry from Ikardja, I ordered a halt to rest the men, after a march of more than 30 kilometres, and to give Ziras' column time to advance to Sinirkeui. After about two hours the advance was continued, and we immediately heard the first shots of the engagement between Ziras and the enemy. From the plain we could watch the progress of the fighting on the hills to our east, and so clearly could the enemy positions be distinguished that I ordered a battery belonging to the brigade of field artillery to get ready to fire, so as to silence the two mountain guns which they were using. The distance was not more than 3,500 to 4,000 metres, and a field battery firing at such a range from the plain could obtain very satisfactory results. After I had given my order to the officer commanding the artillery, Colonel M. Criesis, I went to a hillock close by to follow the action. Impatiently I waited for the firing to commence, because the enemy in the meantime was showing signs of uneasiness and preparing for flight. On turning to see what was happening, I saw Colonel Criesis galloping aimlessly about on the plain at the head of his battery evidently searching for a better fire position, whereas no better place could be found than the plain on which we were. By the time I had managed to stop the colonel's wanderings the enemy had retreated, and the skirmish was over. My object had been to fire a few shells to frighten the enemy, if for nothing else. But this was not understood by Colonel Criesis, who considered it wiser to look for a better position; thus the opportunity of disorganizing the enemy detachment from a safe point of vantage was lost.

Late that night, at about 11 p.m., the division reached Kutuk Djordja, after a march of about 50 kilometres. The enemy detachment was pursued all night long by Colonel Ziras, and very early in the morning of the 13th, on finding himself before Afium-Karahissar, he entered and captured the town, the enemy retiring to the east.

Although this was not a very important military feat, the fact that Afium-Karahissar was taken by the XIIth Division was passed over in silence and attributed to the IVth perhaps because, according to GHQ plans, the capture was to have been effected by the IVth. The fact remains that the IVth Division entered the town at noon on the 13th, after Colonel Ziras' departure.

The retreat of the enemy from his strong positions clearly proved that he had realized in time the menace to his left, and was withdrawing his left wing towards the main body of the army in the district of Kiutahia. This certainly did not mean that our operation had failed, but there was a danger that the struggle would be prolonged, for the enemy was carrying out the only safe plan open to him—namely, a retirement before our superior forces. The vast extent of the country permitted him to withdraw in safety, and to keep his forces intact and ready for future action at a time more convenient and on ground more suited to him. On the other hand, we found ourselves obliged to follow him so as to force him to accept battle, while we were penetrating deeper into an inhospitable and hostile country, advancing all the time further from our bases, and suffering inevitable wear and tear to personnel and material. Of course, it was still too early for us to judge whether this retreat was of purely local significance—i.e., whether the enemy thereby sought to escape the menace on his left—or whether it was a question of a general retreat, for we were in ignorance of the general military situation.

The capture of Afium-Karahissar by Colonel Ziras was the result of his overstepping the orders he had received. His column was the right flank-guard of the division, and after the enemy's retreat from Sinirkeui he was drawn by the pursuit a long way to the east instead of continuing towards Gheislar and Ak Euren. Colonel Ziras' impulsive nature could not resist achieving the glory of the capture of the town; but his action prevented the division from being able to start next morning, for it had to wait for him to come out of Afium-Karahissar, and could only resume its advance in the afternoon.

The march of the 13th was not a long one, happily, for the men were exhausted. In any case, it was impossible for me to go on much further, because, except for the general 'directives' of GHQ, ordering us to turn to the north, I had no information about either the enemy's movements or our own. In consequence of this I marched on to Elpirek, where the division encamped for the night. Colonel Ziras' column, again marching as our right flank-guard, went on to Sipsin, where it went into camp.

At last, in the evening, the orders from GHQ arrived, and we were able to make out the general situation. The advance of the whole army had taken place according to plan; the mission of the XIIth Division was now to speed up its advance to the north, so as to assist the other divisions fighting before Kiutahia. The IVth Division was ordered to remain in Afium-Karahissar, and I received instructions to send my detachment of field artillery to it in exchange for a brigade of mountain guns. This was regrettable, though justified by the very mountainous ground towards which we were advancing.

The march of 14 July, long and wearisome, was carried out without incident, via Hamam–Ak Euren to Beldjemija, where the division encamped in the evening. The right flank-guard, still under Colonel Ziras, marched to Aidemir-Tekekeui, north-east of Beldjemija. During the afternoon, heavy firing could be heard in the

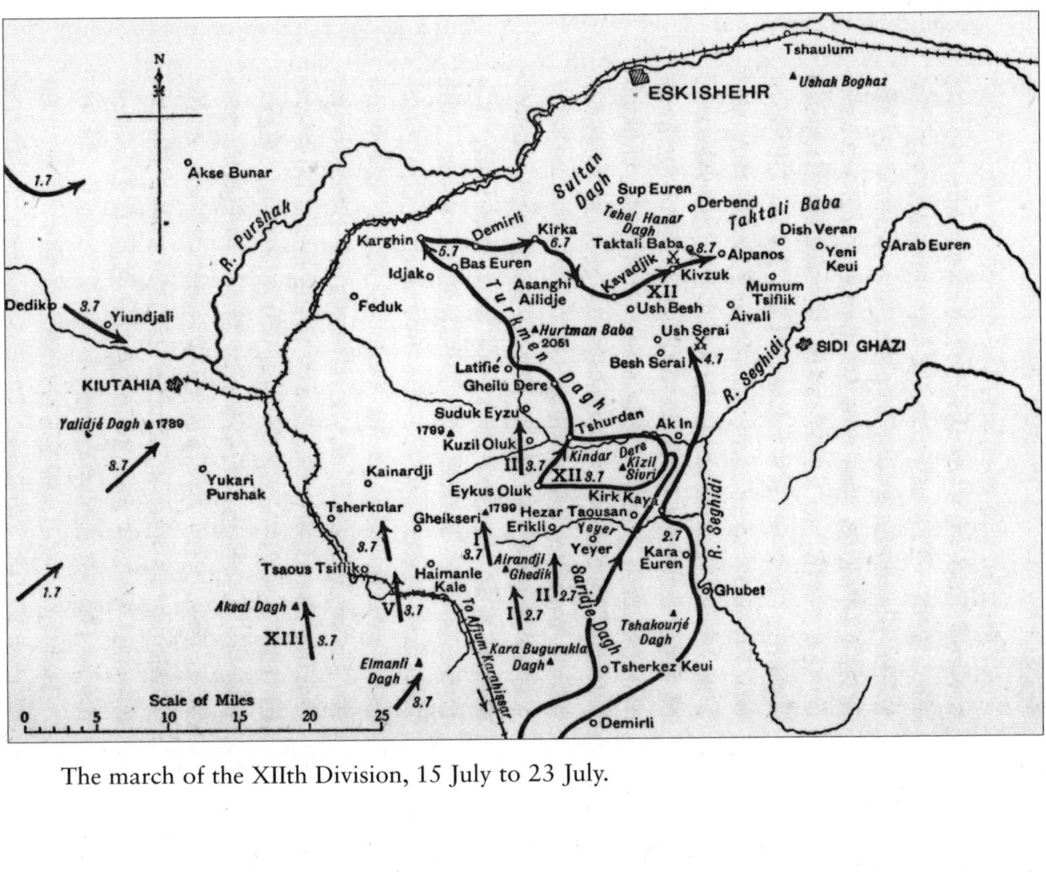

The march of the XIIth Division, 15 July to 23 July.

north—i.e., in the direction of Kara-Buguruklu-dagh, where the IInd Division was in action. In Beldjemija I received an order breaking up the southern group under Major-General Gidas, and placing the XIIth Division under the 1st Army Corps.

Before I continue the account of the operations of the XIIth Division, it is necessary to give a synopsis of the general situation as it was on the evening of 14 July.* After some severe fighting the IInd Division put the enemy on Kara-Buguruklu-dagh to flight. The centre of the army (2nd Army Corps) occupied Elmanli-dagh and deployed on both sides. The mixed detachment, joining the centre to the left wing (3rd Army Corps) occupied the heights of Sousouz Kaya (north of Ghendiz). The left wing (3rd Army Corps) reached the line Tshoukour Keui-Doumtshaïr. The northern group crossed the line Biledjik-Pazardjik. In the northern theatre of operations, one enemy division, attacking probably from the district of Nicomedia, advanced from Nicea and occupied Yeni-Shehr, and inserted itself between the left wing of the 3rd Army Corps and the northern group. But no harm was done by this, either locally or generally.

On 15 July, acting under the orders of the 1st Army Corps, the XIIth Division advanced to Tsher Kezkeui and Saridjé-dagh towards Kirk-Kaya at the northern outlet of the Yeyer Pass. I gave the right flank-guard, under Colonel Ziras, the route Demirli–Ghubet–Kara Euren, towards Hezar-Taousan. Probably this route may appear to be rather far from the main column of the division, but I could find no road nearer than that over the mountain mass of Tshakourjé-dagh. Seeing that I was on the extreme right of the battle front, I could not leave my right wing unprotected, and as the detachment would be accompanied on the march by the Cavalry Brigade (Colonel P. Nicolaides), which had been placed under my orders, it would be capable of defending itself against hostile attack.

At the village of Tsher Kezkeui, about noon, the XIIth Division crossed the IInd, which had been successful in the fight at Kara-Buguruklu and was now making its way to Erikli. We were obliged to interrupt our march for about two hours, to let the column of the IInd Division pass, and we then entered the long pass, which cuts through the Saridjé-dagh. The first part of this defile is easy, the ground sloping gradually on both sides with no steep inclines, but towards its outlet at Yeyer it becomes a steep ravine, down which a deep and rapid torrent flows, and this made progress difficult. In the evening I was marching with the 46th Regiment, which formed the vanguard, and trying to get the column out of the ravine into the plain before nightfall, when a volley of rifle fire warned me that the enemy was holding the exit of the pass. It was reported to me soon after that the half-squadron of cavalry had been fired on near the exit and had been obliged to retire; meanwhile the first sections of the vanguard had deployed, but darkness had already supervened, and it was impossible to distinguish either the positions of the enemy or the situation in general. In consequence, I ordered the

* See sketch, p. 43.

sections of the vanguard to remain in their places all night, and the main body withdrew to a point within the pass, where there was space to encamp. The night passed without disturbance, but it was doubtful if the troops had any rest, as the greater part of the 41st Regiment had been detailed for outpost duty, and was expecting the enemy to appear at any moment.

The dawn of the 16th revealed our presence to a hostile aeroplane, which dropped bombs on us, but without doing any damage. Colonel Panayotakos attacked after sunrise, and after a few minutes' fighting he was able to emerge on to the plain, where he was joined by Ziras' column coming from Hezar-Taousan. It was the appearance of the latter which had caused the enemy to abandon the fight and to retire to the north. The division was immediately reformed, and began the march to Ak In, preceded by the Cavalry Brigade. At some distance south of Ak In, the brigade came under artillery fire and immediately took up the prescribed formations, upon which, having realized that the village and its surroundings were strongly occupied by infantry and artillery, the vanguard of the division (14th Regiment) deployed to the right of the road, the 46th came up on its left, while the 41st remained in reserve. The attack was about to be launched, when an order reached us from GHQ directing the division towards Gheïlu-Deré, all except the Cavalry Brigade and the 14th Infantry Regiment. The Cavalry Brigade, the 14th Regiment, and one mountain battery were ordered to march via Ak In to Sidi-Ghazi, through the valley of the River Seghidi. To appreciate the situation exactly, and to understand the reason for GHQ's decision to order the detachment to march towards Sidi-Ghazi, it is necessary for me to give a short description of the general situation.

On 15 July, the enemy began to realize the great extent of our enveloping movement, and therefore made an attempt to concentrate his forces on his left, with the obvious intention of stopping the rapid advance of the Greek right wing, and, if opportunity offered, of breaking through our battle front, at the point where the right wing joined the centre; and that is why the 1st Division, forming the left of the right wing, encountered serious opposition on the heights of Aïrandji-Ghedik. The right division of our centre (the Vth), in occupation of Tsaous-Tsiflik and Haïmanle Kalé, had to meet violent enemy counterattacks during the whole of that day and the following night. Nevertheless, the enemy's plan failed, since the 1st Division was able to occupy Aïrandji-Ghedik. In addition, the enemy had realized that the extreme right wing of the Greeks was not where he imagined it to be, but stretched even farther to the east, where strong forces were already marching on Erikli and occupying Hezar-Taousan.

On the same day the IVth Division in Afium-Karahissar was strongly attacked from the south and east, but was able to repulse the enemy.

By 16 July, it became clear to the enemy that the two ends of the half-circle, which our army had formed, required but one more day's march to unite, and to form a complete circle round Kiutahia, and that if he wished to avoid surrendering he would have to make haste to abandon his position in front of Kiutahia. This movement was carried out as hurriedly as possible in the direction of Eski-Shehr. The enemy's retreat was executed in perfect order, and he succeeded in extricating the main body of his forces safe and sound from the threatening embrace of the Greeks. The fact that during the fighting of 15 and 16 July the Turks had lost some men, three or four guns, and a certain number of machine guns, does not prove that the defeat was as great as one had hoped for. Personally, I cannot imagine how GHQ came to mistake this retreat for a rout, and to think that the Turkish Army had retired in disorder to Eski-Shehr and thence to the east. In any case the commander-in-chief entertained the idea—or rather Colonel Saryannis, who was the leading spirit of the operations, did—that there was still time to cut off the retreat, if a force was sent to Sidi-Ghazi. The idea was childish, and the proposed method of executing it still more so.

However shaken the enemy appeared, the entire Turkish Army was still intact, and it was absurd to imagine that it would be possible to cut off the retreat with a small force sent in the direction referred to. This small force would be crushed by the bulk of the retreating enemy. An entire army corps might possibly have succeeded in delaying the enemy's retreat, but would certainly not have succeeded in enveloping it, our divisions in front of Kiutahia being still too far away for it to be possible for them to be in time for the necessary encircling movement.

On the heights south of Ak In, which I had reached towards noon of 16 July, I knew nothing about the above-mentioned general situation or the retreat of the Turkish Army. On the contrary, there was an enemy force in front of me, apparently determined to defend itself with vigour. Consequently, when I received the order from GHQ directing me to turn off to Gheïlu-Deré and to leave the Cavalry Brigade and the 14th Infantry Regiment before Ak In, I supposed it was intended to continue the original enveloping movement of Kiutahia, and that the detachment was intended to guard the extreme right wing of the battle front in the direction of the valley of the River Seghidi, which ends at Sidi-Ghazi. Not for a moment did I imagine that one Cavalry Brigade with a mounted battery, and one Infantry Regiment with a mountain battery of 6.5, were supposed to be able to cut off the retreating march of the entire Turkish Army, and this on mountainous and very difficult ground.

I insist on laying emphasis on these details, because later at my trial a great effort was made to put the whole responsibility of the events, which followed, on me.

After communicating the orders of GHQ to Colonels Ziras and Nicolaides, I took the necessary steps to direct the rest of the division on Gheïlu-Deré. The march was carried out in two columns: (*a*) The 41st Infantry Regiment, the half-squadron of cavalry, one half-battery of the remaining brigade of mountain artillery of the XIIth, and a company of sappers marched via Eykus-oluk on Gheïlu-Deré; (*b*) the 46th Infantry Regiment and one half-battery of artillery marched by the valley of Kindar-Deré via Tshurdan on Gheïlu-Deré.

In coming to this decision, I was influenced by the following considerations—firstly, that to cross the mountain Kizil-Sivri in one column only would unduly lengthen out the division; secondly, I was informed by the local inhabitants that the distance between the two roads was insignificant and not as it was represented on the map. I marched with the first column. Late in the afternoon we arrived at Eykus-oluk, where we found the IInd Division marching towards Suduk-Eyzu, and to avoid marching on the same road I turned off to Tshurdan, where I ordered a halt for the night, as darkness had fallen. Tshurdan lies in a deep and extremely precipitous ravine, and above the village rises, steep and forbidding, the great mountain Turkmen-dagh, on the first slopes of which lay Gheïlu-Deré, 1,500 metres from Tshurdan, which is not even marked on the map.

Arrived in Tshurdan, I became seriously uneasy over the non-arrival of the 46th Regiment, which did not reach Gheïlu-Deré till 11 p.m. This delay was due to the impassability of the road at the bottom of the ravine, which ended at Tshurdan.

On the evening of 16 July, the general situation was as follows: The divisions on the extreme right (IInd, XIIth) had reached the district Tshurdan—Suduk-Eyzu. The 1st Division, having gained height 1799 after severe fighting, advanced to the north of Gheïkseri, the enemy retiring towards the railway station at Tsherkular. The losses of this division were considerable. The XIIIth Division (left of centre) was delayed before height 1210, northeast of Aksal-dagh, but finally advanced parallel with the Vth. The mixed detachment, after capturing the first line of defence, continued the attack on the main front line of Yalidjé-dagh. The left wing (VIIth, Xth), advancing on Kiutahia, occupied the line Yiundjali-Dedik. The enemy retired to the east and to the north. The northern group (IIIrd and XIth), occupying Akse-Bunar, was obliged to send a strong force to drive the enemy out of Kiupru Hissar, which he had captured in the meantime.

The above facts were completely unknown to me, when at Tshurdan, on the evening of the 16th, I had to face the problem of the advance for the following day. According to information received before the advance by aeroplane reconnaissance, the whole of the Turkmen-dagh was covered with trenches and fortifications, and we had a serious task before us, with a force weakened by the absence of the 14th Infantry Regiment. Of artillery, I had only one mountain battery, because the 4th Brigade of Mountain Artillery, which on 30 June had been attached to the XIIth, had not yet joined the division—a fact due to the ill-will and incapacity of the major commanding the brigade. Only on the following morning did he finally arrive to continue the march, and then only after I had been obliged to send the commander of my artillery, Colonel Criesis himself, to look for the major, whom he discovered following the IInd Division to Kuzil-oluk. But even with the addition of this brigade, it cannot be said that the division had any really useful artillery at its disposal.

The division was to march via Gheïlu-Deré–Latifié and, after crossing the lofty, thickly-wooded Turkmen-dagh, to continue on to Karghin through the pass of Bas-Euren.

This movement began early on the morning of 17 July over extremely hilly and precipitous ground, causing a great strain on the men from the beginning. About noon, on the height of Latifié, we met the two Skoda mountain guns captured by the IInd Division on the previous day, and beyond the village, far below us, we could see the column of the IInd Division heading towards the north-west.

Here I received news from GHQ that the enemy, after having been defeated, was retreating in disorder all along the line, and that the detachment before Ak In had been ordered to march straight to Eski-Shehr, to prevent him from retreating to the east. In the meantime, violent gunfire was heard to the north-east towards Ush-Serai, from which I concluded that the detachment had managed to pass Ak In, and to advance sufficiently to the north. It was clear, however, that they had been engaged in a fight with the hostile detachment, which was evidently guarding the flank of the retreating army; but the fact that, during the whole of that day, the sound of firing remained stationary, and was always heard coming from the same direction, and with the same intensity, showed that the detachment had not been able to advance further. It was impossible for me to lend assistance, not only on account of the distance, but principally because the disorderly retreat of the Turkish Army—according to the information of GHQ—necessitated my hastening the march of the division to Karghin, so as to cut off the retreat and effect, at any rate, a partial, if not a complete, blockade of the enemy army. It was only natural, for the reasons stated above, that I should feel anxious about the fate of my detachment, which the exaggerated optimism of GHQ had exposed, unsupported and alone, to the full weight of the retreating enemy. At that time, I had not the slightest reason to doubt that the retreat was being made in disorder; but, nevertheless, I considered the task entrusted to this detachment was extremely risky, not to say foolhardy.

The continuation of the march brought us close to the summit of the Turkmen-dagh (Hurtman Baba, 2,051 metres), and towards evening we reached the pass or rather the ravine of Bas-Euren. I marched with the head of the vanguard (41st Infantry Regiment). Just as we were approaching the pass, I saw coming towards me the commander of the half-squadron, Captain Zupas, who reported that, while attempting to reach Bas-Euren, sharp rifle fire had forced him to fall back. He was under the impression, however, that the opposition was not serious, and that the appearance of the infantry would put the enemy to flight. This information naturally did not prevent me from continuing the march. Nevertheless, hardly had the point of the vanguard entered the pass than a volley of rifle fire obliged it to deploy. After a while the first sections of the vanguard deployed likewise, but, unfortunately, the extremely steep slopes of the ravine did not permit of any large numbers deploying freely. This march had resulted in lengthening out the column terribly, and to an extent which was dangerous, and when I wanted to make use of the battery of the vanguard, I was obliged to wait a good hour before it appeared. After a long delay it managed to come up, just as the sun had set.

Notwithstanding this, I posted it at a bend in the pass, and ordered a few shots to be fired, more with the hope of frightening the enemy than of obtaining any real results. Unhappily it had no effect, as the enemy continued to keep up a lively fire, and, darkness supervening, I was obliged to halt where we were, and what was worse, inside the ravine and within range of the enemy's guns. It is remarkable that we had no losses, for the whole night long the enemy fired at us, and the bullets kept falling in the camp.

So far as I could judge, the enemy, retreating from Kiutahia, had observed the march of the division and realized the menace to his flank if it succeeded in debouching from Bas-Euren to Karghin in time. He therefore took steps to prevent this happening, and up to a certain point succeeded.

The division was obliged to halt on account of darkness; but still the presence of such a large force on its flank had caused the enemy some anxiety, as we were able to judge by the result the following morning. Nevertheless, the next day, 18 July, the enemy retired from Bas-Euren before sunrise, and as we came out on to the plain, we were confronted by a wonderful sight. We found eight guns abandoned: four Skoda of 15, three field Krupp of 7.5, and one long 105; all the fields, as far as Karghin, were covered with shells and every kind of materiel.

I arrived at Karghin about 9 a.m., and there received the first reports about the events which occurred in the district of Ush-Serai–Besh-Serai. These described what had happened as a disaster. A captain, belonging to the Cavalry Brigade, presented himself to me and reported that he was present at the death of Colonels Ziras and Nicolaides, of the chief of the brigade staff, Major Papagos, and several others; that the brigade and the 14th Infantry Regiment had been completely destroyed and the few survivors taken prisoners; and that he himself had only managed to escape with difficulty. I confess that I did not doubt the veracity of this officer's statement, in spite of his agitated manner, which was only natural after what had occurred, and of which he had been an eye-witness. Little by little other stragglers arrived from the scene of the disaster, and finally the truth came out.

The truth was undoubtedly bad, but the catastrophe was not such as the panic-stricken captain had imagined. The latter, to be able to flee faster, had ridden a horse which was not his; his own was found wandering on the spot two days later by the officer commanding the Vth Division, Colonel Trilivas, who happened to be passing there, and who kept the horse and rode it till the end of the campaign.

I can only say very little about the misfortune of Ush-Serai, because never to this day has this question been entirely elucidated. Accusations were made, inquiries were held, but the affair was always skilfully hushed up by certain elements at GHQ, because some of those who had been among the panic-stricken were united to the commander-in-chief by ties of relationship.

So far as I could verify the facts, the affair happened in the following way. During the afternoon of 16 July, the detachment had forced the enemy at Ak In to give way, and was thus able to continue its advance to Ush-Serai, near which it halted for the night. Colonel Ziras' character predisposed him to hold the enemy in contempt, and it seems that during the night of the 16–17th, he either did not take sufficient measures for the safety of the camp, or the troops on guard did not take the necessary precautions. In any case, the fact remains that at about 3 a.m. the enemy surprised and attacked the camp with rifle fire. While an attempt was being made to restore order amongst the troops, they were assailed by shell fire, which increased the general confusion. The ensuing action began under bad conditions for us, on account of the suddenness of the surprise; but, nevertheless, our troops fought well, in spite of the enemy receiving fresh reinforcements every minute. About noon some of the sections of the 14th began to give way, and very soon the entire regiment was retreating in disorder, notwithstanding the heroic self-sacrifice of the cavalry brigade and the desperate attempts of Colonel Ziras, who, with the regimental colours in his hand, attempted to stem the flight. The detachment was driven south-west towards the Turkmen-dagh; but, fortunately, the enemy did not pursue it, and the artillery brigade, as well as the battery of the brigade of mountain artillery of the XIIth, were able to save their guns, and to reach Latifié though they were exhausted. Some fugitives were driven to the northern base of the mountain, whence they rejoined the XIIth Division. The losses in killed and prisoners were very heavy, the greater part of the wounded were left behind, and cut to pieces by the Turks, according to the evidence of the Vth Division, which passed there soon after. This was the result of the ridiculous optimism of GHQ.

On my arrival at Karghin I found the general situation was as follows: the XIIth Division in Karghin, the IInd in Feduk, and the 1st a little to the left of the IInd. The 2nd Army Corps on the line Yukari–Purshak–Kaïnardji. The mixed detachment at Kiutahia. The left wing, after the fall of Kiutahia, had turned to the northeast and was pursuing the enemy to Eski-Shehr.

All the same, the main body of the enemy had succeeded in slipping away, in spite of all our efforts, some of his formations following the main road Kiutahia–Eski-Shehr, others by Feduk–Idjak–Demirli towards the north, and the remainder via Latifié to Eski-Shehr.

GHQ ordered a general pursuit, but on account of the new situation they were obliged to change the battle-front of the army. The 2nd Army Corps was ordered to proceed to Sidi-Ghazi via Suduk-Eyzu and Tshurdan, and thus form the right wing of the army. The new centre was composed of a group formed by the IInd and XIIth Divisions, which was placed under my orders, with, as objective, the fortifications of Sultan-dagh, south of Eski-Shehr. The 1st Division was in reserve in the rear. The mixed detachment was on the road east of the River Purshak; and, lastly, the left wing was west of the river, while the northern group remained at In-Eunu (north-west of Eski-Shehr).

On 19 July, for what reason I do not know, the group under my command was dissolved, the divisions of which it was composed being placed under the 1st

Army Corps as before. On the same day the army corps marched via Demirli to Kirka and, as the XIIth Division was at the tail of the column, we did not leave Karghin before 2 p.m. In the evening, as we were approaching Kirka we saw fighting in the distance. It was the two divisions, assaulting the Sultan-dagh. The night of the 19–20th we passed at Kirka.

On 20 July, the 1st Army Corps despatched the XIIth Division to Asanghi Aïlidjé to act as reserve to the other two divisions. We started at 4:30 a.m. and arrived about 11 a.m. at the above-named place. In the meantime, calm had supervened in the north; the enemy was evidently abandoning the Sultan-dagh, but a cavalry reconnaissance reported serious fighting at Ush-Besh. There was no doubt that this was the 2nd Army Corps, which, on rounding the slopes of Turkmen-dagh, had come into contact with that part of the enemy which had remained there after dispersing Ziras' detachment.

The night passed quietly, although we were expecting the enemy to attack the camp any minute. On 21 July, I received from the 1st Army Corps the order to march direct to Derbend, but owing to information that reached us from Ush-Besh that the Vth Division was engaged in a serious struggle, and as heavy firing could be heard from that direction, I decided to lead my division to Kayadjik, so as to come to the assistance of the Vth in case of need. I immediately reported my decision to the 1st Army Corps, informing them at the same time that I was already proceeding in that direction. The answer from the corps approving my action was not slow in arriving. Near Kayadjik I came up with the Vth and was informed that the division, after having forced the enemy to give way, was steadily advancing towards Yenikeui via Aïvali; so I promptly turned to the north and marched in the direction of Derbend.

That day the battle formation of the Greek Army was as follows: the 2nd Army Corps (right wing) lay south and east of Sidi-Ghazi; the 1st Army Corps (centre) was concentrated in the district Tshel Hanar-dagh–Derbend. The mixed detachment south of Eski-Shehr. The 3rd Army Corps (left wing), which had entered Eski-Shehr at 6 p.m. the evening before, had reached the line east of Eski-Shehr, Tshaulum (on the railway line)–Ushak–Boghaz. The northern group occupied Boz-Eyuk (on the railway line west of Eski-Shehr).

The Turkish Army continued its retirement in perfect order to the east, protecting this movement with strong rear and flank guards, thus imposing a great strain on our divisions, who were attempting to check this retreat. GHQ were well aware of the necessity of this, when they ordered a general pursuit, but, unlike us at the front, the Supreme Command considered the defeat of the enemy at Kiutahia to have been complete, and the consequent retreat a disorderly flight. I do not know on what facts GHQ had based a conception so far removed from reality; nevertheless, I do not think that this impression could have been created by the reports from the front, where we were always able to appreciate the remaining fighting capacity of the enemy. I can in all good faith declare that

GHQ had not foreseen as being possible the events of 21 July, when they suddenly found themselves facing a counterattack by the enemy, and if this counterattack was not completely successful, this was exclusively and solely owing to the bravery of the troops, and to the spirit of initiative shown by the leaders. I must also add that this unjustified optimism of the Supreme Command succeeded in diminishing to a certain extent the caution of some of the divisional commanders, who had before been convinced that the last battles had been fought against the main body of the enemy and not the rearguards.

On the morning of 21 July, the divisions of the 3rd Army Corps, near the line Tshaulum–Ushak–Boghaz, were violently attacked, and they only succeeded in repulsing this attack with great difficulty. The enemy's principal effort appeared to be directed at the gap between the 3rd and the 1st Army Corps, but this having been luckily perceived in time, the officer commanding the cavalry brigade, Colonel Nikolaides, was able to delay the enemy's advance until the 1st Division from Sup-Euren could fill the gap. The IInd Division, on the right flank, was attacked near Derbend, before it left its camp, but managed to deploy and to push back the enemy. Still further to the right the XIIth Division, coming out of Kivzuk, came into contact with strong forces, which were obviously attempting to insert themselves between the 1st and 2nd Army Corps. Lastly, the Vth Division encountered strong opposition beyond Aïvali, and on the extreme right the XIIIth Division near Sidi-Ghazi had to face a violent attack from the north.

As I was marching towards Kivzuk I heard from all directions the sounds of the heavy firing of the battle then beginning, but as I had received no information about the situation I was unable to make out exactly what was happening. Hardly had the vanguard of the division (46th Infantry) come out of the village of Kivzuk than it was met by severe rifle and gun fire from the heights on the other side of a valley, which spread to the northern entrance of the village. The whole of the 46th Regiment deployed, and two battalions of the 41st wheeled to the left of the former towards the height Taktali-Baba, which was occupied by infantry and artillery.

The configuration of the ground north of Kivzuk is as follows: A cart track to Alpanos runs in a northerly direction along the bottom of a long and narrow valley, which is crossed at right angles by another; the latter, running east and west, falls towards the east into the plain of Mumum Tsifiik–Dish Veran.

The two valleys form between them the letter 'T'. The valley running to the north is bounded on both sides by fairly steep heights, these being especially steep on its eastern side. The other valley is bounded on its northern side by heights, whose bare earth sides slope very gradually in the direction of Alpanos, but become extremely steep towards the west, where they merge into the high and rocky knoll of Taktali-Baba, which dominates Derbend and the plain lying to the north of it.

The enemy, as I said before, was occupying the Taktali-Baba and a part of the heights stretching to the east of it. The advance of the 46th was carried out without much difficulty, because, as I afterwards realized, the enemy had all his attention focussed on the IInd Division fighting to the south of Derbend. Although I was not expecting to meet the enemy at this point, it nevertheless was obvious that the presence of the XIIth Division was not known to him until the moment it came out of Kivzuk. It was, indeed, fortunate that I had taken my division by this particular route, because if I had marched straight on to Derbend and not via Kivzuk to Alpanos, a large gap would have been created between the IInd and Vth Divisions, into which the enemy undoubtedly would have forced himself.

The battle commenced about 2:30 p.m. The infantry advanced with decision and in excellent heart to the attack of the enemy positions. Unfortunately, I cannot give the artillery (4th Brigade Mountain Artillery, and one battery of the 12th) the same praise. Owing to the characteristic incapacity of their leaders, they were unnecessarily slow in occupying the indicated positions, and when they finally began to fire, sent a few shells into our infantry, who were advancing to the attack of Taktali-Baba.

About 8 p.m. the enemy was defeated and the Taktali-Baba captured, and from the top of the hills, lying to the south of Alpanos, we enjoyed a spectacle of the retreat of the whole Turkish Army. From these hills we could see long columns marching from west to east, and raising clouds of dust crossing the plain far to the east of Eski-Shehr. The distance from us was not great, about 6,000 to 7,000 metres, and bitterly did I regret the absence of heavier guns with which to harass the retreat of the enemy army.

This battle of 21 July was the result of the enemy's attempt to profit by the exhaustion of the Greeks, and the large gaps between the units, which had been created during our pursuit. The rooted idea of GHQ that at Kiutahia we had put to flight the main body of the Turkish Army led to the slackening of the necessary connections between the units, and the impetus of the pursuit had resulted in the creation of gaps between the divisions. It was, therefore, natural that the enemy, having kept his liberty of action, should attempt to profit by them. And that is what occurred; for we found ourselves suddenly faced by a violent counterattack from the main body of the Turkish Army, and though this failed, its failure certainly was not due to the strategy, foresight, or tactical abilities of GHQ, who were still at Kiutahia and consequently unable to direct the battle.

The repulse of the Turkish counterattack was chiefly due to the initiative of the commander of the cavalry brigade, Colonel Nikolaïdes; and, secondly, to the chance intervention of the XIIth Division at a most critical time. By this I do not wish to minimize the actions of the other units, which fought with great courage. I only maintain that if the enemy had succeeded in establishing himself between the 1st and 3rd Army Corps, as well as between the 1st and 2nd Army Corps, all the efforts of the other units would not have been able to prevent a most serious setback to the Greek Army, and possibly a severe defeat.

No pursuit being ordered, the division spent the night on the battlefield. A dressing station was established near a well in the valley, and there the wounded, about 300, were tended, and transported the following day in bullock-carts and by other means to Eski-Shehr. I am here afforded an opportunity to express my appreciation of the capacity and self-sacrifice of the chief surgeon of the division, Bravakos, whose high efficiency and energy conquered all obstacles.

The next day, the 22nd, I wrote the following letter to Lieutenant-General Papulas, as I was desirous of acquainting him with the condition of the division:

July 22nd, 1921.

Sir,

I have the honour to lay before you certain facts with regard to the Division under my command, and earnestly to request that immediate steps may be taken to comply with the indispensable requirements which I enumerate later.

The circumstances in which I was given command of the XIIth Division are well known to you, but strictly speaking I was not given a Division at all.

Of Infantry there were only, properly speaking, two Regiments, the 14th and 41st; the third Regiment, the 46th, being composed of the riffraff of which the various companies in Thrace wished to be rid.

It is an absolute fact that an entire Punishment Training Company was transferred to the 46th Regiment. Cavalry, medical personnel, ammunition columns were non-existent. These deficiencies were made good within a week, but only by collecting the odds and ends of men and materiel remaining in Smyrna.

Of Artillery there was only one Mountain Brigade, and though I received a promise that one Field Battery and one half battery of Skodas would be supplied to the Division, one battery was taken away from me before it had even been used, and the Skoda half battery has never been received. One Brigade of Mountain Artillery was certainly sent me by the IVth Div., but its personnel was so ignorant that for days it was unable even to find the Division, in spite of all my instructions. It was so untrained that in yesterday's action at Alpanos, in which the Division fought for 6 hours against a strongly entrenched force of 8,000 men, only 4 guns of one battery (the other was with Ziras' detachment) supported the attack. The Brigade, during the whole of the action, was engaged in making endless reconnaissances, and when it did fire once, it fired at our own troops.

As to means of communication, the Division is deficient in wireless, heliographs and horses, and it has never received the operation orders in time for action to be taken on them. It has had to regulate its movements entirely by local indications and always has found itself completely isolated.

In spite of all these deficiencies, the Division by immense efforts has accomplished longer marches than any other, having been continually on the move since July 6th.

In following the itinerary Inei–Afium–Kara–Hissar–Tshekes–Ak In, it crossed the Turkmendagh twice, once from the South to support the Vth Division and once in order to reach Alpanos. It came into action against the enemy at Afium–Kara-Hissar, at Kirk Kaya, Akin and Baseuren, where it forced him to abandon 8 guns and a large quantity of matériel. Finally, yesterday it succeeded, with only two Regiments and one battery, in pushing back an enemy force of equal strength, thus facilitating the advance of the Vth Division.

Though the above results have been obtained by tremendous efforts, there is no certainty that this will be possible in the future, as the Division is lacking in the essentials to its continued existence as such.

Today the fighting portion of the Division is reduced to two Regiments and one Mountain Battery, of which the 14th Regiment requires to be reorganized; the other battery of the Mountain Artillery Brigade is with the mixed Detachment, and it also requires refitting. The IVth Artillery Brigade is useless to me, unless a trained personnel is provided.

If, during yesterday's battle, the Division had had some Field Artillery or a half battery of Skoda, it could have put to flight the enemy columns, which were retiring undisturbed, instead of the Division, with its two Regiments and Mountain Battery, having to struggle to dislodge the enemy from the heights of Alpanos.

I lay no claim for anything out of the ordinary to be done for my Division, nor do I demand, though I think it is my right, to command a Division formed like any other. I simply ask for the addition of the absolutely indispensable means to enable my Division to continue to fight, and which in my opinion are as follows:

(1) *Artillery.*—One Brigade of Field Artillery or one half battery of Skodas, one of the two to be in exchange for the IVth Brigade of Mountain Artillery, which is useless to me.

(The IInd Division disposes of 32 guns.)

(2) *Means of Communication.*—At least 2-3 heliographs and a few riding horses. (I am informed that other Divisions, possessing wireless also, have more than 5 heliographs.)...

To this letter, Lieutenant-General Papulas answered as follows:

Sir,

I received your letter and I hasten to answer and to express to you my sincere congratulations on the action of your Division.

I recognize the insufficient means which the Division possesses and the condition in which it was, and that these difficulties have been surmounted entirely according to my expectations.

I have already ordered everything possible to be done to complete the deficiencies, in proportion to the means at my disposal, and the Army Corps will send you field artillery. I will send you one Skoda battery as soon as it arrives, as I have had a telegram that it is being sent. Unfortunately for the present there is no wireless apparatus, but I will send you some, as soon as we are provided with any. But for the present you will receive a heliograph. I have ordered boots and other supplies, which are being sent to us; you will be supplied from these at the first opportunity.

The steps taken by you and your staff give me the assurance that your Division will be rapidly reorganized, so that it can continue once more to show itself worthy of the work entrusted to it.

I hope very soon to give you the command of an Army Corps.

Yours sincerely,
A. Papulas.

On 23 July, the burial of the dead took place. They were buried in graves on the southern slope of the Taktali-Baba in a small wood of low trees. On the graves were placed some stones in the shape of a cross, and the whole was covered with earth, so as to avoid destruction at the hands of the Turks. I do not doubt but that the graves are intact to this day.

During the afternoon, the division was concentrated in a camp near Alpanos, as reserve to the army corps, and there I received the order of the 1st Army Corps to suspend operations, and with this order the first period of the campaign was concluded.

2

From 23 July to 13 August

To show what the views of GHQ were as to the situation after the Battle of Eski-Shehr, I append the report of the commander-in-chief on the military situation of 21 July, and the announcement of the battle made to the government by the minister of war, who was then at Ushak.

Report on the Military Situation,
July 21st

The great Battle of Eski-Shehr ended in a complete and notable victory for our heroic troops.

The pursuit of the fleeing enemy continued during the whole of yesterday, reaching within 45 kilometres east of Eski-Shehr.

From orders found on captured officers of superior rank it appears that the enemy, having collected practically all his forces, attacked, with the intention of retaking Eski-Shehr, thus giving our troops the opportunity of obtaining this notable victory.

The remaining enemy forces, marching by night, are fleeing to Sivri Hissar and to the north. Up to the present 40 guns, machine-guns, many prisoners and a quantity of rifles and ammunition have been reported as taken by our troops, but an exact return of the booty captured, as a result of the rapid pursuit of the enemy, has not yet been received.

C.-in-C. of the Army in Asia Minor,
A. Papulas.

The minister of war, N. Theotoky, who was in Ushak, sent the following report of the battle to Athens:

> I have pleasure in announcing the news of another great victory for our army and I subjoin a report from C.-in-C. Papulas just received.
>
> The army after occupying Eski-Shehr was ordered to occupy the ridge of Tanismas, north of the railway line; another section of the army to occupy Tshilhanar-dagh up to Derbend and to pursue the enemy towards Aksakali-Azakli; another army section to pursue him through the pass of Akin-Sidi-Ghazi towards the east; and yet another section was posted on the extreme left of the army in In Eynu. Thus the whole army is established in position. The enemy profiting by the concentration of almost all his forces, amounting to 14 divisions and 3 cavalry divisions, and counting perhaps on finding our army exhausted by its long marches and in an unadvantageous position as a result of the pursuit through mountain passes, attacked yesterday, 21st, early in the morning, along the whole of our front from a distance of 5 kilometres N.W. of Eski-Shehr to Boz-Eyuk, attempting to envelop our flanks, but principally to break through our centre, with 4 divisions, on the high plateau of Tshil Hanlar.
>
> The army holding itself in readiness, according to orders, repulsed the enemy attack as soon as it developed, and attacking in its turn pushed back the enemy all along the line and pursued him up to the ridge of Boz-dagh in the north, and eastwards beyond Ushak-Boghazik and towards Mahmudié in the south-east.
>
> The cavalry brigade charged the fleeing enemy with the sword. The enemy suffered serious losses, abandoning their wounded all over the battlefield. We captured numerous prisoners, guns, and a quantity of war material, of which the exact amount is not yet known.

The above clearly shows the attempts of GHQ to prove that our undoubted victory of 21 July had ended in the destruction of the enemy. Such attempts are pardonable if they are intended to lend more brilliance to the glory of this military achievement for the purpose of reanimating the sentiments in the interior of the country and the morale of the fighting troops; but between this and the complete misrepresentation of the real situation in an official report to the government, there is, I think, a great difference.

This report states that the enemy lost forty guns and a quantity of rifles and ammunition, and that his remaining forces fled towards Sivri-Hissar. As far as I know, the enemy did not lose more than twenty-seven guns, and the number of captured rifles was proportionately less; on the other hand, the statement about the flight of the enemy is misleading, because those who saw this flight with their own eyes—of whom I was one—saw that it took the form of an orderly retreat. It is no doubt true that a retreat is always a flight, but there is a great difference between an orderly retreat and a disorderly one. What I have just written refers especially to the military report, but neither does the communiqué made by the minister of war respect the truth, for it describes the chance disposition of the troops as being the result of the deliberate calculations of GHQ, whereas (as was well known at the front) GHQ, after the occupation of Kiutahia, judged the enemy's retreat to be a rout, and directed the divisions to pursue him, without taking into consideration the possibility of a counterattack. Everyone is liable to make a mistake, and no one likes to acknowledge having done so, but the communiqué goes on to insist on the complete flight of the enemy when pursued by us, his serious losses, and the capture of numerous prisoners, guns, and war materiel; whereas the truth was that the enemy lost but a very small fraction of all this, and that our pursuit ceased immediately after the battle.

I remember the discussions that took place between various officers, in which they laid stress on the small number of guns and prisoners captured, which showed that the defeat of the enemy was not complete. The military depots of Eski-Shehr were empty, and the capture of twenty-seven guns taken before 21 July surely did not mean that the enemy had lost the greater part of his artillery! There is a vast difference between destroying the enemy and defeating him, and I think that GHQ took a great responsibility upon themselves when, in their report to the government and the general public, they presented the fortunate issue of the operations since 12 July in a light that was far removed from the reality.

It was forgotten that 'the size of the victory is reckoned according to the relatively large or small proportion of the enemy forces destroyed or captured, to the extent of the territory conquered, the importance of the economical resources captured, and the enemy communications that have been seized' (Colonel F. Culmann). Of the above conditions only the one relating to territory had been fulfilled, and that was of no great importance if one takes into consideration the vastness of its uninhabited areas, but with regard to the other conditions these pans of victory are not in any way justified.

In order to make the Turks surrender, they should have been made to suffer the greatest losses in men and materiel; but they were not driven back in flight. They were merely defeated and then retreated in good order, and this fact gave rise to the idea that it would be necessary to push forward as far as Angora to obtain complete success.

If the Battle of Eski-Shehr was such a great catastrophe for the enemy as the reports maintained, the idea of continuing the campaign as far as Angora would naturally not have arisen, as it would have been superfluous, for once the Turkish Army was destroyed the enemy would have been obliged to accept our terms. In spite of this, the plan for this campaign was worked out, and I am, therefore, forced to conclude that GHQ did not speak the truth, either in their communiqué or in their report to the government. It was natural for the government to believe that the military situation had been correctly described by the report from GHQ, and to outline their future policy according to it, for the situation thus presented to the government bore an unexpectedly optimistic aspect.

The enemy, though not entirely destroyed, was reported to be in such a state of dissolution that a slight effort would suffice to complete his downfall, and encouragements from abroad for a complete Greek domination in Asia Minor were being received. In these circumstances, Ministers Gunaris and Theotoky could not be expected to realize that it was imperative to bring the campaign to an end, and formally to declare to those who were urging on the continuation of the campaign from abroad, that Greece could not continue to fight without immediate active support and supplies. How could they realize that the army was in need of being reinforced and entirely re-equipped, so as to enable it to march against the Turkish Army, whose condition was being improved with material received from Russia and other countries? How was it possible, I say, for the government to judge otherwise, when the opinion of its military advisers was in favour of continuing the campaign, and when they thought the army capable of doing so in its present condition? Being politicians, they did not know the state the army was in. For them, the decision to continue represented a definite political line; the army was merely an instrument, and their military advisers assured them not only of the possibility but of the expediency of the execution of this policy. It would in truth have been strange if they had not been convinced by these assurances. Of course, there were many officers who judged the situation as extremely serious, and, when questioned, they declared that unless certain definite measures were taken, all idea of continuing the campaign was, to say the least, risky, but they had no right to express a responsible opinion. They were commanders of army corps and divisions, who could do nothing but submit to the orders of the Supreme Command.

As we shall see later, the decision to continue the campaign was not unanimously agreed upon—one, at least, of the responsible members was strongly opposed to it, and this was the commander-in-chief himself.

Also, it was not decided to extend the campaign merely in the direction of Angora, but to advance and capture that town, as is seen in all the orders of the GHQ.

Major-General X. Stratigos, in his review of the campaign, says that the decision was taken 'with a full knowledge of the tremendous difficulties, as regards topographical conditions and the immense distances which would hamper the task of the Greek Army.' May I be permitted to doubt this? for, judging from subsequent events in which I took part, I could tell how little, from every point of view, the campaign had been studied and prepared for.

Finally, I must remark that the way Major-General Stratigos seeks to introduce the king's person into this question is misleading and out of place. I say this because the king never interfered more than was necessary in this question, leaving the responsibility for the decision and the execution of the plan to his advisers—a fact that Major-General Stratigos knew better even than myself, and it is a regrettable symptom of incompetence to seek to cloak grave responsibilities with the person of the king.

Major-General Stratigos's argument is based on an effort to prove the military necessity for a continuation of the campaign towards Angora. There is no doubt whatsoever that from a theoretical and military point of view, this opinion is correct. But between the military necessity of carrying out certain operations and the possibility of executing them lies a great difference. The execution depends on the means at one's disposal.

Major-General Stratigos tries to show the situation of the army after the battle of 21 July in such a light as to convince us that the continuation of the campaign was logical and easy, as well as essential; whereas it was not so.

Reading between the lines of his book, it appears that Major-General Stratigos well understood that the battle of 21 July was not decisive—that is to say, that the enemy did not suffer such a defeat as was described in the military communiqué; but, in spite of that, he tries to prove that the victory was an important one, and the defeat of the enemy equally great. Whereas, as I have shown, the enemy suffered no serious losses, and retreated in good order, unpursued, to his principal positions, which had been prepared some time before, and where he intended to fight the final battle.

Major-General Stratigos, rightly convinced of the military necessity of the continuation of the campaign, after the 'dissolution' of the enemy on 21 July, was under the influence of GHQ, who, being far from the front, imagined the military situation to be different from what it was. Otherwise it would be difficult to explain how it happened that all the officers at the front considered the continuation to be a perilous and hazardous undertaking unless the necessary preparations were made beforehand. It was perhaps natural for Major-General Stratigos to be influenced by the results which such strategy would achieve, and to hope by this means to bring the war to a successful conclusion, without sufficiently taking into consideration the inexperience and self-conceit of some of those at GHQ; and it was natural for the two ministers to listen to the opinion of their military adviser, who was also a parliamentary deputy.

On 26 July I had a meeting at Eski-Shehr with Major-General Kondulis, commander of the 1st Army Corps, under whose orders I happened to be. I had a long discussion with him on the military situation, and saw to my satisfaction that our views agreed on all points. We were both of the opinion that for the purpose of such a tremendous undertaking—the advance to Angora—it was necessary, above all, for the army to be reorganized, reinforced, and refitted, and this could only be done by ordering a general mobilization, and, if for political and technical reasons this was not possible, then, at any rate, by calling up a certain number of classes of the reserves. Only then did we think that a further advance could safely be undertaken, because it was necessary to strengthen the army with men and regular officers, seeing that the enemy had retired on the 21st with insignificant losses. We also took into consideration that the enemy had retreated towards his base at Angora. From here the railway could supply him with all his requirements of men and material and enable him to make a very strong defensive under the most favourable conditions. It was certainly possible to suppose that a menace on our part would cause him to retire still more to the east to avoid the decisive battle; but this supposition should never push into the background the possibility of a defensive opposition beyond the River Sakharia. Finally, in our opinion, the success of an advance to Angora could only be assured by strongly reinforcing our army.

In any case, it was of paramount importance for the troops to be refitted, as their clothing and boots had been more or less worn out during the first period of the operations, the rifle equipment and field guns needed repairs and in many cases would have to be replaced altogether. In addition to this we had practically no heavy artillery, and what we had was more productive of difficulties than of genuine utility on account of its worn-out material, which had been used by the French and English at Verdun and Salonica. Our air service was in a wretched state. This was not so much the fault of the 'personnel', who worked zealously in spite of being understaffed and inexperienced, as of the very bad and worn-out character of the material. The morale of the men, although fairly good still, was no longer the same as during the attack of 12 July.

I had no opportunity of discussing the situation with Major-General Polymenakos of the 3rd Army Corps, but I learnt through Major-General Kondulis that the former also agreed with what I have just said.

All this would take time and money no doubt, but it would have been far better to impose this fresh sacrifice on the country, than to allow the army to be drawn totally unprepared into such an undertaking. GHQ had distorted the truth after the Battle of Eski-Shehr, and public opinion was convinced that, as things were, a fresh sacrifice was superfluous. I believe that if the real situation had been stated sincerely and openly we should not have had any difficulty in obtaining the necessary means to ensure a successful issue to the campaign.

The military situation was such, that it was impossible for any officer, who was not voluntarily blind, to imagine that the advance to Angora would prove to be easy and comfortable.

On 27 July, I went to Kiutahia, where I met Lieutenant-General Papulas, and I asked him about his intentions. The commander-in-chief, without any hedging, frankly expressed his opinion, that we ought to content ourselves with our present acquisitions, and not take further risks; but he added, nevertheless, that the government had requested, through the Premier Gunaris and the Minister of War Theotoky, that the campaign should be continued until the enemy was completely defeated. The commander-in-chief spoke in blunt terms against these ideas, and announced his intention to resign if he saw that the government persisted in them.

General Kondulis and the author.

I could not do otherwise than encourage the commander-in-chief in his views, as I entirely agreed with him about the dangers of new operations without the necessary measures being taken beforehand. The ideas and views of Colonels Pallis and Saryannis were directly opposed to those of Lieutenant-General Papulas, who was very much upset by this opposition, and protested that they not only did not take his views into consideration, but attempted to make him radically alter them.

Colonel Pallis's opinion was that everything said against a further advance was exaggerated, and that the enemy could not oppose any serious resistance.

As to Colonel Saryannis, this officer, a legacy of the former commander-in-chief Paraskevopulos, was, as I have already mentioned, considered to be the only man who understood the situation in Asia Minor, and without his advice the whole campaign was doomed to shipwreck. His views and opinions were the gospel of every operation. No one took into any consideration his behaviour in London, where he sealed the mouths of Maréchal Foch and General Georges, when they attempted to give their opinions, and he became the principal cause of the disasters of December and March. In spite of his conduct as military adviser to the Greek Mission in persuading it to order those fateful operations, he was kept in his place, and his advice continued to be taken seriously.

After my interview with Lieutenant-General Papulas, I saw the minister of war, who, with much energy and at great length, explained the necessity of going to Angora, so that we should be rewarded by the final destruction of the enemy. The minister could see by my answers and objections that I did not agree with these ideas, and asked me if I did not consider that the enemy had been destroyed after the battle of 21 July. I explained to him that theoretically—i.e., from a military point of view—it was impossible for me not to agree with the continuation of the campaign, seeing that the result of the Battle of Eski-Shehr had not been decisive. It was not sufficient, however, to continue the campaign in theory. It had also to be continued in practice, and this was not feasible, according to my mind, without first taking certain definite measures—and I gave my views as to what measures I considered indispensable under the conditions. The minister answered that, as regards the re-equipment of the troops, supplies of every kind were to be had in abundance in Athens and Smyrna, but he deemed it superfluous to call any more classes of the reserve to arms, seeing that the enemy had suffered a severe check. The advance to Angora was imperative in his opinion, because the enemy not having yet been destroyed it was absolutely necessary to complete his destruction. He added that our action would not be very important, as it would be more in the nature of a 'raid' (*sic*).

The foregoing conversation convinced me that the minister had not grasped what the military situation was. He considered that the enemy, if not actually destroyed, had been severely shaken, and that our existing forces were sufficient to continue the operations; and, finally, this use of the foreign word 'raid' moved my curiosity to discover how much he had understood of the situation. I therefore asked him what he meant by the words 'raid to Angora', and if by this he meant an action by the cavalry brigade, perhaps strengthened by an infantry detachment, and I received the reply that this meant the entire army taking part in the 'raid' to Angora. I did not insist further, my opinion not having any authority beyond explaining the situation in regard to the XIIth Division; besides, I had expressed my opinion when questioned, and I had no right to go beyond that, or to insist on my views being taken against those of the responsible military advisers of the government.

I left Kiutahia disheartened with all I had heard, and with a strong presentiment of trouble to come.

I afterwards learnt from Lieutenant-General Papulas how a final decision to continue the campaign to Angora came to be taken. Much has been said and written about this decision more or less approaching the truth, but my own knowledge of it is derived from conversations with the commander-in-chief and Colonel Pallis, the chief of the staff at GHQ.

Lieutenant-General Papulas, as he confessed to me, absolutely refused to give his consent to this operation, and even threatened to resign in the event of his staff and the government insisting on their views. The commander-in-chief showed his disapproval before the council, but, in spite of that, he agreed to act against his personal conviction. When I met the commander-in-chief after the retreat, I well recollect the bitterness with which he expressed himself against the government and certain members of his staff—especially against Colonel Saryannis —who had lured him into acquiescence.

Unfortunately the members of the staff at GHQ understood the commander-in-chief's character pretty clearly, and played on the strings of his well-known egotism and ambition with great dexterity; for while Lieutenant-General Papulas was not lacking in all-round common sense, his ignorance of the science of war forced him to follow blindly the advice of his staff, especially when they tried to overcome any opposition on his part induced by his own logical reasonings, by making use of arguments which brought visions of victory and glory before his eyes. Colonel Pallis, on the other hand, though he did not share the views of those who judged the expedition to be dangerous under the conditions proposed, still considered the undertaking far from easy from a technical point of view, nor did he think it could be lightly undertaken.

Unfortunately, the Ministers Gunaris and Theotoky, who were in Kiutahia discussing the military situation with Colonel Saryannis, formed a very optimistic view of it, and this probably influenced the manner in which they put the question of the continuation of the operations to Angora before the commander-in-chief and his staff. While Lieutenant-General Papulas listened, Colonel Pallis expounded his opinion at length, accentuating the difficulties of such an expedition, especially of the transport of supplies, owing to the great distances, the nature of the ground, and the fatigue which the troops would have to endure. To the prime minister's remark that some of the staff thought that this expedition would be easy to carry out, he replied that the views he was giving were neither personal nor theoretical, but represented the responsible opinion of the Supreme Command.

After a long discussion, the Prime Minister Gunaris, who was very properly considering how to profit politically by the military situation, put the following three questions to Colonel Pallis, always in the presence of the silent commander-in-chief:

(*a*) Was the present situation such as to permit the government to base their future line of policy on it—that is to say, was the destruction of the enemy such that our army could hereafter remain safe and undisturbed in the occupied territory?

(*b*) Did the present situation permit of a gradual demobilization of the classes of reserves under arms?

(*c*) Should the answer to the above questions be in the negative, what further action did the commander-in-chief propose?

The chief of staff answered the first two questions in the negative, defining the task the army had still to execute as follows:

> The advance will have to be continued until contact with the enemy has been established; and in the event of his having retired beyond Angora—towards Sevastia or Cesarea—the army will at any rate have reached his capital. But if the Turkish army should not have retreated far, we shall have to attack them, and Col. Pallis had no doubt but that we should be victorious. But if the enemy should elect to remain where he is, the two armies would meet and then the advance of the army to Angora will depend on the condition of the weather. Nothing could be done, however, unless more means of transport were provided, especially motor lorries, so as to minimize the difficulties of the great distances.

These were the opinions of the Supreme Command. The ministers were in accord, and the premier announced that the government would place at the disposal of the army the requisite number of motor lorries and the different kinds of supplies required.

The commander-in-chief did not take part in the discussion—the presence of the king, he told me, made him speechless. The decisions were taken without his co-operation, and if he finally accepted the views of his staff, he did so out of ignorance and because he had not the moral courage to persist in his views, which would have entailed his resignation from the post of commander-in-chief, and this would not have suited his blind ambitions.

The opinion of the staff was drawn up in a written report to the government in the following form:

> Memorandum on the Operations of the
> Army in Asia Minor.
>
> (*a*) With the occupation of Eski-Shehr and the breaking up of the enemy on the front Eski-Shehr–Afium-Karahissar, the first period of the campaign was concluded.
>
> (*b*) The aim of the second period is the disruption of the Kemalist forces, or their removal from the Eski-Shehr front in such a manner that their concentration before it will either be rendered impossible or will demand a great amount of time and means which the enemy does not possess at the present time.

(*c*) To attain this, the army must carry out raids on Angora, and if it should come into contact with enemy forces, the latter must be crushed, the enemy supplies concentrated in Angora must be destroyed, and if after that the enemy does not surrender, the army must return to Eski-Shehr after completely destroying the railway line, as to remain longer in Angora will be of no advantage.

(*d*) After this incursion it is improbable that Kemal will be able to keep together a large force, much less an entire army, which, deprived of means of transport, would be unable to leave the railway line and approach the Eski-Shehr front in force.

(*e*) The expedition to Angora presents certain difficulties such as the great distances to be covered (Eski-Shehr to Angora via Sivri-Hissar is 265 kilometres, via Tshiftelar-Inlar is more than 300 km.), the bad condition of the roads, the impossibility of crossing the rivers Sakharia and Purshak except by bridges, and the season of heavy rains which begins in September causing, among other disadvantages, the principal difficulty of supplies.

(*f*) The study of the undertaking made up to the present has led G.H.Q. to the conclusion that it would be possible to advance as far as the eastern section of the Sakharia, viz., the line Beilik-Kiopru–Kavak.

(*g*) If, in that march, the army should meet the enemy and crush him, then the pursuit towards Angora by a portion of the force will present no difficulty. But if on the contrary the enemy should retreat beyond the Sakharia, the army will either have to advance or halt according to the conditions which prevail at the time. That is to say, if, for example, the railway line is captured undamaged and the roads and motor lorries are in good condition, etc., the advance can continue; otherwise the army must return to Eski-Shehr after destroying the railway line from Beilik-Kiopru up to 100 km. east of Eski-Shehr.

In Kiutahia July 28th, 1921.
The C.-in-C. of the army in Asia Minor.
A. Papulas

The above was submitted to HM the king, the prime minister, and the minister of war on 28 July 1921.

That which characterizes or ought to characterize a military document—i.e., clearness and accuracy—are conspicuous by their absence. The above memorandum is not clear, and betrays some uncertainty on the part of those who were responsible for it. It is certainly correct to say that the first period of the operations was over, but it is incorrect to say that the enemy had been broken up, because this had not been done. It would be more correct to say that the enemy had been pushed back. This inaccuracy makes the breaking up of the enemy appear to have been the result of the first period of the operations, and that the subsequent dissolution of the enemy, or his removal from the Eski-Shehr front, is to form part of the plan of operations for the second period.

Which of the two was implied? If it was a question of the enemy having been broken up, there would be no necessity for plans to drive him back, because an enemy who has been broken up is not able to concentrate or attack. If, on the other hand, it was a question of removing the enemy from the front, there remained no other means than to attack him; consequently, in either case, an attack on the enemy is understood by this. If this is true, why does paragraph (*c*) refer to this in the words 'if it should come into contact with enemy forces'? This implies, I imagine, that GHQ were vague as to whether the enemy was still in front of us or not, which ought to have been an impossibility, considering that the army possessed an air service, and intelligence bureaux, and that there was available the information from prisoners and deserters who arrived daily.

Why is use made of the word 'raids', and even in the plural? This word was used by the minister of war when he spoke to me at Kiutahia. As far as I know, this word in open warfare means an action on a large scale, chiefly by cavalry, or cavalry accompanied by infantry, a destructive action, but principally a rapid action, destined to create a disturbance at a given spot in the enemy's country. It anyhow does not mean an operation by nine divisions of infantry against a fortified enemy. The use of this word in the plural is incomprehensible, for 'raids' on Angora could not possibly be undertaken by a whole army acting as if it consisted only of a brigade of cavalry with horse artillery. The idea of these raids on Angora makes the defeat of the enemy forces a secondary matter, the only remark referring to this being that he is to be crushed when encountered. The principal objective is stated to be Angora and the destruction of the enemy's stores there; whereas, as we know, the principal aim of every military operation is to meet the enemy and annihilate him. The vagueness of the phraseology of the Memorandum leads one to believe that the Turkish Army had withdrawn to a point not in the direction of Angora, and that we are to neglect him entirely and advance carefree to Angora. Such an absence of clearness is always unpardonable, especially when it occurs in a document intended for the use of two ministers anxious to understand the military situation and the commander-in-chief's views.

Further on the Memorandum seems to take for granted that the enemy would surrender after the destruction of his stores in Angora. How so? It suffices to cast a glance at the map for even the most inexperienced person in military matters to see that the distance between Eski-Shehr and Angora is so great, that the enemy would have plenty of time to remove his stores elsewhere at the first sign of our intention to attack. This is what actually had been done, for the town had been emptied of stores, except for the contents of some railway carriages, which could not be removed, as there was no railway line beyond that town. In the event of our having entered Angora, we should, therefore, have found nothing except these railway carriages and a few empty depots, as had been the case in Eski-Shehr. In any case, it is impossible to destroy 'matériel' on such a scale as to paralyze one's opponent completely; such a thing is only possible in combination with his decisive defeat on the battlefield. I consider that the authorities were in error when they thought that the destruction of the railway line to Angora would prevent an eventual concentration of the enemy before the Eski-Shehr front. In Asia Minor, except for the few railways, there were only tracks, passable in summer for heavy-wheeled traffic, but impassable in winter when only the local carts, and especially the springless ones drawn by oxen, could be used. The Turks had only the smallest quantity of motor-transport at that time, so all transport was carried out by the above-mentioned methods, which, as we found, did not detract from their mobility. On the other hand, the country east of Eski-Shehr was partly desert-land and barely cultivated; consequently the absence of railways had hardly any influence on the movements of the Turkish Army. If the latter had no desire to give battle, he could retreat, and contrariwise could follow us when we retreated. And this is what occurred later, when a large section of the railway line was damaged—100 kilometres and more. The enemy followed us when we retired from the Sakharia, hampered us in every way, and even attacked us at the end of September after we were established on our definite front at Eski-Shehr.

In describing in the Memorandum the difficulties that might be expected, the most important was omitted—that is, the crossing of the salt desert, the Axylos desert of the ancients, where there is not a drop of water. This desert was crossed by the 2nd Army Corps with incredible sufferings.

In paragraph (*f*), the statement is made that 'the study of the undertaking made up to the present'. It is quite obvious, I think, that what is written in the first portion of the Memorandum—that is to say, about the raids to Angora, the crushing of an elusive existing enemy, and the destruction of the enemy stores at Angora—was written without having been studied at all, and that all this was put down for the edification of ministers and for the sake of using pompous phrases without any real meaning; but if this is true of those paragraphs, the last one puts the crown on the whole work. Once again mention is made of the hypothetical presence of the enemy, but this time with even greater disdain, for, after he is annihilated, only a portion of the army is required to pursue him to Angora. The rest of the paragraph cannot be taken seriously, and it is surprising that the ministers did not return the Memorandum to the compilers with a request for greater lucidity and less vagueness of expression to cloak their doubtful meaning. It is truly amazing for a document of the kind to show so much uncertainty about a definite action. As regards the conditions—all the factors of the situation referred to were well known; the railway line, partially destroyed by the retreating enemy, was being actively repaired by the military railway service (Major Mich. Vlangalis); the condition of the roads and the amount and condition of the motor transport were all well known.

The purpose of this document was not so much to enlighten the government as to fix on them the eventual responsibilities of GHQ, and that this was the case was shown later when, after the expedition had failed, the commander-in-chief, with the Memorandum in his pocket, showed it about as a proof that his action had been in accordance with the intentions of the government.

After the meeting was over, the premier, M. Gunaris, sent off the following telegram to the government in Athens:

Smyrna, July 7, 1921.

> Confidential. This morning a council was held under the presidency of H.M. the King. Were present beside myself and Minister of War, C. in C. with Chief of Staff Pallis, Chief of G. Staff Dusmanis and Major-Gen. Stratigos. I communicated Government's opinion on military question, with which you have been made acquainted by Theotoky's telegram before my departure.
>
> I took the stand that the Government had decided and ordered the military operations with intention to destroy the enemy, the proof of whose destruction will lie either in their offers to negociate [*sic*] and accept a peace which we consider advantageous or in the dissolution of their forces, which will permit us to proclaim the end of the conflict through the annihilation of the enemy and then proceed to regularize the situation and transform it to one of semi-official peace by ordering demobilization. The enemy has not shown a disposition to negociate [*sic*] and accept peace. I asked G.H.Q. if it considers the annihilation of the enemy to be an accomplished fact and to permit of the above-mentioned action being taken. G.H.Q. declared that the enemy, having suffered significant losses, finds himself in a situation closely approaching dissolution, but that he cannot be described as being annihilated in the above sense.
>
> To the question what action would ensure the success of the desired result, all agreed that success could undoubtedly be attained, but in any case it was quite sufficient after pursuing the enemy to reach Angora or the river Alys at the most. This undertaking would take 20 to 40 days. There is a probability that if the enemy remains on the defensive line of Sivri-Hissar or the Sakharia to the east of it, he will be defeated and destroyed. After this the continuation of the operations was unanimously decided on. It requires 10 days to prepare the commencement of the movement on account of the necessity of re-equipping divisions especially with boots and clothing.
>
> Papulas left to-day for Eski-Shehr. H.M. the King and ourselves leave day after tomorrow, when H.M. King will review troops and bestow decorations on regimental colours, officers and men who have distinguished themselves. After that we will return here, relying on a further stay of H.M. King, within next week.
>
> Gunaris.

This summary of the prime minister is clear and lucid, the reverse of the military document. That he could be convinced that the continuation of the campaign was possible as well as in our interest is not surprising.

It must be confessed that if the government desired the continuation of operations, it did so with the hope of emerging successfully from the impasse in Asia Minor by destroying the enemy's resistance. This would have the effect of a speedy demobilization, greatly desired by the army and public opinion in Greece. But was the manner in which the government carried out this solution the correct one? Would the plan of GHQ satisfy these views? The advance to the Sakharia, and the destruction of the railway line, presupposed a decision to establish our line of defence east of Eski-Shehr, otherwise, if the enemy was not annihilated, we should not be able to hold this with a reduced force.

I do not know how or why the idea was started that the enemy would defend himself east of Sivri-Hissar, for he could not offer any serious resistance from this side of the Sakharia, so his line of defence would more likely be established on the heights on the further side of the river. The latter form an ideal position for offering a serious and effective defence, as it necessitates the crossing of the Sakharia by the attacking force, and our army on reaching this place would have to decide if it should go on or stop. If, 'according to the prevailing conditions', the army had to stop, what impression would the enemy receive? This operation on such a great scale—for the whole Grecian Army would be there—would give the same impression to the enemy which he would get if he were to repulse a real attack—that is, the result of such an operation would be the contrary of what was intended. On the other hand, if the army is to advance 'according to the conditions which will be prevailing then', how can one guarantee the success of such a military operation with absolute certainty, especially as it would entail enticing the army more than 100 kilometres away from its base into a wild, half-desert country? It is known that a strong army can surmount most obstacles, but there are obstacles before which everything is powerless, and one of these is the desert. The region east of Eski-Shehr is more or less desert country, but to the south and east of the Sakharia it is practically all desert, and such villages as are to be found at rare intervals are more like the habitations of animals than those of men. No serious measures were taken to enable the army to cross this waterless tract of land, hundreds of kilometres in extent, though it was obvious that an area of such vast expanse, entirely lacking in means of communication or transport, presented the greatest obstacle to an advancing army. GHQ did not sufficiently take into consideration the condition of the country, nor, what was still more important, the knowledge and ability of their opponent. He was not believed to have any military capacity or strategical knowledge, but, as we have seen, the enemy had not been vanquished during the first period of operations, and though badly shaken he had known how to avoid destruction, and therefore showed that he possessed great military ability. An army with an unlimited extent of friendly country behind it, which knows how to avoid, through a timely retreat, the enveloping manoeuvres of its opponent, is practically in no danger, as subsequent events proved was the case. Our army advanced, came into collision with the enemy, stopped, and finally retreated to the line before Eski-Shehr. The advance took place with great labour and under indescribable privations. The battle was delivered at the point selected by our opponent, and under conditions most favourable to him. The subsequent halt and the fatal retreat were owing more to the lack of ammunition and food than to the climatic conditions and the superiority of the enemy. I think that this proves conclusively my contention that GHQ did not take sufficiently into consideration the difficulties of that country. The Greek Army, above all, was not defeated by the enemy on the other side of the Sakharia. The retreat was due to the want of proper preparations for the campaign, to the ignorance of certain elementary facts of war, and to the absence of an experienced directing mind. The result of all this was the collapse of the morale of our army and the consequent revival of that of the enemy.

There is not the slightest doubt that what the government had desired and had decided to do was theoretically correct. That is to say, that the enemy had not suffered serious damage during the first period of operations, and not having proposed either an armistice or a capitulation, it was necessary for us to continue the campaign and impose our will on him, so as to ensure peace and demobilization as soon as possible.

The military problem did not admit of any other successful solution, and, as always happens, there is only one correct solution to a military problem. It only remained to see if its execution was possible; and it is just this possibility which I dispute, for we had neither the necessary numbers nor sufficient means at our disposal. Those who decided on the continuation of the campaign did not take these factors sufficiently into consideration; and because of the ease with which the first part of the operations was accomplished, they allowed themselves to be persuaded by the arguments of the intelligent though inexperienced Colonel Saryannis into making a disastrous decision.

I thought then, as I think today—justified as unfortunately I am by the events—that the definite establishment of the Greek Army on the line Eski-Shehr–Afium-Karahissar was imprudent, and the expedition to Angora worse. I was told, when discussing the situation with the minister of war and Colonel Pallis, that my doubts and arguments were not based on facts, that they had information, chiefly from so-called deserters and prisoners, which showed that, in spite of appearances to the contrary, the situation of the enemy was desperate, and that it was impossible for Greece not to reap some benefit from her sacrifices and struggles. They believed that Turkey would soon submit to our conditions of peace; and for this purpose, it was not sufficient to occupy the railway centres of Eski-Shehr and Afium-Karahissar, which would only have the effect of isolating Angora. The Greek Army must enter and occupy Angora, the capital, in order to make Turkey submit. To the above was added the information that one of the Great Powers had unofficially advised that the campaign should be pushed to the farthest possible limit, promising, if things turned out well, to grant Greece a loan and every kind of war material, as well as the recognition of her right to annex the land conquered by her.

No doubt this political argument was worth consideration, but I confess that I was unable to attach an exaggerated significance to it, because I considered that if one of the Great Powers had really shown such disposition to help, there was no reason for it to wait for the final outcome of the campaign, instead of immediately offering the means indispensable to the continuation of the war, in the way of money and material, especially as the Turks were being generously supplied by other powers. I considered that it was in our interest to inform that Great Power that without these indispensable articles any idea of continuing the campaign was out of the question, and that we must take only such measures as we considered necessary for the protection of Greek interests and the safety of the troops. I have no doubt that such a clear and open declaration would have forced the Great Power in question to disclose its real intentions, but this was considered to be neither politic nor to our advantage, because, according to the minister, we could not possibly show mistrust in the word of a Great Power.

I confess that I was not convinced by any of the foregoing arguments, either military or political, because I foresaw the situation dragging on endlessly, and the indefinite maintenance of the army under arms, while awaiting the inevitable reorganization and the consequent offensive of the Turkish Army. No action of ours, not even the occupation of Angora, would, to my mind, bring sufficient pressure to bear on Turkey to make her accept our conditions, nor would it prevent her from reorganizing her resources sooner or later.

My opinion was that it was imperative to abandon the mountain-plateaux of Asia Minor and concentrate the army on another line—either inside or outside the zone of the treaty of Sevres. I will not go into the question here as to which line would have been the best, as it would lead me too far from my subject; but the line chosen should have been one which would have permitted the demobilization of a certain number of classes. No doubt in this case the Baghdad railway would have had to be so thoroughly destroyed, that it could not have been repaired for a long time to come, but this would have been comparatively easy, because of the vulnerability of the numerous railway engineering works, etc. All idea of annexing the occupied territory was, to my mind, impossible, because that part of the country was entirely hostile to us, and its occupation would require an army disproportionate to our strength; while the Greek population beyond Philadelphia was not so numerous that it could not be transferred to the zone occupied by us.

It may be said that, if this plan had been carried out, the fruits of victory would have been lost to us; we should have had to abandon the Baghdad railway, captured at the cost of so many lives, and finally the enemy would have regained confidence on our withdrawal, which he would have considered as equivalent to a retreat. But as I said before, it was impossible to maintain the army indefinitely on a war basis; while, on the other hand, I think that the morale of the enemy would not have been restored as much as it was after our retreat from the Sakharia, for the simple reason that in July we were undoubtedly the victors, in spite of the incomplete defeat of the enemy, whereas in August we broke off hostilities and withdrew, leaving the enemy still occupying the positions which we had attacked, and able to follow us in our retreat. It may be that such a decision would have diminished the good will of some of the Great Powers, but as those powers had only given us a purely theoretical support, how could we, for the sake of keeping this support, give up the Greek interests which, as is well known, consisted above all in economizing the forces of the army?

I do not mean to say that the enemy would not have attacked us in a year's time, but I do maintain that it was possible to choose a line of defence which had the advantage of economizing the forces of the army, whereas the decision to hold the line Eski-Shehr–Afium-Karahissar was, to say the least of it, dangerous, and the expedition of the Sakharia foolhardy. The argument that, by withdrawing our forces, we should have left the enemy free to use the Baghdad railway to transport and concentrate the troops to attack us is not sound, as was subsequently proved; for when the enemy attacked and routed us in August 1922, he was not in possession of the railway line, or even of the main railway centres. The July operations were rightly undertaken, because there was a chance that the enemy would be destroyed or forced to accept our peace conditions. But when this did not occur, and it became impossible to strengthen the army immediately, the situation should have been appreciated as follows:

(*a*) The continuation of the campaign is indispensable to ensure the complete submission of the enemy, but to obtain this it is absolutely necessary to reinforce the army and to equip it with the indispensable articles of which it is deficient, all of which will require time and money to accomplish.

(*b*) If it is found impossible to reinforce the army in a short space of time—that is to say, before the autumn—temporary establishment on the line of Eski-Shehr–Afium-Karahissar until the reinforcement has been successfully accomplished might be considered. This would not be before the spring, when the season is again favourable for making a fresh attempt on Angora. Naturally such a delay would be useful to the enemy also, in strengthening and reorganizing his army, but his task could not be compared to ours, for we had the sea and the railway lines in our hands; nevertheless, this loss of time was preferable to our continuing the campaign under the existing conditions. There are examples in military history which prove what I have just said. For instance, if Napoleon, during his Russian campaign, had decided to winter in Smolensk, establishing himself firmly in Poland for the winter, he could have occupied Moscow the following summer and kept it. But even so the occupation of Moscow would not have put an end to the war. The Russia of 1812–1813 had many points of similarity with Asia Minor. There were no large and prosperous towns which could be of any real use to the invader. In the event of the Russian Army being defeated, it was easy for it to take refuge in inaccessible places in the country. The climate was rigorous, trade in the interior was very scarce, and the population would not notice the conqueror's presence. To hold such a country by force is difficult, if not impossible, and Napoleon, with all his genius, was unable to accomplish this, and it must be remembered that Napoleon invaded Russia at the head of half a million veterans, experienced in war.

(*c*) If for one reason or another it was not possible to reinforce the army, then it was imperative to abandon the Baghdad railway line, and to hold a shorter line further to the rear.

I remained some days longer at Eski-Shehr, before my nomination to the 2nd Army Corps was gazetted, and I soon realized that all military prudence had vanished. Then I understood the true meaning of the Greek proverb: 'Those whom the gods wish to destroy, they first drive mad'.

There were serious thoughts of definitely annexing the country already under occupation and of creating a strong kingdom of Armenia, whose purpose would be to prevent the ragged remnants of Turkey from troubling our Asiatic State. I have seen the plans which Major-General Stratigos seriously drew up for settling the boundaries of our state in Asia Minor, long reports on safeguarding these new frontiers, plans for increasing the army by the formation of new units, and for the distribution of these units in the new countries.

The prevailing idea of GHQ was that the enemy no longer existed, and that an advance to Angora was only a military promenade. All the details of this operation were freely discussed in public, and Colonel Saryannis declared that as there would be some difficulty in victualling the troops, they would have to take measures to provision themselves with supplies found in the country—this in a waterless desert country, where all the villages were seven or eight hours apart, and their inhabitants had not even enough to feed themselves. This colonel, who was the directing brain of the army, to show off his great professional capacities, issued serious instructions to the army corps and divisions on attack and defence, on vanguard and rearguard actions, and on the proper use of artillery. These instructions contained a complete treatise on tactics, which may have been a credit to the *École Supérieure de Guerre* in Paris, whose pupil the colonel once had been, but were entirely useless to an army about to undertake operations in a desert. The mania of the officers of GHQ for the continuation of the campaign was remarkable; for instance, Colonel Vernardos, directing the 3rd Bureau, one day threatened to have an artillery colonel court-martialled, because he dared to express doubts as to the possibility of crossing the desert. Only one man on the staff had any hesitations, and he was, if I am not mistaken, Colonel Spiridonos, directing the 4th Bureau.

On 5 August, I arrived in Sidi-Ghazi, having been nominated to the command of the 2nd Army Corps (Vth, XIIIth, IXth Divisions). I replaced Major-General Arist. Vlachopulos in this command, nominally on account of my seniority, which had only just been discovered by GHQ, but principally because GHQ judged him incapable of commanding a large formation, on account of an episode which happened at Aksal-dagh during the first period of the operations. The failure was due to the orders of GHQ and to the half-hearted action of some sections of the XIIIth Division, and was not the fault of the GOC; this explains why no one at GHQ has ever dared to accuse him officially of any fault. On the contrary, Major-General Arist. Vlachopulos has in his possession letters from the commander-in-chief expressing his complete satisfaction with the manner in which the general commanded the 2nd Army Corps. This is what the commander-in-chief wrote to him, but to me and to others he spoke of the total incapacity of Major-General Vlachopulos to hold a high command. Unbelievable as it sounds, the insincerity of the commander-in-chief was such towards those under him that no one could ever be certain as to where he stood.

A few days after this Colonel Pallis, chief of HQ staff, came to visit me at Sidi-Ghazi. We discussed at length the impending operations, and I expressed the hope that we should not remain long in Angora, on account of the advancing season and the danger of the rains. Here I must explain, that on the tablelands in the interior of Asia Minor (Eski-Shehr is about 1,000 metres above sea-level) winter begins early in September (and sometimes, but rarely, earlier), when the rains begin and the roads, which are only cart-tracks, are transformed into immense muddy swamps, impassable for heavy wheeled traffic; consequently, it was natural that I should feel anxiety for the safety of the field artillery, and much more for the heavy artillery and the motor lorries which supplied the army.

Colonel Pallis, with characteristic calm, replied that it was not possible for us to remain a short time in Angora, as it would give rise to suspicion abroad that we had been forced to abandon the enemy's capital; we ought, on the contrary, to stay as long as possible so as to destroy all the stores we should find there, especially railway material, and he added that, in his opinion, we must even advance beyond Angora, as far as the River Alys (60 to 70 kilometres east of Angora), in order to show our superiority by pursuing the enemy as far as this point. Colonel Pallis added that GHQ hoped to persuade Lieutenant-General Papulas of the necessity of this advance, so there was still a faint hope that the commander-in-chief would oppose this madness. Alas! at Sidi-Ghazi there is an ancient Byzantine monastery transformed into a Turkish Tekke; in this Tekke lies the tomb of Sidi-Ghazi, a great Turkish general and saint; this tomb is 10 metres long, because the more important the person buried the longer is his tomb. When, some days later, the commander-in-chief visited SidiGhazi and was informed of the history of the tomb, he said: 'Then my tomb will be 20 metres long'. After that, hope vanished.

Old Byzantine monastery converted into a Turkish tekke.

During the time I was at Sidi-Ghazi, 5–13 August, I cannot say that any systematic work towards re-equipping the army was undertaken. Boots and clothing were sent, but not in sufficient quantities to replace the waste of the first period of the campaign. It was naturally impossible to replace all the worn-out rifles and guns in such a short time, even if this had been decided on.

At this time, the 2nd Army Corps was on outpost duty east of Sidi-Ghazi with the Vth Division (Colonel of Infantry Trilivas) at Tshetshegues, the XIIIth (Colonel of Artillery Digenis) at Arab Eyren, and the IXth (Colonel of Cavalry Kalinsky) forming with the IVth the southern group under Major-General Tricupis, whose HQ were temporarily at Idje-Karahissar about 25 kilometres north-east of Afium-Karahissar.

On account of my short stay at Sidi-Ghazi, it was unfortunately impossible for me to inspect in detail all units of the army corps; but the impression I carried away of the 33rd Infantry Regiment belonging to the Vth Division under Colonel Rokka, of the 2nd Infantry Regiment belonging to the XIIIth Division under Colonel G. Ziras, and of the 2nd Field Artillery under Major N. Papadimas, was perfect from every point of view.

At Sidi-Ghazi I once more had occasion to gauge the depth of the abyss which separated the corps of officers of 1916 from the others, and to realize to what a high pitch some people can be goaded by their passions.

When I took over the command of the 2nd Army Corps, I found at the head of the artillery and the engineers Colonel of Artillery Merenditis and Colonel of

Engineers N. Botsaris. Colonel Merenditis deeply resented, it seems, my taking over the command of the corps, and from the first seized every occasion to create difficulties. He found an opportunity in the fact that the chief of staff of the army corps, Colonel of Infantry Gavallias, was junior to him in the rank of colonel. The chief of the staff, as one knows, has to follow and be cognizant of every detail of the service of the staff and, for the smoother working of the service, the chiefs of the various departments and other staff officers bring their papers to the chief of the staff for his information, and for him to make suggestions on the various subjects contained therein. Not much importance is attached to the difference in seniority between the staff officers, and occasionally it happens that the chief of the staff is of lower rank than some of the officers directing the bureaux or departments; but this does not prevent the chief of the staff from being made acquainted with the whole of the staff work and his being fully informed. At all events, between officers of the same grade no notice is taken, or rather should not be taken, of the difference in seniority, especially during the course of operations. Such a case occurred on the staff of GHQ where Colonel Vernardos, director of the 3rd Bureau, was senior to the sub-chief of staff, Colonel Saryannis, and some years older than him.

Colonel Merenditis, deeply resenting this fact, submitted a report, in which he complained of the injustice done to him, and expressed a desire to know what measures of satisfaction would be given him. It was characteristic of the man that he addressed himself to me in writing on the subject, whereas the question could have been solved verbally more easily. I answered in writing that I recognized his rights, and ordered that in future all service documents were to be brought to the chief of the staff by Colonel Merenditis' aide. Next day Colonel Merenditis reverted to the affair, complaining this time that my decision was not just, because, being senior, he could not tolerate the control of the chief of the staff over his work, and that, in consequence, his position on the army corps staff had become impossible. Before this extraordinary complaint just on the eve of operations, I considered that, according to the regulations, the measures I was permitted to take to enforce discipline in this case were not adequate, and I sent him with a report to GHQ, and placed him at the disposal of the commander-in-chief. The latter punished him with two months' imprisonment, the sentence being carried out in Mudania.

Fortunately, other officers who may have shared Colonel Merenditis' political opinions held in check their annoyance and hid their want of discipline. Excellent work was done by many, including Colonel Botzaris, who carried out his duties everywhere and always with zeal and genuine ability, never shrinking before any danger or difficulty. Colonel Merenditis' successor, Colonel of Artillery Papaioannu, also showed exceptional ability, and during the difficult days beyond the Sakharia invariably assisted me loyally and efficiently.*

* See sketch, p. 85.

The ideas of GHQ on the further advance might be summed up as follows: GHQ had principally in view two probable lines of defence of the enemy (the line Kismet–Tepe-Tchal–Tepe-Mandra eastwards, occupied by a cavalry screen, was simply an outpost and not a defensive position). The first line might perhaps be in the district immediately to the east of Sivri-Hissar, but this was extremely unlikely, because in the rear of this line was the Sakharia, and a retreat of the Turks at that spot might be turned into a catastrophe. The more probable line of defence would consequently be to the east of the Sakharia. This position was the most advantageous to the enemy; for it would have the effect of drawing the Greek Army further away from its base, and lengthening its lines of communication. Secondly, the river, a serious tactical obstacle, the crossing of which it was easy for him to prevent, ran in front of his line of defence. Lastly, this position would bring him closer to his base in Angora.

The daily aeroplane reconnaissances, as well as information obtained from deserters, confirmed the concentration of the main forces of the enemy behind the eastern bank of the Sakharia, where he had organized a strong defensive front at a short distance from the river. Our numerical superiority was not such as to enable us to force a crossing of the river, and to make a subsequent frontal attack on the enemy's line. Such an attempt, though not impossible, would have meant disproportionately heavy sacrifices on our part. GHQ, considering that the possibility of the enemy putting up a defence west of the Sakharia in the district of Sivri-Hissar should not be overlooked, ended by deciding that the advance of the army should be regulated in such a manner as would enable it to deal with either alternative. It was, therefore, considered necessary that the main group of the Greek forces should march inside the area bounded by the Purshak on the north and the Sakharia on the south, as far as the probable line of defence east of Sivri-Hissar, in order to make certain that the enemy had really retired to the east of the river, and the 1st and 2nd Army Corps were detailed for this purpose.

The mission of the 2nd Army Corps, encamped in the district of Sidi-Ghazi and south of the source of the Sakharia, was to follow the river on the right flank of the advance, in order to cooperate in the fight, or to outflank the enemy's positions from the south, as circumstances would suggest. The above measures of dealing with the situation were thought sufficient until it was conclusively proved that the enemy had concentrated all his forces east of the Sakharia.

In this event, the whole army was to emerge from the area enclosed by the rivers, so as to avoid having to attack the enemy's front across the Sakharia.

A division of the forces on both sides of the river was dangerous, because the enemy's superiority in numbers would have enabled him to attack and destroy any isolated section which should venture to approach him from outside the rivers. It was necessary for the army to concentrate for the attack while the eastern bank of the river was held by a mixed detachment which it was unlikely that the enemy would cross the river to disperse.

As soon as these questions were settled, it was necessary to examine the point at which the army would come out of the zone of the rivers.

The topography of this district is as follows: The River Sakharia, having its source southeast of Sidi-Ghazi near the village of Tshiftelar, flows eastwards at first and later turns to the north, and finally takes a north-westerly direction, thus forming a large loop intersected in the centre by the River Purshak, flowing (from Eski-Shehr) from west to east parallel with the southern arm of the Sakharia. The loop formed by the course of the Sakharia is thus divided into two long zones. The northern zone is mountainous; the few existing cart tracks are impassable for heavy wheeled traffic, and still worse is the ground north-east of the upper arm of the Sakharia. The ground in the southern zone between the Purshak and the Sakharia is of a hilly nature, and passable everywhere for all arms in summer-time. South of the Sakharia the ground is undulating, composed of very fine sand mixed with salt, waterless, destitute of all forms of life and means of subsistence, and bears in general the character of a desert.

The decision having been taken for the army to advance into the zone formed by the Purshak and the southern arm of the Sakharia, the question remained whether the flanking movement of the mass of the Greek forces against the enemy established on the east bank of the Sakharia should be carried out from the north or the south.

The advance of the main body of the army by way of the northern zone provided two important advantages. Firstly, an attack from that side—that is, from north-west to south-east—would have the effect of immediately threatening the retreat of the enemy to Angora; and, secondly, the lines of communication of the army would lie closer to the Eski-Shehr railway line, which was being thoroughly repaired. On the other hand, firstly, the nature of the ground and the state of the roads did not permit of, or rather rendered doubtful, any movement of vehicles, consequently the advantage of the proximity to the railway was considerably reduced; secondly, the crossing of the northern arm of the Sakharia would have to be made under enemy fire, an operation which we particularly wished to avoid, for it was impossible to suppose that the enemy would not perceive this movement and hasten to present a new defensive front behind the river. It was easy for the enemy to make such a movement, as this would bring him still closer to the Angora railway.

It now remained to consider an advance outside the loop and to the south of the Sakharia. Here the enemy would be likely to effect a concentration in the desert south of the Sakharia, so as to prevent a possible advance on our part from that side. At GHQ it was said that the Turks, with full knowledge of the topographical conditions, considered an operation from the north impossible, and that they were so certain that we should attempt to operate from the south that from the very first—i.e., from the month of April—they had established a defensive salient on their main front facing south, along the Rivers Gheouk and

Katrandji, tributary to the Sakharia. Subsequent events proved this information to be correct.

It is true that an operation via the desert presented certain advantages, but it also contained serious disadvantages, such as an exaggerated extension of the lines of communication, and the necessity of undertaking extremely fatiguing marches through the heart of an arid waterless country. GHQ did not take these difficulties sufficiently into consideration, and consequently the troops were left repeatedly without ammunition or food.

After a consideration of the above factors, GHQ decided that the mass of the army should advance in the zone between the Rivers Purshak and Sakharia, and cross the southern arm of the latter when it was absolutely certain that the Turkish Army had concentrated east of the Sakharia.

During the time the army stayed near Eski-Shehr, necessary measures were taken to create fresh bases of supplies, because the Smyrna base had been isolated by the action of the retreating enemy in destroying all the bridges of the railway section, Afium-Karahissar–Eski-Shehr, and until those were repaired, no transport by this line could be carried out. Part of the large collection of stores at the Smyrna base was sent by sea to Mudania; from there the supplies were transported by the narrow-gauge railway line to Brussa, thence again by motor transport to Karakeui (a station on the Baghdad railway), and from Karakeui by rail to Eski-Shehr, where the new supply centre for the army had been established. At Eski-Shehr all the ovens for baking bread were put into use, and military field ovens also were employed for that purpose. In Sidi-Ghazi, a large bakery was built, which supplied the whole of the 2nd Army Corps with bread.

The enemy in his retreat had destroyed a large part of the railway-line, Eski-Shehr–Angora; it was, therefore, necessary to repair this to facilitate the advance. The work was undertaken by Major Vlangalis and completed with great efficiency. In ten days, he had repaired the section of the line as far as Alpikeui, which included a bridge 30 metres long. The repairs to the line more or less kept pace with the advance of the army, finally reaching the station of Akhor, where the most advanced depot of stores was established which supplied the troops first via Sivri-Hissar, and afterwards, when the army had advanced further, by the bridge of Kavukjé.

All this took time and necessitated a great deal of labour, but it was essential to create a new base sufficiently large to provide the army with all that was needed for prolonged operations. Much time, however, was lost, and this, of course, was an advantage to the enemy, as it enabled him to reorganize and strengthen his front.

The intentions of GHQ are made clear by the above preparations. There is no longer a question of a simple raid; it has now become an operation of some magnitude, with the object of attacking the main body of the enemy, of annihilating him, and capturing his capital. The commander-in-chief, in the operation order for 14 August (not in my possession), issued on 7 August, expresses himself as follows: 'The whole army will attack so as to annihilate the principal enemy forces, will pursue them until they are dispersed, and will advance to Angora to destroy the enemy's stores there and the railway-line'.

This order obviously refers to a decision lately made, and is not in accordance with the Memorandum submitted to the government, in which it is clearly defined that 'if the enemy should retreat beyond the Sakharia, the army will advance or stop according to the conditions which will prevail at the time'. It was known by now that the enemy had retired beyond the Sakharia, and the order referred to above lays down beforehand that the enemy should be crushed and pursued as far as Angora, without taking into consideration the prevailing conditions—i.e., that the railway line should be intact, and the roads and motor transport in good condition. The 'favourable conditions' were not so favourable, because the railway line had been destroyed up to the Sakharia, and the amount of motor transport was not sufficient to ensure the troops receiving their supplies easily and regularly. As to the roads, it is unnecessary to discuss them, as we know that in summertime they were everywhere passable, but were totally impassable in the rainy season.

After the campaign was over, great efforts were made to make it appear, both at home and abroad, that no definite decision to capture Angora had ever been come to, whereas at the beginning of August, it was understood by everyone that the operations were aimed at the capture of the enemy's capital. The army was convinced that this was intended, for efforts had been made to revive its fighting spirit by allowing it to believe that this would be the last attempt, and its successful issue would be followed by demobilization. Public opinion at home, and abroad as well, was induced by appropriate press articles to believe the same.

The official communications published after the campaign by GHQ and the Ministry of War all show the same tendency to try and prove that there was never any question of capturing Angora. The GHQ Memorandum of 28 July provides a panacea, as it is composed in such a way that every person can draw his own conclusions as it pleases him. In this category of official communications must be included Major-General Stratigos' treatise, 'General Review of the Operations during the Period of July 22nd to September 23rd, 1921', which is nothing but a skilful defence of GHQ, designed to conceal their responsibility on this point, and written in great haste (Brussa, 26 September), with the intention of disarming beforehand any criticism and comments.

In closing the present chapter, I feel certain that every impartial critic will agree with me that—

(*a*) It was, if not impossible, nevertheless very risky to undertake these operations, considering the state of our army.

(*b*) That once the decision was taken, it was cowardly, for those who were responsible, afterwards to attempt to deny their responsibility on this point. The denials which were made after the event are merely absurd; for if we take them seriously, we must then accept the idea that the advance on Angora occurred of itself without being ordered or prepared for by anyone, and that the army corps had marched automatically to capture the enemy's capital.

3

From 14 August to 30 September

The position of the Greek Army on the eve of the expedition to Angora was as follows:

The 1st Army Corps (Ist, IInd, XIIth Divisions) and the cavalry brigade were at Eski-Shehr.

The 2nd Army Corps (Vth, XIIIth Divisions) was in the district of Sidi-Ghazi, with outposts to the east of it.

The 3rd Army Corps (IIIrd, VIIth, Xth Divisions) was in the district of Alpikeui, with outposts about 35 kilometres to the east of EskiShehr. The IVth and IXth Divisions, under Major-General Tricupis, were in the district of Afium-Karahissar–Idje-Karahissar. The XIth Division (Colonel of Artillery Kladas) was east of Brussa.

The beginning of the advance was fixed for 14 August, and was executed in conformity with the GHQ operation order of 10 August, which is given below:

ARMY IN ASIA M.

General Headquarters.
August 10th, 1921. 9.30 p.m.

General Order of Operations for August 14th.

I. The information given in the plan of operations has not altered. The general disposition of the enemy is unchanged.

Supplementing this, we have information from various reliable sources that the enemy's IXth Division, brought from Cilicia, has fortified itself on the line Yashan–Tchiflik–Ulun Bunar (15 km. N.W. of Ak-Shehr), thus covering supplies and reinforcements from Ak-Shehr by Tsherkezkeui–Eurenkeui–Piribeili to Bolatli. These reinforcements are transported by rail from Koniah to Ak-Shehr.

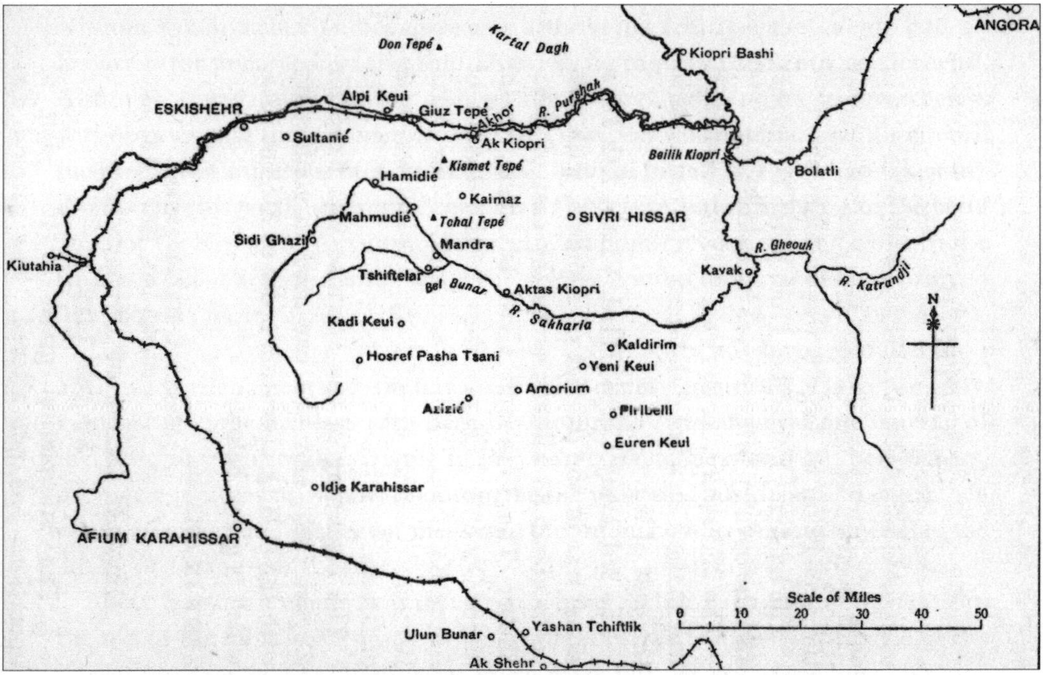

To illustrate 'General Order of Operations', 11 August.

II. Operations will commence on Sunday, August 14th.

III. No change in the operations as laid down in the plan.

IV. The zones of operations are as laid down in the plan of operations. The vanguards of all the Army Corps are to cross the line of out-posts at 5 a.m.

(*a*) The 2nd Army Corps (Vth and XIIIth Divisions) will proceed to the line of heights Kadikeui—slopes N.W. Bel-Bunar–Tshiftelar (inclusive).

The IXth Division of this Army Corps, starting from the district of Idje-Karahissar the same day (August 14th), will proceed via Azizié by regular daily marches (25 km. and will there join the right of the 2nd Army Corps. By reason of the distance it is probable that the Division will not receive the order of operations. It will therefore not wait for these, but continue without interruption until its arrival at Azizié and Amorium, where it will receive orders from the 2nd Army Corps. This Division must take measures of safety, more especially for its right flank, and push forward a reconnaissance in the direction of Tshai, while advancing on Eurenkeui. In the event of a late arrival of some of its units delaying its start from the district of IdjeKarahissar, it will be necessary to execute longer marches so as to reach the district of Azizie by the evening of August 16th.

(*b*) The 1st Army Corps will proceed to the general line Varakes (E. of Mandra)–Zafaramei (5 km. S. of Kaimaz) inclusive, and will try to occupy the bridge of Mandra as quickly as possible.

(*c*) The 3rd Army Corps will proceed to the general line Kaimaz–Ak-Kiopri–Don Tepé, and must hasten to occupy the bridge of Ak-Kiopri in order to save it if possible.

The IIIrd Division will seize Don Tepé with strong forces, in order to ensure the safety of its left flank, as well as operating during the following days principally on the Kartal mountain to try and capture the enemy's position in order to cut off his retreat to Kiopribashi and Kamam.

A strong force with a party of engineers will be posted along the road on the right (southern) bank of the Purshak to assist the IIIrd Div. in case of necessity by building a bridge.

(*d*) The cavalry brigade starting very early will precede the 2nd Army Corps into its zone of operations and will try to prevent the destruction of the bridge of Aktas Kiopri and to hold it.

Reconnaissances towards Amorium, Yenikeui and Kaldirim.

(1) Headquarters of the 2nd Army Corps with the column marching on the road Sidi Ghazi–Tshiftelar.

(2) Headquarters of the 1st Army Corps with the column marching on the road Sultanié–Hamidié–Tjonker.

(3) Headquarters of the 3rd Army Corps with the column marching on the road Alpikeui–Ak-Kiopri.

(4) Headquarters of cavalry brigade with the cavalry brigade.

(5) G.H.Q. will be at Eski-Shehr.

(6) Telephone centres of Army as follows:

(*a*) For the 1st and 2nd Army Corps, Mahmudié from 4 p.m. onwards.

(*b*) For the 3rd Army Corps, in Giuz Tope from 10 a.m. onwards.

(*c*) The cavalry brigade will maintain liaison with the nearest Division.

(7) Liaisons. As defined in the plan of operations.

PART II

(1) *Supplies.*

(*a*) For the 2nd Army Corps (except IVth Div.) and cavalry brigade, by motor transport. Point of distribution, Tchetchenges.

(*b*) The 1st Army Corps, by motor transport. Point of distribution, Hamidié.

(*c*) The 3rd Army Corps by railway, afterwards by Army Corps transport. The supply station is Alpikeui.

(*d*) IXth Division. Will ensure its own supplies from Afium-Karahissar as far as Azizié. After Azizié it will be supplied by the 2nd Army Corps.

(2) *Transport of Prisoners.* According to plan of operations.

The Commander-in-Chief of Army in Asia Minor,
Anastasius Papulas.

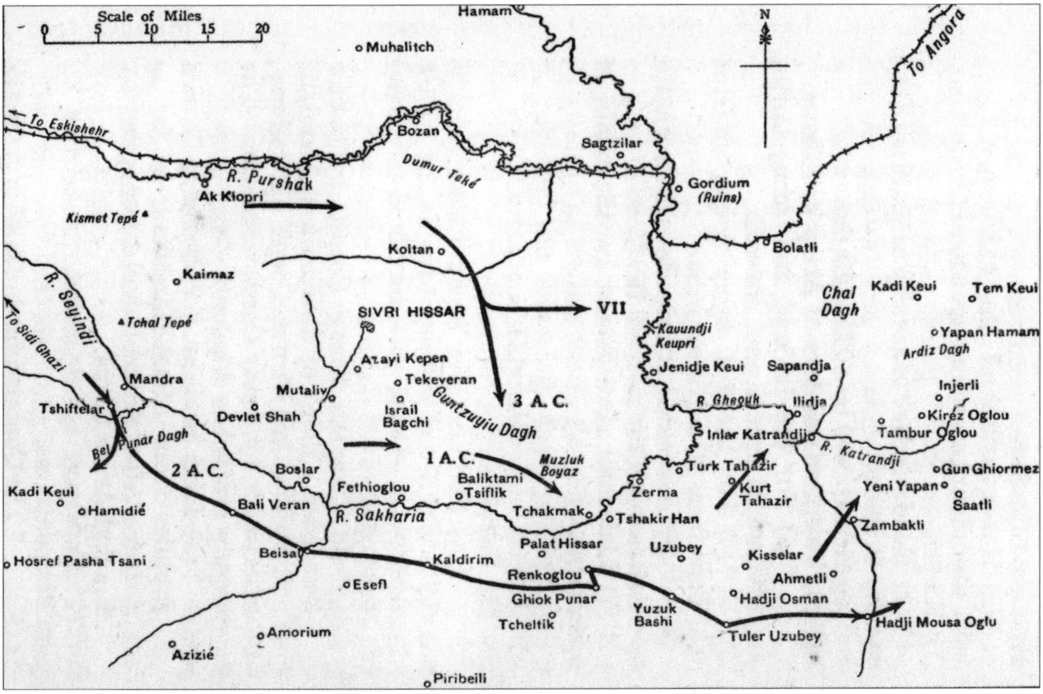

The operations from 14 August to 23 August.

The enemy cavalry screen was in touch with our troops on the line Kismet Tepé–Tchal Tepé–Mandra, and to the south. The mass of his cavalry was between Tshiftelar and Azizié.

The march of 14 August was accomplished by the XIIIth Division unmolested, and in the evening it reached the heights south-east of Tshiftelar (Bel-Bunar). The Vth Division reached the line, the heights of Bel-Bunar to Kadikeui–Hamidié, and was all day in touch with hostile cavalry, which endeavoured to delay its march; towards evening the enemy cavalry drew off to the south-west in the direction of Hosref Pasha Tsani, thus menacing Sidi-Ghazi and our communications. There were no troops in Sidi-Ghazi capable of resisting a sudden attack by the enemy, and had he surprised what few were there, he would have thrown our lines of communications into confusion and seriously hampered the subsequent advance of the army corps. I could not allow such a state of affairs to continue, and in the absence of instructions from GHQ (which, judging the situation from afar, had ordered that no forces were to be detached to cover the exposed wing) decided to send a mixed detachment composed of one regiment of infantry and one mountain battery of the Vth Division, under Colonel Alexandru, in the direction of Hosref-Pasha, until the whole corps had passed by and measures had been taken by GHQ to cover Sidi-Ghazi.

In the evening, at about 10 p.m., I was informed by telegraph that the advance would continue the following day, and that the line of outposts was to be crossed at 5 a.m. The 2nd Army Corps was ordered to proceed to the heights 5 kilometres east of Devlet Shah. The cavalry brigade was ordered to precede the army corps and occupy the bridge of Boslar. About midnight the order regulating the advance on the following day was received.

On the morning of 15 August, the march of the two divisions continued to Veli Veran, advancing parallel to each other, and all day the enemy cavalry continually harassed both divisions. The march was extremely trying, because besides the heat and suffocating dust the men suffered terribly from want of water, as we were already marching over the plains of the salt desert.

During those first days of the advance, the monotony of the operations was most wearisome to all of us; long marches (35 to 40 kilometres a day) on sandy soil with no vegetation—for one could not call the dry khaki-coloured grass of the district, which no animal would touch, vegetation. On the other hand, the continual harassing by the enemy cavalry necessitated the constant deployment of sections to repulse these attacks, a proceeding exceedingly tiring for the troops, afflicted as they were by the great heat, dust, and thirst. The cavalry brigade alone was not sufficient to repulse the constant attacks of the enemy cavalry, amounting to three divisions at least, which, by reason of its great mobility due to the small native horses used, seemed to be ever-present. It is true that the Turkish horsemen never ventured to attack our cavalry, though this certainly was not due to lack of courage or incapacity on their part, but to the difference in size of the horses of the two opponents. A collision between the two bodies of cavalry, though often attempted by ours, was never brought off, as the Turks realized that their small horses would have been crushed by ours. On the other hand, lack of barley and forage had reduced the speed of our horses, many of which were getting old, having seen the battlefields of Macedonia and Epirus (1912–1913). The inevitable result of the inactivity of our cavalry (in no way due to inefficient handling or inexperience) was that the army corps found itself surrounded the whole time by a swarm of hostile cavalry, which hampered its movements and especially those of the transport.

In the evening, the army corps and its staff occupied the line Veli Veran, and about midnight orders from GHQ, of which I give a summary, were received:

Enemy, estimated at about 14,000 strong, appear to be arriving from Cilicia, and advancing northwards via Isakli–Karapunar–Eurenkeui. Advance is to be continued tomorrow.

2nd Army Corps to area heights south-east of the bridge Fethioglu—heights Esefl. Detachment at Hosref-Pasha will be recalled. In the event of an enemy advance from the south, the army corps will order the cavalry brigade to attack and drive them back.

1st Army Corps to area Savilak–Tekéveran Israil Bagchi–Asayi Kepen–Mutaliv.

3rd Army Corps to heights Kalé Tepéveran Koltan–Bozan.

IIIrd Division will push back the enemy in front of it, and endeavour to cut off his retreat to Sagtzilar.

Cavalry brigade will gain contact with enemy moving northwards from Karapunar, and delay them so as to give 2nd Army Corps time to attack them and push them southwards. If army corps attacks, the cavalry brigade will place itself under the orders of the army corps.

The march as ordered was executed on 16 August, under the same conditions as before. No enemy forces were reported to the southward, and the army corps occupied the indicated line (with the staff at Beisal).

That evening the positions held by the army were:

2nd Army Corps.—Heights east of Beisal, south of the Sakharia.

1st Army Corps.—Bridge Fethioglou–Guntzuyiu mountains, heights east of Sivri-Hissar.

3rd Army Corps.—From Mount Dumur Teké to the village of Bozan.

IIIrd Division.—Advancing towards the enemy in the direction of Muhalitch.

The army had now reached the area whence, according to the decision taken, it had to cross the southern arm of the Sakharia, to deploy and execute its change of front to the north. This movement, seeing that it was a flank march in the face of the enemy's front, was naturally a delicate operation, and would have to be carried out with care and circumspection. The 2nd Army Corps, from its position south of the river, was the one which would have to cover the passage of the 1st and 3rd Army Corps across the Sakharia by pushing forward and extending to the right. But before executing this it would be necessary for the IIIrd Division to clear the situation at Muhalitch and in the zone formed by the union of the Sakharia and the Purshak.

A preparatory order was received in the night which clearly reveals the intentions of GHQ to push forward the 2nd Army Corps to the line Palat-Hissar–Tcheltik, to keep the 1st Army Corps stationary, and to concentrate the IIIrd Division towards the River Sakharia.

In accordance with this order the 1st and 3rd Army Corps executed only slight movements next day, in preparation for the wheel to the south. The IIIrd Division, not encountering any serious resistance at Muhalitch, was able to push back the enemy, who in retreating crossed the north-western arm of the Sakharia by the bridges of Hamam and Kiopribashi.

I established my HQ east of Kaldirim, and towards the evening went out to inspect the outposts of the XIIIth, a duty entrusted for that night to the 5/24 Evzones. I was surprised to find that, during the time I spent on the outpost line,

The author's H.Q., village of Ren Koglu.

the commander of the regiment, Colonel N. Plastiras,* avoided presenting himself to me, as it was his duty to do. Although he was breaking the elementary rules of discipline, I did not demand an explanation from him, because I did not wish to give anyone a pretext for saying that I was persecuting this officer on account of the opinions he was known to hold; but I cannot conceal the painful impression this incident made on me, for, after all, we both were facing a common enemy and, it is supposed, were fighting for the same idea and the honour of the Greek Army, whose uniform we wore.

On 18 August, the 2nd Army Corps reached the line Tshakir Han–Yuzukbashi (IXth Division Tcheltik), the pontoon section having bridged the Sakharia at Tchakmak. The mixed detachment of the IXth Division remained at Piribeili, covering the line of communications of the army corps against any attack from the south.

The other two army corps completed their movements preparatory to crossing the southern arm of the Sakharia, and on this date were disposed—

1st Army Corps in area Muzluk Boyaz–Balik-tami Tsiflik–Silivak.

3rd Army Corps in area Sivri-Hissar and southwards, with a detachment at Muhalitch.

Southern group of divisions in area Ishai Bulavadi and Lake Eber.

As for some time I had received no news of the general situation, I sent a staff officer, Captain Skylakakis, to GHQ, at Azayi Kepen, to obtain information, and

* Later head of the military mutiny which shot the six ministers in 1922.

to verify the intentions of the Supreme Command. Captain Skylakakis, on his return, reported to me that he found General Papulas and his staff rather worried because the present conditions were becoming unduly protracted and uncertain about the enemy's intentions, as they had calculated that the army would have completed the passage across the river and the turning movement to the north, by the 23rd, and then be ready for the offensive. The truth is, that no one at GHQ knew anything positive about the enemy. They had merely vague information that he was drawn up behind the tributary rivers Katrandji and Gheouk; beyond that their ignorance was complete.

On the 19th, the advance was continued without any serious opposition beyond the usual annoyance from the enemy's cavalry, and by that evening the positions of the army corps were:

2nd Army Corps.—Tuler Uzubey and the heights on each side.
1st Army Corps.—Tshakir Han-Muzluk Boyaz–Renkoglou–Palat-Hissar.
3rd Army Corps.—Silivak–Baliktami Tsiflik. The Skoda Brigade of Artillery being dispatched to Tuler Uzubey to join the 2nd Army Corps.

After establishing my HQ at Ghiok Punar, I returned in the afternoon to Renkoglou, some few kilometres off, to meet the commander of the 1st Army Corps, whose divisions had been occupied since the morning in crossing the river at Tchakmak and Baliktami. I found Major-General Kondulis beside himself with rage and using forcible language about what he considered to be the lack of judgment of GHQ in throwing the army into this fatal expedition in the desert, an operation due to the unwarranted optimism and inexperience of Colonel Saryannis. The general considered the idea of an enveloping movement from the south to be entirely wrong, as well as dangerous, on account of the difficult conditions of that district, and ended by stating that an operation from the north, in spite of its mountainous character, would have been preferable, by reason of the proximity of the railway line, which more or less counterbalanced the want of good roads; whereas any mishap occurring while crossing the Salt desert must end in the destruction of our forces.

In addition to the above, the fact that GHQ took it upon itself to settle the HQ of the army corps, and even of the divisions during the march, without consulting the corps commanders, roused the ire of Major-General Kondulis, who complained that in this manner the commander of an army corps was allowed no initiative at all.

He was certainly right in expressing himself with force against that foolish expedition in the desert, though, to my mind, once the continuation of the campaign to Angora had been decided upon—rightly or wrongly—there could be no doubt about the choice of the route to be taken. Seeing that in the north the enemy held the heights east of the Sakharia, it became imperative to take the southern route through the desert, because it was possible though difficult to feed the army along this route, whereas by the northern route the provision of supplies would become entirely problematical.

The order for the advance on the 20th laid down the movements of the army as follows:

> *2nd Army Corps* to areas Hadji Mousa Oglu–Ahmetli.
> *1st Army Corps* to areas Kisselar–Uzubey–Yusukbashi.
> *3rd Army Corps* to areas Muzluk Boyaz–Ghiok Punar–Ortoklar.
> *VIIth Division* was to be prepared to attack Bolatli as main objective, making a feint against the bridge Kavundji—the object of the feint being to cover Sivri-Hissar, the object of the main attack being to cut off the enemy's retreat when he began to withdraw after the main attack by the army. For this operation the VIIth Division was to be under the direct orders of GHQ.

Harassed as usual by the hostile cavalry, the 2nd Army Corps advanced on the 20th to the line Tuler Uzubey–Hadji Osman. I do not exactly remember for what reason, as the documents relating to this are not in my possession, but the advance of the army corps did not reach the line laid down in the order. I suppose this was owing to the fact that during the day aeroplane reconnaissances announced the concentration of large enemy forces north of the River Gheouk in the district of Inlar Katrandji–Kirez-Oglou, and that this necessitated a more complete concentration of our forces. In any case an order was received from GHQ to stay the advance, which caused the Vth Division to halt on the heights east of Tuler Uzubey, the XIIIth Division near Hadji Osman, and the IXth Division at Tuler Uzubey. In this village I met the commander of the IXth Division, Colonel Kalinsky, who complained to me of the risky dispersal of the forces of his division, of which three battalions were at the disposal of GHQ, and two battalions with mountain artillery had been left at Piribeili; the division commander himself was at Tuler Uzubey with four battalions and one mountain battery. Besides that, the boots and clothing of his troops were in a wretched condition, and he was not satisfied with the professional ability of some of the senior officers, who, as a result of the difficulties and dangers of the last marches, had lost their nerve. No doubt the complaints of the commander were well founded, but I was unable to remedy them in view of the circumstances.

When I met Colonel Kalinsky, a characteristic incident occurred. I was standing near a hut, when the commander, followed by his staff, approached me, and as I advanced to greet him, I saw that some of his officers, instead of following him, turned and went behind the hut. At the end of our conversation, I requested that the officers of his staff should be presented to me, and, strangely enough, only two officers came forward—the chief of staff, Colonel Lefas, and Captain Platis. The remainder, who had disappeared, included the commander of the infantry,

Colonel Tsiroyannis, and the commander of the artillery, Colonel Philippu, who had gone behind the hut to avoid meeting me. I reported this fact to GHQ, but the commander-in-chief merely recalled Colonel Philippu and placed him in a post of confidence with the Supreme Military Command in Smyrna; Colonel Tsiroyannis was not removed from his post, and later was given the command of the IXth Division.

On 21 August, except for minor readjustments of the position, there was a day of rest, and most welcome to the troops. The HQ of the 1st Army Corps was at Tuler Uzubey, and I profited by this to go and see Major-General Kondulis again for an exchange of views on the situation. I also seized the opportunity of this pause to send my chief of staff, Colonel Gavallias, to GHQ at Renkoglou to gather information. This was that the enemy positions beyond the rivers Katrandji and Gheouk were very strong, and that at GHQ there no longer reigned the unclouded optimism of the early days.

The whole of the 1st Army Corps had been transferred to the south of the Sakharia, and had advanced in the district of Yuzukbashi–Uzubey–Kisselar. The 3rd Army Corps had pushed the Xth Division beyond the river to Ghiok Punar and the IIIrd Division was concentrated at Musluk Boyaz north of the Sakharia. This division crossed the river on the 21st and thus the entire army found itself south of the Sakharia with its left wing at Zerma on the river and its right at Tuler Uzubey. Only the VIIth Division remained opposite the left bank of that arm of the Sakharia, which flows in a northerly direction.

According to all appearances, the army, after having been exhausted by the march through the Salt desert, had reached the locality where the enemy had decided to accept the decisive battle. The moment was also propitious for the enemy, for our lines of communication had become extended to an exaggerated degree, and the army was no longer capable of the same exertions as during the July operations. The time spent by us in re-organizing and re-equipping our forces was also of use to the enemy in his work of reconstruction, but with this difference, that we did nothing to reinforce our army in men, whereas he, by employing drastic measures, had managed almost to double his forces. Although for the moment we still had a numerical superiority over the enemy, it was not such that we could look forward with absolute confidence to the task barely begun.

I think it might be of interest if I give in full the directions which GHQ considered it advisable to issue on 21 August. These directions, a complete lesson in tactics in themselves, are no doubt flawless, but somewhat unnecessary perhaps, because if they were addressed to trained subordinates, such directions were superfluous, and if the recipients of these directions were men inexperienced in questions of that nature, they were useless, as being beyond their understanding. I rather think that GHQ, having realized the intentions of an enemy whom until that moment they had considered incapable of making a decision, and being

Artillery on the march in the salt desert.

justly disturbed by the seriousness of the situation, had composed these directions with the forlorn hope, at the last moment, of showing the troops the manner in which the operations were to be conducted.

General Headquarters,
August 21st, 1921. Noon.
Order-Directions.

(1) According to information by aeroplane reconnaissances, the enemy has extended the left of his organized defensive position from a point 3 km. S.W. Sapandja parallel with the River Gheuk as far as Kirez Oglou Idjirli. The probability is that this extension will be continued to the east until the day of our attack. This will necessitate the 1st and 3rd Army Corps, and perhaps a part of the 2nd Army Corps, undertaking an offensive against these defensive positions which are protected by barbed wire.

(2) Accordingly I give the following general directions relative to the conduct of such an offensive:

The army corps which are to attack and capture a particular section of the front of the enemy's positions will not attempt to capture the whole of this front at the same time by uniformly dividing the forces of the infantry and artillery. This would bring about a dispersal of efforts, doomed to failure, and would deprive us of the principal advantages of this offensive—viz., the selection of the most suitable point for a concentration of superior forces in order to effect a breach. On the contrary, after the staffs and the artillery commanders have thoroughly reconnoitred the position on the eve of the offensive, they must select the points, or rather those sections of the front, where the principal effort shall be made. For the choice of those sections the two following main factors must be borne in mind:

(*a*) Facility of approach and of attack for our infantry.

(*b*) The existence of positions at a good distance away suitable for concentrated artillery support of the infantry attack.

After this choice has been made the concentration of the various attacking groups will be effected, and they will be assembled opposite those sectors where the principal attempts will be made. This will in no way affect the other sectors, where the attack will be carried out as energetically as possible with the smaller forces available.

I draw special attention to the non-dispersal of the heavy and field artillery.

The whole of the artillery must occupy its positions and be ready to support the infantry before they begin their advance. The infantry attack must be conducted without exposing too many men at the start. This would only serve to increase our losses uselessly and to exhaust the men prematurely, rendering them incapable of further efforts. The progress of the attack will, on the contrary, be followed by the methodical support of the artillery, the ground will be properly utilized, and the attack will be pushed on by a gradual reinforcement from the reserves kept in the rear. It is indispensable, at the moment of capturing a section of the front of the enemy's position, to send out strong forces accompanied by artillery so as to repulse a probable counter-offensive of the enemy. As soon as a breach is successfully made it is necessary to widen it and to obtain the mastery of the whole of the front by straining every effort to attack it from the flanks of the successful breach.

The front then mastered, the line must be consolidated, the forces reorganized, and the whole of the artillery brought forward so that we can prepare to continue the offensive against an eventual second position. The above is intended for divisions and lower units, to be applied in the sector of the enemy front assigned to them.

(3) In accordance with the above, the Army Corps will push on until they come in touch with the enemy position, where they as well as the divisions will make the necessary reconnaissances and issue the orders for the offensive.

(4) I must remind you of my orders regarding the protection of the officers and men during the offensive by making a suitable use of the ground as well as of those relative to the use of artillery during the offensive against an organized position. It must be borne in mind that economy in ammunition is indispensable in view of the extraordinary difficulties in getting up supplies.

The Commander-in-Chief of the Army,

A. Papulas.

The front occupied by the army was not sufficient to allow of its full expansion; it was consequently necessary for the 2nd Army Corps to plunge still further into the desert.

On the 22nd, a further short advance was made by the army to the line heights, 4 kilometres north of Turk Tahazir, on the right bank of the Sakharia; heights, 8 kilometres east of Turk Tahazir, immediately south of Kurt Tahazir; heights, 6 kilometres south-west of Zambakli; each army corps being allotted a zone of advance. The 2nd Army Corps being ordered to move to its right, and to take up a position in echelon on the right flank.

When these moves were completed, the 2nd Army Corps was disposed in echelon. Vth Division, north-east of Hadji Mousa Oglou; XIIIth Division, north-east of the district Seit Ahmetli; IXth Division, to the rear of the Vth, and the cavalry brigade on the right of the Vth Division.

I followed the march of the Vth Division, and can bear witness of what such an advance meant to the troops. Added to the usual trials were the flames and smoke of burning grass, which poisoned the already stifling atmosphere. Those were days of horror.

On the same day the two other army corps advanced a short distance to the line about 5 kilometres from the rivers Gheouk and Katrandji; the 2nd Army Corps consequently formed an echelon to the right and a little to the rear. Thus, on the evening of the 22nd, the army was ready for the offensive against the fortified front of the enemy.

As is clearly seen, the enemy had full knowledge of our intentions and movements, and our efforts to avoid, by intricate encircling movements, the necessity of an offensive on his fortified front, which was protected by the Sakharia—a sufficiently serious tactical obstacle—had been made in vain, because the enemy, after vigilantly following the evolutions of our approach march, had changed his front and established himself in new fortified lines facing south and well protected by the rivers Gheouk and Katrandji. Though these obstacles were not serious, the rivers being everywhere easy to cross, the position was in other ways extraordinarily strong owing to its precipitousness.

I think—but this is an entirely personal judgment formed by later events—that the strength of the VIIth Division was not equal to the task entrusted to it; and if for this task one more division or the whole of the 3rd Army Corps had been used, perhaps the results would have been different.

In that case our attack from south to north would certainly not have had the same breadth which it afterwards assumed, but it would have had the advantage that the enemy, feeling the menace of large forces on his flank and rear, could not have defended his front with the energy that he did. Given also that the operation towards Bolatli did not meet any serious obstacles—as actually was the case, for the VIIth Division advanced without difficulty in that direction—the concentration of a larger force on that flank would have brought relief to the southern offensive against the enemy's principal positions. This would also have released the 2nd Army Corps from the almost useless task of attempting to encircle the left wing of the enemy.

The order of operations for 23 August is given below:

General Headquarters,
August 22, 1921. Time 11.30 *p.m.*

Order of general operations for August 23rd.

(1) The enemy is concentrating nearly all his forces on the entrenched front of the River Gheouk (north bank) from Yenijekeui to Kirez Oglou. His principal forces are being concentrated to the rear of his left flank in the district Kirez Oglou-Injerli. Aeroplane reconnaissance estimated this evening's concentrated forces at 20,000. A special reconnaissance noted an enemy force of 3,000 men at Yok Bayir, probably constituting an advanced position.

(2) Tomorrow at 10 a.m. the army will advance and occupy the ridge directly south of the rivers Gheouk and Katrandji (whereon lie the enemy's advanced positions), from which the day after tomorrow, August 24th, it will assault at 5 a.m. the main enemy position without further orders from me.

(3) My intention is to make the main attempt at breaking through the enemy's position, in the district of Anderis directly to the east of Ilidja (the section of enemy's front 4 km. N.E. of Inlar Katrandji), and at the same time to envelop the part east of Injerli.

The 3rd Army Corps will attack, in the zone between the river Sakharia and the road Uzubey–Inlar Katrandji (exclusive to 5 km. S. of Inlar Katrandji inclusive from there)—the heights 2 km. east of Sapandja.

To retain on the western bank of the Sakharia a detachment strong enough to prevent the enemy from moving troops over the bridge of Hodja Atsili (1 km. S. junction river Gheouk) and thus attacking our flank. A bridge will be built by the pontoon section at Turk Tahazir. The Army Corps will direct its main attack on the enemy positions between Sapandja, Ilidja and Inlar Katrandji heights. On the rest of the front, an attack to be made, more to the west, so as to hold the enemy forces on this section of the front and to be ready to repulse a possible counter-attack of the enemy from there.

The 1st Army Corps will attack in the zone between the right of the 3rd Army Corps.

and the line road Tuler Uzubey to Zambakli (inclusive)—2 km. AV. Ghun–Ghiormez—road Injerli–Yapan Hamam–Kadikeui. The main attempt to be executed W. of Tambur Oglou in conjunction with the main attempt of the 3rd Army Corps.

> After the reconnaissance from the ridge south of the river Katrandji, the Corps Commander will decide as to whether the attack is to be made as above ordered, or whether it should be made in the right half of the Army Corps zone. The 2nd and 3rd Army Corps will be informed in time and a report made to G.H.Q. This will not influence the 3rd Army Corps in the execution of the mission entrusted to it. To strengthen the main forces engaged in attempting to break through the front, the regiment of heavy artillery will be placed at the disposal of the 1st Army Corps at Uzubey from today. The regiment of heavy artillery must be used solely to co-operate from its positions as much as possible in the struggle on the right of the 3rd Army Corps.
>
> *The 2nd Army Corps*, attacking on the right of the zone of the 1st Army Corps, will try to envelop the enemy's position east of Injerli and occupy the heights between Mount Ardiz and Temkeui. It will keep strong reserves in echelon on its right as long as possible. Tomorrow, August 23rd, it will advance its left wing to the heights 4 km. S.W. Yeni Yapan, from which it will start the day after tomorrow, August 24th, at 5 a.m.
>
> The Cavalry Brigade will continue to be at its disposal...
>
> The Army Corps will issue orders only for tomorrow, August 23rd, and after the reconnaissances which they will execute tomorrow afternoon from the S. of the river Gheouk–Katrandji ridge, the orders for the day after tomorrow, August 24th, will be issued ... etc.

To follow the operations on the map from now onwards would be extremely difficult, as the map is incorrect; also, it does not indicate the formation of the ground or the exact location of the various positions. The line to which the army corps proceeded lies about 5 kilometres south of Saatli. The corps was disposed in echelon formation with two divisions on the front (Vth and XIIIth), and the IXth with the cavalry brigade in the rear and to the right, and still further to the right, one company and one squadron had been detached under Major Tsangarides. This formation was used because it conformed to the position of the army corps, which became the extreme right of the whole battle front, and also because we were informed that the enemy had concentrated large forces on his extreme left.

When I had taken the measures laid down in the above GHQ order, I issued my orders to the divisions under me on the afternoon of the 23rd, and after that went to my HQ at Kerpoglou, easy in my mind over the next day's attack.

On the 23rd, some collisions took place during the advance of the other army corps in the district of Ilidja–Inlar Katrandji, which were unimportant in the case of the 3rd Army Corps, but more serious for the 1st Army Corps, south of the Katrandji at Kirez Oglou. These were the advance positions of the enemy, for the defence of which he made no serious resistance; while his decision to relinquish this position may have been helped by a severe thunderstorm which burst in the evening, accompanied by violent rain, under cover of which he retired.

The enemy forces concentrated in front of me did not cause me much anxiety, because I considered that the attack of the 1st and 3rd Army Corps on the following day would be sufficient to ward off any eventual hostile menace to the 2nd Army Corps, which, in case of such attack, would easily be able to repulse it.

Consequently, it will not seem strange that I was astonished, when, late that evening, Colonel Vernardos, head of the 3rd (operations) Bureau at GHQ, arrived at my HQ at Kerpoglou, agitated and anxious, and described the situation as being serious and almost tragic.

According to the information of GHQ, the enemy had withdrawn almost the whole of his forces from the fortified line and concentrated them opposite the right wing of our army, with the evident intention of attacking and encircling us. As a result of this information, the order for the action on the following day was no longer valid, and the question was whether the 2nd Army Corps by taking up a defensive position was capable of holding back the enemy.

I explained to Colonel Vernardos that I did not consider the situation to be so dangerous, because I thought that the concentration of enemy forces facing our right had not been made with the intention of attacking there, but rather that he desired to safeguard his left from the menace of our enveloping movement, which he had discovered in time. In my opinion, if the enemy made an attack at all, it would be against our left, for if this succeeded it would have incalculable consequences, as it would cut off the army from the Sakharia and throw it into the desert. On the other hand, if the enemy had really concentrated nearly all his forces—25,000, according to Colonel Vernardos— opposite the right wing of our army, there would remain but a weak force opposite to the 1st and 3rd Army Corps, and the latter would consequently be easily able to improve the situation. I finally gave it, as my considered opinion, that in any case the 2nd Army Corps, composed of 15,000 rifles and seventy-two guns, would undoubtedly be able to hold the Turks for two or three days at least, when the pressure of the two other corps would be felt by the enemy. This seemed to allay Colonel Vernardos' nervousness.

About midnight, however, a second messenger from GHQ arrived at my HQ in the person of Colonel Saryannis, sub-chief of the staff of the army. The information which he brought was more or less the same as that of Colonel Vernardos, only with this difference, that he was not so anxious and agitated as the former had been. Colonel Saryannis announced to me, amongst other things, that the order of operations for the following day had been cancelled, and that I would shortly receive a fresh order for the defensive disposition of the 2nd Army Corps. Colonel Saryannis also announced the serious news that the 1st Army Corps had asked for the attack to be delayed a whole day, on account of the IInd Division not being able to reach the front in time.

Such a delay under the existing conditions was, to my mind, extremely dangerous, and I think that GHQ ought not to have considered it; on the contrary, if the situation was as serious as was pictured, then the 1st Army Corps should attack without waiting for the IInd Division, which would anyhow soon reach the battle-line.

I cannot conceal here the fact that this sudden change from optimism to pessimism, as well as the nervousness displayed by GHQ in sending two of the most important members of the staff to my HQ, amazed me as much as it did those with me. This was clearly the result of the mistaken idea under which GHQ laboured, that there were only two courses open to the enemy—either to remain in his entrenched position, where we hoped that he would be enveloped and crushed, or to retreat without fighting. But as soon as it was thought the enemy was taking the initiative and intended to attack, the indispensable *sang-froid* and calm judgment, without which no army leadership is possible, were shattered. Unfortunately, from that day until the end of the operations, the mental barometer of GHQ varied with rapidity from optimism to pessimism and *vice versa*. This was revealed in the contradictory orders issued, and I can unhesitatingly state that from then onwards the operations were no longer controlled or directed in the proper sense of the words.

It must not be thought that this wavering to and fro of the Supreme Command remained unknown to the troops, for, according to a well-known psychological phenomenon, the state of mind of the commander-in-chief (even in the case of Lieutenant-General Papulas, who did not interfere with the operations), his strength of will, and his firm decision to win, or contrariwise, were transmitted instantaneously and mysteriously to all ranks. One cannot commit a greater error than to imagine that the incapacity of a leader can be balanced by the capacity of the chief of his staff; sooner or later, and more often sooner than later, the troops will infallibly realize who commands them and how.

I immediately gave out, on the strength of Colonel Saryannis' statement, orders to the divisions, that the offensive had been deferred, but I was afraid that these would not be received in time, on account of the rain which had begun. What I feared nearly occurred, because the motorcars of the liaison officers stuck in the mud, and the bearers of the orders were obliged to continue on foot, reaching the divisions, one a little before the departure of the XIIIth, and the other just as the Vth was starting.

On 24 August, there was a day of absolute calm for the 2nd Army Corps. The inactivity of the enemy forces facing the corps showed that the concentration opposite the army's right was not very important, for if it had been as GHQ imagined, the enemy would undoubtedly by noon have attempted to profit by the inactivity of the other two army corps.

The situation was uncertain by reason of the enemy's inactivity, though, to my mind, it excluded all idea of a retreat on his part.

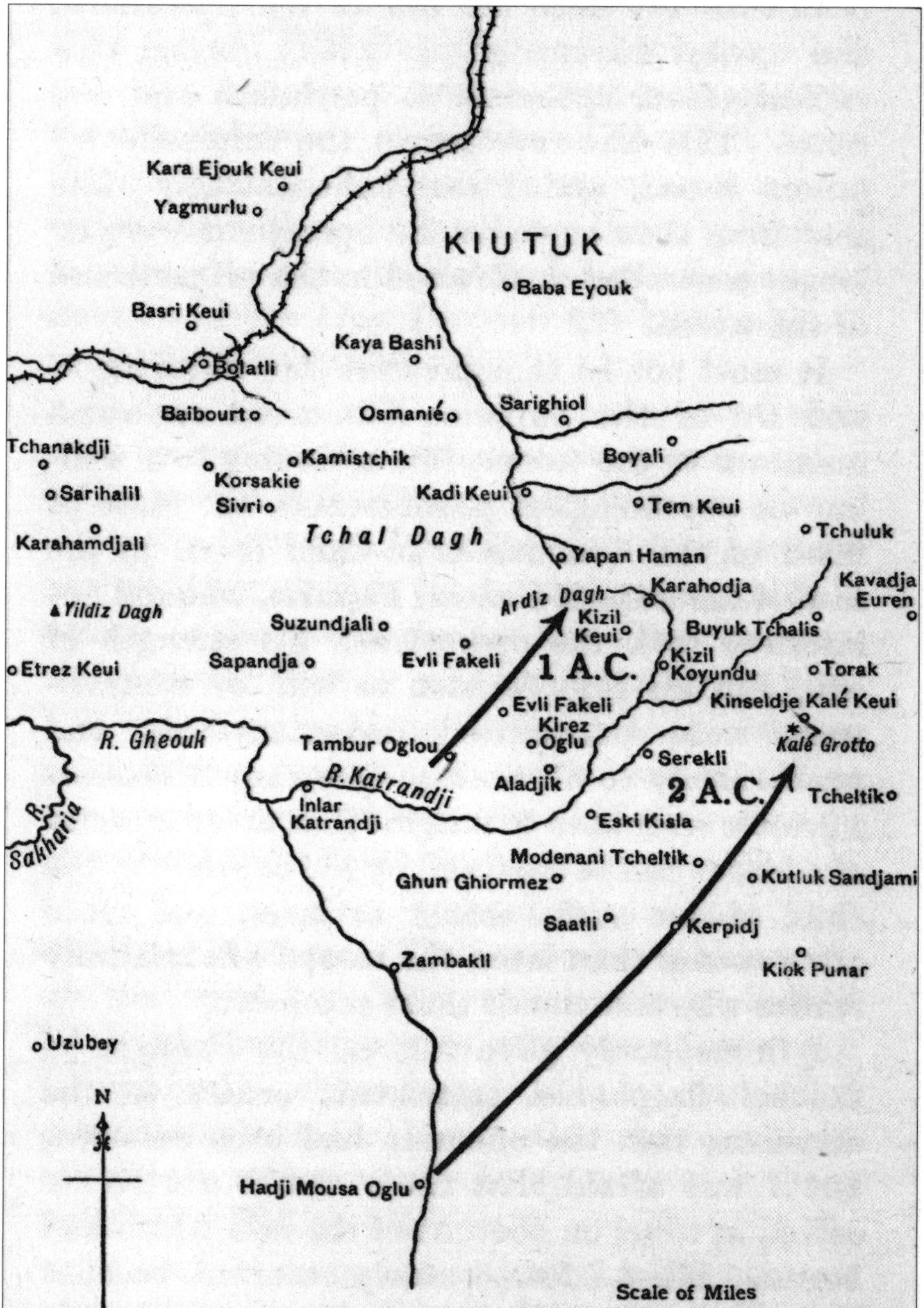

The operations from 24 August to 11 September.

Shortly after noon I received a telegraphic communication from GHQ, ordering the 1st and 3rd Army Corps to advance towards the north-east; the 2nd Army Corps to be the pivot of this movement.

As soon as the advance of the 1st and 3rd Army Corps began, it became apparent that the information as to a concentration of large enemy forces on the enemy's left was not correct, because these army corps immediately encountered strong opposition.

During the night, the following order was received from GHQ:

GENERAL HEADQUARTERS,
August 24th, 1921. Time 9.15 p.m.

THE 1ST, 2ND, AND 3RD ARMY CORPS.
Mixed detachment Edipidou.

> Enemy has abandoned trenches E. Etrezkeui. When 1st Army Corps has captured trenches W. Tambur Oglou and has reached line Ghun Ghiormez–Evli–Fakeli near Kirez Oglou, as ordered, it will continue main attack in the general direction Kinseldje–Kalekuei with its right wing towards Kutluk Sandjami and its left towards Kizil Koyundu. 3rd Army Corps will attack on left of 1st in the general direction Kizilkeui as ordered. 2nd Army Corps will attack when advance of right wing of 1st Army Corps commences, with XIIIth Division towards Kiok Punar in conjunction with right wing of 1st Army Corps, and the remaining divisions to the right and in echelon to the rear. Mixed detachment Edipidou of IXth Division proceeds tomorrow 25th inst. to Kerpoglou, where it will be placed under orders of 2nd Army Corps.
>
> The Commander-in-Chief of the Army,
> A. Papulas.

The struggle continued all night, and towards the morning of the 25th, while I was still waiting in inaction, as the right wing of the 1st Army Corps had not yet advanced, the counterattacks of the enemy on the latter became so violent that the 1st Division—fighting on the left flank of the 2nd Army Corps—found itself in a critical position, and was obliged to ask me for reinforcements. I immediately ordered the XIIIth Division to go to their assistance by moving a little to its left. This division had later to be reinforced by the Vth.

Thus the 2nd Army Corps, with the exception of the IXth Division, found itself involved in the conflict, in spite of the orders of GHQ, for I had not asked their permission for my action.

I merely informed them of it, after I had thrown my divisions into the attack. I draw attention to the fact of my not having followed the orders of the commander-in-chief, because it escaped the notice of my subsequent accusers.

The intervention of the XIIIth Division was crowned with complete success, for by the evening it had repulsed the enemy, about 8,000 to 10,000 strong, and forced him to retreat.

After this turn of events and the evidence that the enemy had not transferred any forces to his left, the spirits of the commander-in-chief—or rather his staff—revived, and they returned to the original plan of an envelopment by the right wing and ordered the 2nd Army Corps to advance towards Kinseldje Kalé, an advance which would eventually necessitate the capture of the mountainous group of Kalé Grotto.

The advance began early on the morning of 26 August, and at about noon the corps found itself strongly opposed, the enemy defending himself with energy and executing violent counterattacks. Within two hours we had 1,300 out of action, fifty-four officers and 800 men from the XIIIth Division alone. But our troops fought well, continually gaining ground.

During the afternoon, at the moment the enemy was making a fierce counterattack against the XIIIth Division (left of army corps), my chief of staff, Colonel Gavallias, received the impression, through not hearing any firing on our left, that the 1st Army Corps was not in action. He expressed regret that GHQ did not co-ordinate the efforts of all the army corps, for whereas during the two previous days, the 1st Army Corps was struggling fiercely, the 2nd Army Corps was idle, and today the 2nd was fighting and the 1st was idle. This was said in my observation post in the presence of Colonel Vernardos, who accompanied the army corps as GHQ liaison officer. The colonel's opinion was just the contrary, for he considered it was quite correct that the 1st Army Corps should not be moving, for if it had moved, he, as representative of the commander-in-chief, would have ordered it to remain where it was, as only thus would the enemy's envelopment be attained. The fact that the enemy did not continue his counterattacks against the 1st Army Corps, and that the 2nd Army Corps was gaining a little ground, was at once considered by Colonel Vernardos to be a retreat on the part of the enemy, though at that very moment a violent counterattack was being launched against the XIIIth Division. The director of the 3rd Bureau at GHQ went further still, and proposed that I should send the IXth Division—if it could be called a division—beyond Karadja Euren, and, by a wide encircling manoeuvre from the right, cut off the enemy's retreat, which the colonel imagined to be an accomplished fact.

I told him that I did not consider that the enemy showed sufficient inclination to retire as to justify such a decision on my part. The action of the Vth Division in advancing along the ridge south of the Kalé Grotto range, as well as the advance of Tsangarides' mixed detachment on the right of the Vth, while the XIIIth Division was meeting with serious opposition a little north of Modenani Tcheltik, constituted a sufficiently encircling movement to facilitate the advance. Anyhow, I was not disposed to risk sending the four battalions of which the IXth Division was composed on such a wide movement in order to cut off a retreat which only

The author's observation post at Kalé Grotto.

existed in Colonel Vernardos' imagination. Besides, in conformance with the orders from GHQ, I kept this division in reserve to protect the flanks and rear of the advancing corps.

The colonel then tried to break down my refusal, which he imagined was due to my fear of taking the responsibility for such a hazardous encircling movement, by suggesting that he should give me a written order 'by order of the Commander-in-Chief', based on a letter to him from the chief of staff of the army, which he showed me, and in which he wrote: 'And I also agree with your opinion that this is the moment for an encircling movement'.

This suggestion showed Colonel Vernardos' chivalrous spirit in offering to assume the responsibility for the proposed action, but I replied that in any case I would not accept this ingenious scheme, for the execution of which I would rather bear the entire responsibility myself.

Colonel Vernardos based his opinion that the enemy was retreating on the concentration by the enemy of forces on his left. As I have stated already, GHQ, four days ago, considered this concentration of the enemy to mean an attack, but as the attack did not materialize this signified, according to Colonel Vernardos, that the enemy was retreating.

The events justified my predictions, because the enemy not only did not retreat, but strengthened his resistance against the 2nd Army Corps; and a strong cavalry detachment with artillery skirting the right wing of the corps marched towards the rear of the army. I was later informed that they very nearly captured the commander-in-chief and his staff at Uzubey.

It seems that GHQ had conceived the idea that the enemy, fearing that his left would be outflanked, was leaving the Sakharia in a general direction towards the north-east—that is to say, he was trying to escape to Angora. I do not exactly know what gave rise to that impression: perhaps it was the ease with which the VIIth Division crossed the Sakharia, thus cutting off the enemy's right from all touch with the river. The retirement of the whole enemy front after that, I suppose, was believed to be inevitable, and probably this belief had influenced Colonel Vernardos when he made the above proposal to me, without taking into consideration the local conditions in which the 2nd Army Corps found itself. He appeared in person at my post of observation behind the XIIIth Division, and could see not only what opposition the enemy was putting up, but also his furious counterattacks, and could realize the terrific consumption of ammunition by the field and heavy artillery. This ought to have been enough to prove to him that this engagement was anything but a rearguard fight aimed at delaying our advance, so as to give the enemy time to withdraw the main body of his forces unhindered towards the north-east. I had the distinct impression, and so had the officers of my staff—an impression not caused by local influences—that we were facing the main body of the enemy, who had finally selected the suitable hour and place, and had interrupted his retreat to give battle under the best conditions for himself. It was no longer a question of simply arresting our advance, it was a question of fighting a decisive battle. A still greater proof of this fact lay in reports by captured Turkish officers, who assured us that, two days before, Mustapha Kemal Pasha himself had been in the lines facing the 2nd Army Corps encouraging and urging his men to a last desperate fight. And at that moment, when I was in need of the whole strength of the corps to face this situation, appears Colonel Vernardos, the commander-in-chief's representative, and proposes an entirely fantastic scheme, containing neither common sense nor correct judgment. To my mind there is not the slightest doubt that the weak IXth Division isolated in this way, would have been destroyed, and of necessity would have drawn the whole of the 2nd Army Corps with it into the desert and to consequent capture. The result would have been the same, but on a larger scale, as the disaster to Ziras' detachment on 17 July, which also was caused by the lack of judgment of GHQ. What consequences such an event would have had for the army in general I leave to the reader's imagination.

The battle continued on the 27th, the enemy defending himself with energy, and the losses on both sides were serious. In spite of this, our divisions were able to gain ground towards the rocky group of Kalé Grotto, which towered above us, and was strongly fortified on the south side. During this day the 1st Army Corps, fighting on my left, did not attack, for what reason I do not know; or if it did so it made no appreciable advance, but the serious part was that it remained inactive on my rear and left, thus both flanks of my corps were exposed. On the night of 27 August, the following order from GHQ was received:

1st, 2nd, 3rd Army Corps and VIIth Division

2nd Army Corps advanced today pursuing retreating enemy to line Kinseldjé Kalé–Serekli. 1st Army Corps occupied fortified line Tambur-Oglou–Aladjik. 3rd Army Corps occupied fortified positions on its right to Sapandja. Tomorrow, 28th, at dawn, army will continue energetically to attack as follows, 3rd Army Corps will turn Xth Division towards the West, covered on the North by mixed detachment, when it will occupy the Western position in conjunction with IIIrd Division and drive enemy out of it.

1st Army Corps will attack energetically to the North with as right limit line Eski Kisla–Kizilkeui. 2nd Army Corps will continue enveloping movement directly right of limit of 1st Army Corps with enveloping direction Kara Hodja covering right. Army Corps to take into consideration that tomorrow and the day after they will not receive ammunition.

27/8/21. 8.20 p.m.
Papulas.

On the 28th, the XIIIth Division (reinforced by some units of the IXth) encountered such strong resistance and such energetic counterattacks, that it was compelled to ask the 1st Division for assistance to protect its own left flank; which was in the air owing to the 1st Army Corps not having advanced. Colonel Frangu unhesitatingly advanced without orders. I could not use the whole of the IXth Division to reinforce my left, because it was on the extreme right, and it would have required many hours to transfer it to the left, a loss of time of which the enemy could have taken advantage; in addition, I could not possibly leave the exposed right flank of the corps (Vth Division) uncovered. On the same day the Vth Division, after a hard struggle, reached the last spurs of the rocky mass of Kalé Grotto.

The impression I received of the fight of the 28th was not very favourable, because I could not help noticing several large gaps between the army corps, and I realized that there was no co-ordinated action between them.

As it was difficult for me to intervene at GHQ and acquaint them with my anxiety, I thought that in any case it would be useful if I established a close liaison with the neighbouring 1st Army Corps, so that we should obtain an exact knowledge of each other's situation and possibly be able to co-ordinate the actions of both, and I sent Colonel Botsaris for that purpose to Major-General Kondulis.

The cavalry brigade could not be used any more, except for protective duties. Owing to the exhaustion of the horses, caused by overwork and lack of barley, not to mention their age, reconnaissances could not be carried out because the wretched animals could not even move at a trot, and for the same reasons, when our men met the enemy's scouts alone, they were frequently captured.

In addition to the want of barley there had been for several days a lack of every kind of food, except meat, and the latter could only be prepared with great difficulty, as there was no wood in the district. Another very serious matter was the want of petrol, and the motor ambulances carrying the severely wounded were reduced to being drawn by buffaloes to enable them to follow the advance of the fighting units, as it was extremely dangerous for them to move without escorts. The slightly wounded men were transported by means of mules, springless carts, and camels, by long marches to Inlar Katrandji, exposed to the dust, the almost unbearable heat, and the constant danger of capture by enemy cavalry who butchered our wounded when they found them. To ensure their safe transport strong detachments were sent to escort them, thus depriving the fighting line of a considerable number of necessary rifles. We were also deficient in medical stores, and the treatment of the 15,000 to 20,000 wounded at Inlar Katrandji was so utterly wretched and inhumane, that the commander-in-chief himself was jeered at by the wounded when he went to visit them and give them a word of comfort. After that, the members of the staff at GHQ at Inlar Katrandji, close to the temporary hospitals, studiously avoided all contact with the wounded, who greeted any passing staff officer from afar with shouts and curses. The state of the medical service was so bad that the attitude of the wounded in Brussa became menacing, and a mutiny was only with great difficulty averted by the personal intervention of the minister of war. The real causes of this deplorable state of affairs are to be found elsewhere, especially in the despicable action of some of the officers of the medical corps and others, as well as in the neglect to take the necessary sanitary measures.

Even more serious was the rapidly approaching lack of ammunition, for on 28 August, at the most critical period of the operations for the capture of Kalé Grotto I was told by GHQ not to expect any ammunition to arrive for another two days.

To the honour of all those who served in the 2nd Army Corps, I here wish to emphasize the fact that, in spite of all the privations and difficulties which the troops had to face, they never murmured or made complaints; on the contrary the men fought with heroism and indomitable perseverance. It fills one with disgust and surprise that those who decided on the advance to Angora, for which they undertook the responsibility (though they later tried to shift it on to other people's shoulders), did not take even elementary precautions to ensure the delivery of ammunition, petrol, bandages, and food. The excuse they made, that the lines of communication were attacked by enemy irregular cavalry 'Tchets', does not hold good, because they ought to have known this was certain to happen when they hurled our army into the desert hundreds of kilometres from its base.

The order for 29 August is as follows:

General Headquarters,
August 28th, 1921. Time 11.30 *p.m.*

1st, 2nd, 3rd army corps, and VIIth division.

3rd Army Corps after a brilliant attack occupied positions defended with barbed wire on its left, and on its right 5 successive lines of trenches, capturing guns and heights W. Sapandja. 1st Army Corps advanced after brilliant attack to line Soyuntsli–Evli Fakeli north, 1 km. S. Kizilkeui.

2nd Army Corps fighting splendidly reached line S. Kizil–Koyundu–Torak. Tomorrow, August 29th, 5 a.m., all Army Corps and VIIth Division will continue in accordance with my last order. I forbid preparation by artillery before infantry attack.

The Commander-in-Chief of the Army,
A. Papulas.

The last phrase of the above order is calculated to make the reader thoughtful, and to bring before his eyes a characteristic picture of the situation. I do not think that the commander-in-chief and his staff (Colonel Vernardos had already left my HQ) could have followed the course of the fighting during those days, because if they had, they must have realized with what obstinacy and with what an astounding expenditure of heavy and field artillery ammunition the enemy was defending himself, and they could never have given an order which reversed all the rules of modern warfare. There certainly was a lack of ammunition, but did this justify the above paragraph which, if it had been carried out, would have produced a regular slaughter of the infantry?

'I forbid preparation by artillery before infantry attack.' A decision by men who were completely out of touch with the situation. I do not know, nor do I desire to examine, what decision the commander-in-chief ought to have taken under the circumstances. I only know that the above order was the very last that he was justified in giving, for it is well known that it is impossible for infantry to make an attack on entrenched troops without an artillery preparation, as it would at once be stopped and then rapidly destroyed. This sentence completely negatives the rest of the order, which demands an energetic attack.

The following day, the 29th, the stubborn struggle continued, and I had to use up the whole corps in the assault before the last spurs of Kalé Grotto were captured. Colonel Botsaris returned that day from the 1st Army Corps, where I had sent him as liaison officer. He reported that that corps had also encountered great opposition, and that the losses of the IInd Division especially were very severe. According to the colonel's information complete optimism, derived from some unknown source, reigned at GHQ.

1st, 2nd, 3rd Army Corps, and VIIth Division.

> Tomorrow, August 30th, the 3rd Army Corps will occupy Mount Yildiz, clear the district, and proceed towards N.E. 1st Army Corps will remain on the line it is occupying and organize the defence and prepare an assault for the following day for the capture of Mount Ardiz. 2nd Army Corps will proceed toward the left to the heights on the right of 1st Army Corps and will keep an entire division in reserve. VIIth Division will continue pressing the enemy.
>
> General Headquarters, 29/8/21.
> 9.45 p.m.,
> Papulas.

The left wing was pushed forward according to the above order on the morning of the 30th, but as to keeping an entire division in reserve it was impossible even to think of it. During the course of the morning a new order (not in my possession) brought by Colonel Vernardos directed me to take two divisions to Inlar Katrandji to reinforce the 3rd Army Corps, leaving only one division and the cavalry brigade to hold the sector which I was leaving. The bearer added that the order was issued in the morning so as to allow the corps time to get ready to move during the night, but that I would receive a definite order by 5 p.m.

In order to understand this decision of GHQ, we must take into consideration the fact that the 3rd Army Corps was meeting great opposition at Mount Yildiz on the extreme left, and it seems that at GHQ, from information received, they feared a strong concentration of enemy forces on our left and the consequent destruction of the 3rd Army Corps, which would cut us off from the Sakharia. This decision of GHQ, in my opinion, was correct up to a point. If one takes into consideration how our forces were scattered and the wide intervals between the different units, one realizes that it was imperative for us to collect our units and to co-ordinate the actions of the three corps. The army was spread out over a front of over 55 kilometres with distinct gaps between the corps. The battle had somehow been transformed into local engagements, each corps fighting on its own account, and it often happened that one corps found itself involved in a fierce struggle while its neighbour was idle. The original plan of an enveloping movement on the right could no longer be executed; on the one hand, because the enemy, having realized this intention in time, had taken the necessary steps to prevent it on ground most suitable to their purpose; and, on the other hand, because of the dispersal of our forces. If the 2nd Army Corps had advanced to the north and north-east after the capture of Kalé Grotto, the distance between it and the 1st Army Corps would have been still further increased, with the result that the former would have been isolated and soon destroyed. What would be the repercussion of this event on the rest of the army? As things were now, GHQ no longer disposed of any troops as reserves (*masse de manoeuvre*), and what they had were too weak to make a counter move to an initiative of the enemy. The latter possessed reserves, small it is true, but still complete units capable of bringing about direct results at any given point on our front selected by him, and, in my opinion, there was not the slightest doubt but that he would choose the point of our contact with the Sakharia. A successful counteroffensive on his part in this locality would mean the destruction of our whole army. It would be cut off from the river and consequently from its lines of communication, and would be literally hurled into the desert, where, without ammunition, food, or water, it would surely be destroyed.

For the reasons given above, the idea of GHQ of contracting the front by placing the 2nd Army Corps between the other two corps or behind the 3rd Army Corps, and the formation thereby of an important *masse de manoeuvre* could not but have my entire approval.

The removal of the whole army corps and the cavalry brigade was indicated, because there was no object in keeping one division and the cavalry brigade to protect the right wing of the 1st Army Corps. Only for reasons of sentiment might we hesitate to abandon ground, but one cannot take sentimental reasons into account in wartime. As long as we could safeguard our left wing on the river there was no immediate danger, and it was possible to consider a fresh action with our left which, in all probability, would find the enemy unprepared, as he was directing all his attention to our right.

I have said that this decision was correct up to a certain point; in fact the order brought by Colonel Vernardos was only an outline of an order. It was a document which ill-concealed the doubts of its author as to the course to be pursued, his uncertainty about the situation and the terrible indecision of the commander-in-chief. If the information of GHQ about the concentration of enemy forces on our left was correct, there remained no doubt as to the course to be pursued; if the enemy had really taken the decision to operate from there, the indication of this would be perceived by us the moment we realized that his forces were being concentrated there, and it was not permissible for us to think that it was an easy matter for the enemy, in a few hours, to take another decision which would have entailed a fresh transfer of troops. Troops are not pawns which can be moved in a moment at random from one end of the battlefield to the other.

An indecisive order for the 2nd Army Corps to be moved would have brought confusion into the regular routine of its services. Were we to go or to remain? To move a whole army corps, and especially when in contact with the enemy, is not a simple matter. There is an entire transport service with motor lorries, and transport of every kind and description; several thousand beasts, etc., which, as conditions were in the 2nd Army Corps, could not be attached to the tail of the column to follow the march. The corps had to be withdrawn when in actual contact with the enemy, a very delicate undertaking, and one requiring great freedom of action. For instance, the whole area and all the roads on receipt of the order had to be cleared immediately of every obstacle that could hamper the free movements of the troops; but the order gave no directions, and thus I found myself in a dilemma; for if I issued orders beforehand, there remained the possibility of receiving a counter-order before 5 p.m., when the transport, having been sent to a distance of several kilometres, would be obliged to return.

These were my thoughts in regard to the general idea of the order. I confess that it is very difficult to comment on the second part of it, which bade me leave—or rather abandon—at Kalé Grotto one division and the cavalry brigade. After several days of bloody fighting, involving three entire divisions, the enemy had moved and retired to a new line of defence. GHQ regularly received our reports on the operations; they were consequently in a position to judge the tactical situation. How it was possible after that to think of leaving, except in a position which had been prepared for defence, only one division and the now entirely useless cavalry brigade in a sector held until now with great difficulty by three divisions, is to me an unfathomable mystery.

The operations of the divisions that morning (30th) went smoothly, and the information that reached me was, that a movement of troops and peasants towards the north had been observed. I did not attach much importance to this last news, for I recognized the customary tactics of the enemy, who, after having obliged us to make an organized attack, and after having caused us serious losses by an amazing expenditure of ammunition on his part, was withdrawing to resume the game on another position which had been prepared beforehand. It made, however, a deep impression on Colonel Vernardos, especially as, soon afterwards, we received news by aeroplane that along the crest of Mounts Ardiz and Tchal there were only a few enemy scouts with a force in their rear of only 2,000 in all; that Yapan Hamam had been abandoned; that no movements were visible in the entire region; and, finally, the aviator expressed an opinion that the enemy was retreating to the north. This convinced Colonel Vernardos that the victory was won, and he impatiently requested to be allowed to go and announce the event to GHQ. The fact that a bitter struggle was still being continued along the front, as we all could see from my post of observation, made no difference to Colonel Vernardos, who took the envelope from the pilot and departed in haste.

I can imagine what a poor opinion the director of the bureau of operations must have had of my military knowledge and my personal courage, as even with such convincing proofs of the enemy's flight I was unable to show any keenness. At my trial, about a year later, Colonel Saryannis, the immediate superior of Colonel Vernardos, deposed that, as he himself had noticed, I was entirely under the influence of my staff and incapable of forming views and judgments of my own. But perhaps, as to the latter, Colonel Saryannis and his friends, accustomed as they were to guide the footsteps and opinions of Lieutenant-General Papulas, and knowing how much one is influenced by the environment in which one lives, thought that mine was a case in point.

As I expected, I received a telephone order at 2 p.m. cancelling the one regarding the move of the corps, and ordering a general pursuit of the retreating enemy to the north by all the army corps. The order added that the pursuit was to commence at once and to continue the next morning without further orders. This order, which was evidently the result of Colonel Vernardos' easily roused and uncontrolled enthusiasm, could not be executed by the 2nd Army Corps, for the simple reason that the enemy opposite us was still maintaining a stubborn defence and contesting every inch of ground. It was only towards evening that the whole rocky group was captured after very heavy losses had been inflicted on the 2nd Army Corps. I do not know in what manner the above order was executed by the other corps, if at all; I only know it was not executed by the 2nd Army Corps, because this was impossible. One is filled with wonder as to how it was possible for such an order to be issued by GHQ, considering that but a short while before their liaison officer had been at my HQ and, in spite of the aviator's report, saw with his own eyes that the fighting was still going on. It is not for me to say which of the two, Colonel Vernardos or myself, had formed a correct opinion of the situation. I can only say that my view was based on the evidence of my eyes, and that the whole of the staff of the 2nd Army Corps agreed with me; whereas Colonel Vernardos' view was based on the aviator's report alone. It was a curious fact that, in spite of the recognized incapacity of our air service, GHQ invariably relied on their faulty reconnaissance's and information, putting aside the information supplied by the divisions and army corps at the front, though the latter could be verified on the spot by the members of the GHQ in the same manner as Colonel Vernardos had the opportunity of doing more than once.

The truth of what I have just said is, unfortunately, fully proved by the fact that another reconnaissance carried out by a different aviator a little later on the same day (30th), over the same area, reported the presence of some 26,000 enemy troops. This information I only received from the 1st Army Corps on the following day, and was too late, unfortunately, to influence Colonel Vernardos' view of the situation.

At 7 p.m., when we at last succeeded in capturing the whole of the Kalé Grotto range, the exhaustion of the troops, after several days of continual fighting, with insufficient food, was such, that all thought of moving any units (and there were none who had not been put into the assault) for the purpose of pursuing the enemy during the night was impossible. My last infantry reserves had been absorbed in the capture of the sinister rock, which, like a volcano, was vomiting flames and smoke from both our own and the enemy's shells bursting on it, and it was impossible to make use of the cavalry brigade on account of the poor state of the horses. If I undertook the pursuit under such conditions, I would have exposed the army to the danger of dispersal, for if the enemy had possessed even a few intact units he could have brought about a catastrophe. Even if I had eventually ordered an immediate pursuit with my exhausted troops, the pursuers would have at once stumbled on to fresh fortified lines, for we had been informed, even before our advance on Kalé Grotto, that the Turks were working on another strongly fortified line about 8 kilometres to the north.

I confess that on that evening of 30 August, I did not feel the relief that I ought to have felt after a great victory which once more had covered our troops with glory. For the reality was terrible, as terrible as it must have appeared to King Pyrrhus after the Battle of Heraclea against the Romans (280 BC). Our losses were entirely out of proportion to the strength of the army corps; the available strength of the three divisions was not more than 8,000 to 9,000 bayonets; there was very little ammunition left, and it was doubtful if this could be replenished, and there was still less food. The enemy had retired, it is true, but without any losses in prisoners and material, only to halt again 8 kilometres further north, where fresh efforts and more fearful losses awaited us. Under such conditions, what would our situation be when we finally reached Angora?

After a quiet night, the following order was received next morning, the 31st:

1st, 2nd, 3rd Army Corps.

Enemy began to retreat, in all probability, during the night of yesterday. He left strong rear-guards on line Mount Ardiz, heights Karahodja, heights Tchuluk, to guard the passage of his right flank retreating to the east.

3rd Army Corps succeeded in uniting with VIIth Division, advanced today Sivri. Tomorrow, August 31st, 5 a.m., all Army Corps will attack enemy in accordance with my order for today, and will proceed to the line given below, where they will take up defensive positions, so as to be re-formed and re-organized.

3rd Army Corps, to which VIIth Division returns, is to hold heights Yagmurlu, heights N.E. Bolatli, heights Kayabashi to road Kamistchik–Baba Eyouk (inclusive), and will protect left flank and advanced position on heights N.E. Kara-Eyoukkeui.

1st *Army Corps* heights Osmanié (N. Tchal) to heights S.W. Temkeui (inclusive.)

2nd Army Corps heights S.W. Temkeui (exclusive), heights S.E. Koyundu and heights Kinseldjé Kalekeui.

General Headquarters. 30 /8 /21.
10.54 p.m.
Papulas.

The above order was undoubtedly prepared under the influence of the latest information by air. The directions by telephone ordering an energetic pursuit, even though the corps was still fighting desperately, were the results of the first information. I lay stress on this point, so as to show how little importance was attached by GHQ to information received from the staffs of the army corps.

I especially want to draw the reader's attention to the first paragraph of the above document, because the way in which the enemy's movements and actions are described is of much significance in view of subsequent events, and it gives an accurate picture of the views of GHQ on the military situation.

As appears from the map our front was swinging little by little towards the east, with the 2nd Army Corps tied down at Kalé Grotto as a pivot. This was caused by the advance of the 3rd Army Corps, which, in conjunction with VIIth Division, had been able to clear the country near the Sakharia. The situation was very different on the front of the 2nd Army Corps, because, absorbed as it was by the bitter struggle for Kalé Grotto, it could not keep up with the advance of the 1st Army Corps, the result being that a noticeable gap (8 to 9 kilometres) had been created between its own left wing and the right wing of the 1st. To fill up this gap it was not only necessary to push forward the left wing, but also to sideslip the entire corps, an operation which was not acceptable to GHQ, who at that time rightly insisted on the capture of Kalé Grotto. Independently of the above, the advance of my left wing was in any case necessary to enable us to join up with the 1st Army Corps, but more especially in order to improve the position of my corps. To explain the matter in detail is unfortunately impossible, because the map in no way reproduces the actual formation of the ground.

The crest to be occupied was unapproachable, as it was dominated by crossfire from another curved ridge not marked on the map, and lying more to the north between Karahodja and Buyuk Tchalis. This last range of hills was fortified by rows of trenches (belonging to fortifications prepared before the advance on Kalé Grotto), and it was held by strong forces. There was no doubt as to the latter, as all the aeroplane reconnaissances, carried out by different aviators from 24–29 August, are agreed as to the presence of an enemy force of 10,000 to 15,000 men. To this I must add, that I, as well as the officers of my staff, saw with our own eyes that the enemy was continually fortifying himself in successive lines.

For this necessary as well as difficult operation, I detailed the IXth Division, which had been the least severely tried, to capture the ridge, and to prolong the left of the XIIIth Division, which had suffered the heaviest losses; the latter I ordered to cover the right flank and rear in place of the IXth.

The IXth Division attacked and, advancing under severe shell fire, and with very heavy losses, to a depth of 2 kilometres, was under the impression that it had captured the indicated ridge. I and my staff, as far as we could judge from our post of observation, were, on the other hand, of opinion that only the first row of hills in front of the actual objective had been occupied. This was afterwards confirmed from the observation post of the Vth Division.

Before deciding to push my left wing on further at the cost of renewed expensive attacks, I sent Captain Skylakakis of my staff to GHQ to explain the situation, as well as the great differences between the actual formation of the ground and the way it is shown on the map. The pushing forward of the left wing by itself would have necessitated appalling sacrifices, and artillery support by the Vth Division from the right would be impossible on account of the conformation of the ground. The advance of this division, besides the fact that there was no question of pushing the right wing forward, would result in the whole army corps being implicated in the struggle for the capture of the designated ridge, which was strongly fortified, and held by forces superior to those of the depleted 2nd Army Corps. It must also be remembered that this corps, like the others, was very short of artillery and small arm ammunition. In addition, the fortified front of the enemy extended towards his left, thus circling round the right wing of the corps in such a way that any move on the part of the Vth Division towards a common action rendered it liable to be entirely surrounded. The further advance of the corps was only possible in the event of a general advance on Angora, in which case the lines of enemy fortifications facing my front would be turned by the advance of the 1st Army Corps. This was also the opinion of the 1st Division on the extreme right of that army corps, with whom I was in communication.

There were factors affecting the situation, leaving out the question of the advance of the left, which had also to be carefully considered from other aspects:

1. The enemy's defence up till now had been very energetic, and he had always retired in good order with all his material.
2. He was liberal in his use of ammunition.
3. Our losses were very great, a third of our available forces were out of action.
4. The privations and general exhaustion after six days' uninterrupted fighting began to affect the morale of the men. They still advanced, but not with the same élan as during the first days.
5. The prestige of the Supreme Command had fallen in the eyes of the officers, especially as a result of the alternate contradictory orders, and, lastly, the noticeable lack of essential material.

I charged Captain Skylakakis to learn if GHQ insisted on a fresh advance from the left—which was not indispensable to my mind—and in general to inform himself of the commander-in-chief's intentions, because, and this was one of the amazing features of this campaign, the leaders of the army corps were not kept informed of his intentions.

The order for 1 September directed the continuation of the operations without any change of plan.

Later in the morning of 1 September, I received a new order from GHQ (not now in my possession)—a fresh example of the Supreme Command's regrettable tendency to change its views—to send a division to Sapandja to strengthen the 3rd Army Corps, which had not been able to advance as much as it might have done. This order, besides the acute anxiety which the hesitations of the leaders inspired in me, disturbed me by the fact that my three divisions barely sufficed to hold the sector. Nevertheless, I sent off the IXth Division, which was again replaced by the XIIIth and to cover the flanks and rear, for which the latter had up to now been responsible, I detailed unmounted sections of the cavalry brigade and sections from each of the remaining divisions.

Captain Skylakakis returned from GHQ the afternoon of the same day (1 September), and reported as follows: GHQ had at last realized the danger of the large gaps between the army corps, and desired us to move closer to the 1st Army Corps—from which we were separated by 8 to 10 kilometres—and to abandon Kalé Grotto if necessary. The lack of ammunition and food caused GHQ to decide to suspend all further operations for two days, and thereby to give the men a rest. Reliable information brought the enemy's forces up to nineteen divisions of 2,000 to 3,000 bayonets each. Further than this Captain Skylakakis could not enlighten me, for the reason that the different members of GHQ were in evident disagreement with each other. Even the sub-chief of staff, Colonel Saryannis, did not conceal his anxiety, and said openly to Captain Skylakakis: 'We have lost the game'. It must be remembered that the colonel was the prime instigator of the raid to Angora. The chief of staff, Colonel Pallis, was calm as usual, and did not wish to express any opinion contrary to that of Major-General Stratigos, who considered the continuation of the advance to Angora as absolutely indispensable, in spite of our heavy losses and great difficulties, unless perchance it could be foreseen in time that we were going to destruction. If I add to the above that the commander-in-chief was much troubled by the discord amongst his advisers not knowing what view to adopt, we have a complete picture of the situation at GHQ. To crown all, the commander-in-chief, General Papulas, transmitted through Captain Skylakakis his desire that my chief of staff, Colonel Gavallias, should go to GHQ to discuss the situation, and if this were not feasible to write his opinion to him freely. This last, amazing as it seems at first view, may be explained by the fact that the relations between Lieutenant-General Papulas and Colonel Gavallias were not only purely military, but they were united by a great friendship dating from the time of the wars of 1912–1913, when my chief of staff was adjutant of the 10th Infantry Regiment, then commanded by Colonel Papulas, and these close relations had subsisted ever since. Notwithstanding all that, it is astonishing for a commander-in-chief to reach such a degree of perplexity as to request advice from an officer—apart from his ability—who was a stranger to his staff.

Of the various items of information brought, only two concerned the 2nd Army Corps—namely, the two days' rest and the move closer to the 1st Army Corps, abandoning Kalé Grotto if necessary. The first was undoubtedly urgent, but it had the great disadvantage of leaving the enemy at liberty to take in fresh supplies of ammunition, to fortify himself, and to move about freely and undisturbed. In regard to the second part, I invited the commanders of the two remaining divisions to come and arrange the details of a move towards the 1st Army Corps.

I prefer to pass over the rest of Captain Skylakakis' information in silence.

But what was said to Captain Skylakakis, nevertheless, did not form the basis of the order issued for 2 September. I give it here:

General Headquarters,
September 1st, 1921. 9 a.m.

1st, 2nd, 3rd Army Corps.

1st *Army Corps*, after brilliant attack, occupied Mount Ardiz, eastern section Mount Tchal, and heights S.W. Temkeui, capturing entire enemy battalion.

3rd Army Corps remained in its position, not having progressed.

2nd *Army Corps* report not received yet. Tomorrow, September 2nd, the Army Corps will continue the advance and attack as they proceed on lines given in my order. 2nd Army Corps will push forward its left to the support of right 1st Division and come to a direct understanding with it for this purpose. It will continue to occupy heights Kinzeldjé Kalé with mixed detachment.

The Commander-in-Chief of the Army.

A. Papulas.

It can be seen from the above that the situation was not as favourable as GHQ imagined it to be when they issued the order of 30 August, but, in spite of that, they insisted on their point of view, thinking, I suppose, that they still had to deal with a rearguard action. The bearer, Captain Papathanasiu, informed me that at GHQ they were enthusiastic, that 'things were going very well'. Also, the chief surgeon of the corps, Dr. Papavassiliu, before returning from GHQ where he had been questioned concerning his department, had been directed by the commander-in-chief to tell me that 'the situation had improved and things were going well'. I can only give one explanation for this sudden enthusiasm—namely, the fact that the day before, one division of the 1st Army Corps had captured an 'entire' (this is the word in the order) enemy battalion—that is to say, 200 men (reduced strength), and this, I suppose, made Colonel Saryannis change his mind about the 'game'.

The bearer of the above-mentioned order reported also that he had been instructed to stop the IXth Division on the road, wherever he should meet it (this division had been sent in the evening to strengthen the 3rd Army Corps), and to transmit an order to its commander to ask for orders immediately by wireless from GHQ. This last information gave me hope that the IXth Division might possibly be returned to me, in which event I had planned to place it between my corps and the 1st to fill the gap, which would render the abandonment of Kalé Grotto unnecessary. Probably surprise may be felt that this action—that is to say, the filling of the gap by the IXth—was not accomplished before this division was detached from the army corps. The project had more than once been under consideration, but it had never materialized, for one reason because all the forces of the army corps were engaged in the struggle for the capture of Kalé Grotto, and, secondly, because of the reiterated orders of GHQ who, judging from afar, had decided on the retention of strong reserves. The very moment that I had finally decided that it was possible to use this force to stop the gap without abandoning Kalé Grotto, GHQ deprived me of the only means with which the stopping of the gap was made possible.

I urgently submitted these views to GHQ, but in vain, for I received the answer that the IXth Division would not be returned to me.

In an order issued at 8:30 a.m., 2 September, GHQ ordered a two days' rest for all the corps, but reverted to the idea of my pushing forward the left wing of the corps, always with the intention of supporting the right wing of the 1st Army Corps in case of danger, but with a difference this time that in the order occurred the words 'if possible'. What troubled me most was the idea of the gap between the two army corps, whereas GHQ were chiefly occupied with the plan of supporting the right wing of the 1st, which certainly was not in greater danger than mine, completely exposed as mine was.

Thus I continued to hold the sector, and to ensure the protection of the space between the two corps it was found sufficient to transfer two regiments of the Vth Division to the rear and left of the XIIIth—that is to say, my extreme left—ready to resist any chance attempt on the enemy's part to penetrate there; I also detailed a cavalry squadron to patrol the gap, and established a close contact with the 1st Division (extreme right of 1st Army Corps) by means of these patrols and telephone. In this manner I avoided the heavy losses which an isolated advance of my left, without the support of the IXth Division, would have cost us. I was also enabled to give the corps the (so-called) two days' rest which had been ordered. Subsequent events proved that the measures taken for the defence of the gap were adequate.

The order for the corps to remain inactive, in order to organize defences, to rest, and take in fresh supplies, did not last long for the others; as for the 2nd Army Corps, it might as well not have been issued, for a rest was not possible, as small engagements never ceased, and there was firing along the whole front for the greater part of the twenty-four hours. On account of the reduction in our strength caused by the departure of the IXth Division, the greater part of the remainder found themselves in the first line. The cavalry brigade could only be used mounted for short patrols, but the troopers were used as infantry for outpost duty. As regards supplies, during the last four days only a quarter of the bread rations had been received and very little ammunition. The rations consisted only of meat and boiled corn, and this was prepared with difficulty as no firewood was obtainable.

Day by day, the situation grew worse on account of these privations, and a most disquieting situation was caused by the rumour spread amongst the men about the appalling losses and the total absence of provisions, ammunition, etc.—tales which were accentuated by their enforced idleness and inflamed by deliberate criminal propaganda. But all this was less disquieting to my mind than the total absence of information and general ignorance of the intentions of the Supreme Command.

The truth is that we had reached a deadlock. GHQ, having started the operations with a complete underestimate of the strength and capacity of the enemy, had not taken sufficiently into consideration the character of the country into which they intended to lead the army, or the means of transport necessary for supplying the troops. They now suddenly found themselves faced by the stern reality of facts. Already the losses were very serious, if not entirely disproportionate to the original strength of the army; and the mobility of the troops was seriously diminished because of the difficulties of transport; also, the morale of the men, although not exactly bad, had changed to a degree which made it very different from that during the first period of the operations. The enemy, on the contrary, had given proofs of decision, courage, and mobility—proofs which convinced me that we had before us the main body of the Turkish Army, at last willing to give battle at the time and place chosen exclusively by themselves, and that they had decided to defend their capital to their utmost capacity.

Was the continuation of operations under the above-named conditions possible, and was it in our own interest? It might be possible if we were to suffer still more terrible losses and an eventual arrival in Angora with divisions of 800 to 1,000 bayonets each; but it certainly was not in our interest, seeing that our weakness was such, that we should be obliged to abandon that town before the approach of winter with the certainty of the impossibility of returning to Eski-Shehr without being seriously harassed by the enemy, against whose activities we were no longer in a position to defend ourselves effectually. Lieutenant-General Papulas, having been drawn into accepting this undertaking, in spite of his originally expressed refusal, now found himself in a state of embarrassment and indignation difficult to describe. His counsellors, who in the beginning were so certain of the necessity and the success of the expedition, and who forced him to alter his prudent opinion about the insufficiency of the personnel and materiel at that time, now stood before him and requested him to make decisions, and wanted him to take over the future direction of operations. The commander-in-chief retired into his tent like a wrathful Achilles and, for some days, refused to see anybody but his aides-de-camp, and with reason, for now in their hour of need his counsellors asked for his approval as commander as well as for his official signature to orders of operations, whereas, when things went well, they did not even vouchsafe to submit the written orders to him at all.

All this is comprehensible and human, but quite unsuitable to an army leader, especially in the difficult position in which the Greek Army found itself during those serious days of September 1921.

On 3 September, profiting by the order which Lieutenant-General Papulas had transmitted to my chief of staff through Captain Skylakakis on the 1st, I ordered Colonel Gavallias to write to the commander-in-chief and place before him our views on the situation. The following is a summary of what this letter contained. The chief of staff begins by asking the general not to misunderstand him, but, relying on their former friendship, he now states his views frankly. He continues by saying that one must carefully examine which of two cases had to be considered. First: did the enemy's retreat from his first fortified line constitute a general retreat? If this is proved, he asks the commander-in-chief to order a general attack, regardless of our need of rest and of our requirements, for to satisfy these would demand too much time, and meanwhile the enemy would have time to recover. This offensive, however, should only be ordered if established on thoroughly reliable information, and not on such as GHQ had, up till now, based its views—namely, the reports from aeroplanes and Turkish deserters—causing the contradictory orders which had considerably lowered the commander-in-chief's prestige. Second case: if, on the contrary, there was sound information that the enemy intended to defend himself on successive lines—and this at least we could see from his fortifications—then it was necessary for the commander-in-chief to consider deeply before deciding to continue the operations for the capture of Angora. Even before the first line of defence had been captured, the Greek Army had lost one-third of its available strength; if it was a question of capturing a second and a third line, the remainder of the army would be lost, and the commander-in-chief would end by entering Angora alone. The primary question was: Was it absolutely necessary to capture Angora? So far as we knew at the beginning, we were only supposed to go as far as the Sakharia, and there new plans were to be made according to the circumstances. Why, then, was this advance being made? If it was done with the intention of destroying the supplies in Angora, it was known that the enemy had already evacuated the town. It is true that there remained the railway coaches, which the enemy had not been able to remove, but was it worthwhile to sacrifice so many men for a few coaches? There is no doubt that the capture of Angora would have great significance from the point of view of prestige; but it would be well to examine if it was possible to gain even this after the information received by GHQ that the enemy had nineteen divisions at his disposal, and without having suffered any disproportionate losses. Above all, if by any chance the occupation of Angora had originally been decided upon, it should not now be pursued only because public opinion expected it. The commander-in-chief should do what he thought was right, irrespective of public opinion. The question of not sacrificing the army should be borne in mind first, and the impression to be created was a question of editorial management. Colonel Gavallias then added: 'As I am almost certain that it is impossible for you to procure reliable information, either in the one case or in the other, so that you can make a decision, may I be permitted to submit to your judgment another mode of action?' And he went on to suggest that the idea of an envelopment with the right wing of the army should be abandoned, and that this movement should be made with the left. For this purpose, the 1st Army Corps, well-fortified in its naturally strong positions, should remain stationary, and an offensive should be undertaken against the enemy's right wing, as GHQ had originally decided, by the 3rd Army Corps on the extreme left, supported by the 2nd Army Corps, which should be closed in to the 3rd for this purpose. After the execution of this enveloping movement, which was bound to be successful—because the enemy had in some places on his right only few fortifications and at others none—GHQ would be in a position to decide, according to the situation, whether to advance to Angora or to return to the Sakharia. The advantages to be gained by this flanking movement would be: (1) to bring the army closer to the railway line; (2) to ensure the safety of the lines of communication to the Sakharia, which were in danger; (3) to avoid all risk of the 2nd Army Corps with its weakened forces being defeated, if the enemy, seeking to obtain a local success, should attack it. In this case, should the enemy succeed, we might be forced to withdraw to the Sakharia, and this would be looked on as a defeat of the whole Greek Army. The letter also stated that, if the decision to make this enveloping movement were made, it would be necessary for this to be done as soon as possible, so as to allow the 2nd Army Corps to be transferred before the enemy should show any signs of attacking. At the end of the letter, he stated that it would be desirable that we should have definite proof that the enemy was really retreating, so that we could advance immediately and reach Angora rapidly, which is what we all wished for, and then to return before the commencement of the rainy season. A postscript said that we all, officers and men, were ready to brave everything for success, and that the morale was perfect.

Eyewitnesses have told me that Lieutenant-General Papulas was deeply moved when he read the letter, and showed it to his staff, saying: 'Gavallias always loved me and told me the truth'. The members of the staff with difficulty concealed their dissatisfaction, which was only natural. Out of the whole contents of the letter, these officers only took into consideration the reference to the difficulties of the advance to Angora, and consequently inclined to the idea of an immediate retreat beyond the Sakharia. The crown prince (afterwards King George II), who was present, asked the very pertinent question, 'Why do you base your argument only on that part of the letter and neglect the part where he speaks of the enveloping movement from the left and also the part where he says that the morale is perfect?'

On the 5th, my chief of staff received a letter in answer from Lieutenant-General Papulas, which read as follows:

> Dear Aleko,
>
> As to the question of Angora, I am sending you a written exposition of my views, which Gunaris asked me for, so that you can see that in this question also the position I have taken up is the correct one.* Tomorrow I will send you another report, in which I set out the situation in detail. We have no information as to whether the enemy is going to retreat or if he will defend himself in retreating. I admit that the information brought by deserters and aeroplanes does not agree, but on what do you want us to base our orders? We have no means other except the information of the above and that of the Army Corps, who are in contact with the enemy. Some days ago the 3rd Army Corps reported the situation very favourable, as it appears from my order based on the report of the above corps.
>
> Lastly, dear Aleko, what lies in my power to do I will do with the greatest prudence, for I feel the responsibility that I bear.
>
> The plan which you wrote to me is being studied and we will carry it out in five days, because it is necessary for the men to rest first and for the corps to be supplied with abundant ammunition.
>
> The 1st Army Corps will remain in its position well fortified, and with the 2nd and 3rd we will execute an enveloping movement against the opponent's right wing: firstly, to avoid losses, and secondly to reach Angora soon, so as to finish, because it is as necessary for us to finish soon, as it is for us to march to Angora to gain a complete victory.
>
> But as to this plan, we will examine it attentively, and if we find that we can execute it with few losses we will advance; otherwise we will await the decision of the Government to whom, as I wrote to you, I am sending a report tomorrow ... etc., etc.
>
> I embrace you.
>
> A. Papulas.

I do not suppose that a commander-in-chief could state his views more clearly or the intentions he had in mind.

The first paragraph of the letter is characteristic of Lieutenant-General Papulas, for there was no reason for him to touch on the question of Angora and the report that he submitted to the premier, M. Gunaris, if he was not consumed with anxiety for the present and with doubts for the future.

---

* In reference to a memorandum of GHQ about the continuation of the campaign to Angora.

The commander-in-chief was already trying to exonerate himself from the responsibility of the advance to Angora, and accordingly gave out that he had been constrained by the government to undertake this expedition against his will. It is also clear that his aim was to leave the responsibility of ordering the continuation or not of the campaign to the government. This attempt on the part of Lieutenant-General Papulas certainly does him no credit, but it must be taken into consideration that, drawn as he was into this operation in spite of his originally expressed opinion, the evolution of events found him greatly embarrassed by the result, which he had dimly foreseen, and he tried to justify his action by transferring the responsibility for it to the government. Any attempt at justification was superfluous, because the commander-in-chief's position was not correct. It would only have been correct if, when the expedition to Angora was decided on against his expressed opinion, he had resigned from the command of the army with the declaration that he would not take such a responsibility against his own convictions. No government could ever compel a commander-in-chief to undertake an expedition which he thought impossible or so risky that he considered it bound to end in disaster. The government may suggest that such an operation is necessary for political reasons, and the commander-in-chief can reply that, in his opinion, the operation is not feasible. If then the government insists, the commander-in-chief must resign the command to whoever will undertake the responsibility of its execution. A commander-in-chief worthy of the name does not require councils of war and special advice from purely outside individuals to help him bear a responsibility which is his alone, and which never can be shifted on to anyone else. In this particular case the operation had not yet been brought to a conclusion, either in our favour or otherwise, and consequently the decision to be taken was in the exclusive jurisdiction of the commander-in-chief.

I have gone into this question a little more fully perhaps than necessary, but I think it advisable to present Lieutenant-General Papulas as he really was, so as to enable my readers to understand, if possible, why a year later he was gripped by the tempest and tossed about like an autumn leaf in the wind.

I confess that I read this letter with relief and satisfaction, for I saw that GHQ were at last emerging from their state of inactivity and considering the only solution which, in my judgment, could extricate the army out of the difficult position in which it found itself. The question was not yet solved by any means; but it gave me an indication of the orientation of the commander-in-chief 's thoughts, which was important, because it enabled me to regulate my actions in accordance with his views. It is possible that I may be opposed in this view of the question, as I was by the worthy president of the Revolutionary Tribunal which condemned me, who considered that I attached more importance than was necessary to a friendly and personal letter, and that what was written to Aleko by A. Papulas did not represent the official opinion of the commander-in-chief and of GHQ. He also considered that it was not in the nature of an official army order, the only document which I was obliged to carry out. This objection is, theoretically, no doubt, not to be rejected on first inspection; but if one considers the circumstances under which this letter was composed, the fact that the commander-in-chief does not write about the weather, but receives opinions submitted to him and answers them, and if one also considers that the commander-in-chief was addressing himself to the commander of an army corps, or to his chief of the staff (which is practically the same in such a case), then I maintain that the letter should be taken as indicating a plan which the commander-in-chief meant to carry out. Besides, are there not cases in military history of a commander-in-chief writing letters to those under him on the general situation have only to refer to the bulky correspondence of the great Napoleon—and as is well-known, whenever possible, a commander-in-chief holds a conference of his commanders, and explains to them verbally his ideas and intentions, which those present accept as instructions to be confirmed later by the issue of orders? Letters and verbal directions certainly do not bear the character of official documents; the official order follows later, and simply confirms the written or spoken words. All these facts are so elementary and well known that I hesitate to mention them; but I do so because of the objection made by the president of the Revolutionary Tribunal, who by this remark proved himself to be lacking in the most elementary knowledge of the science of war.

My chief of the staff, on my order, answered the commander-in-chief the same day, thanking him for not having misunderstood the tone of his letter, and begging him to shorten the five days' delay, during which no rest was possible, and no supplies could be taken in—during seven days only a quarter of a ration of bread was received—whereas it was possible that the enemy would attack on observing our idleness. An enemy attack against the 2nd Army Corps would result in a local defeat only, but against the 3rd the result would be to cut off the army from the Sakharia and consequently from its lines of communication. This second letter was taken to GHQ by Captain Skylakakis, who telephoned that we would probably receive the order to move that night. Captain Skylakakis returned the next day (6 September) and reported that the chief of staff, Colonel Pallis, told him, firstly, that the enveloping movement would only take place if the continuation of the advance to Angora was decided on; secondly, in that case only one division would move up to the 3rd Army Corps, the other would remain to defend the sector of the 2nd Army Corps.

The order for 6 September is brief and for once to the point:

No. 19233/6133/3 5/8/21. 8.20 p.m.

2ND ARMY CORPS.

Tomorrow, September 6th, the Army Corps, including the 3rd, reformed and revictualled, will remain in their positions organized for defence.

A. Papulas.

I have already explained why the enveloping movement indicated in my chief of staff's first letter—irrespective of the decision to advance to Angora or not—was necessary. It was also made clear, I think, with what difficulty two divisions were holding the sector of the 2nd Army Corps, and yet the idea was formed that the sector could be held by the weakened forces of one division and the cavalry brigade, which was only that in name—that is to say, GHQ reverted to the plan which had been impressed on me by Colonel Vernardos on 30 August. I leave aside the fact of the complete dispersion of the 2nd Army Corps during this critical period of the battle over the whole front. I ordered Colonel Gavallias to write to the chief of the staff at GHQ and submit the above arguments, but no answer was received.

I do not doubt that some will criticize my action and the manner in which I interfered with the duties of the Supreme Command. I do not hesitate to accept these criticisms. I will even go further and say that any other commander-in-chief worthy of the name would have either imposed silence on me at once or dismissed me instantly from the command of the army corps; but as I am supposing here that any other commander-in-chief would have acted thus, I go further in my supposition and say that in that case I never would have acted as I did, for under any other commander-in-chief the staff would have been kept in its right place and GHQ made a proper instrument of command in the hand of the commander-in-chief. Criticisms after an event are always easy, and a judgment formed in a safe and peaceful study differs radically from one formed on the field of battle, and in the face of events on which the salvation or destruction of an army depends. The Greek Army found itself in an extremely critical position during those September days when I proceeded to act as I did, occupying as it did a front from Kalé Grotto to Bolatli, the whole of its forces in action, without any reserves (except the weak IXth Division), with large gaps between formations, losses out of all proportion, extreme fatigue after more than ten days' fighting, very little ammunition, and insufficient food seldom forthcoming.

Facing us was an enemy full of energy and initiative, and determined to use every means in his power for the defence of his capital. In these circumstances the result of one strong sudden attack of the enemy against the left wing of the army would be the cutting of our communications; against the right, the retreat of the 2nd Army Corps, and the subsequent throwing of the whole army into the desert. Seeing that a further frontal advance was very difficult, if not impossible, because of the enemy's successive fortified lines, there was only one way out of this impasse, and that was (*a*) to reinforce strongly the left wing of the army; (*b*) to ensure the safety of the lines of communications; (*c*) to attack from there against the enemy's right, where there were no important fortifications. An attack from that direction would not cause the march to Angora to be abandoned; on the contrary this would assure it, and perhaps cause the decisive defeat of the enemy. Any other operation would inevitably be doomed to failure unless the abandonment of the whole campaign was decided on, when the consequent withdrawal of our troops, which might be successfully carried out, would give the impression of a forced retreat. It must not be thought that I was the only officer who viewed the situation in this way; the whole of my staff, the division and cavalry brigade commanders, thought as I did, and I have reason to believe that the 1st Army Corps likewise judged the situation in the same light. Only GHQ, far to the rear, sometimes saw the situation from one aspect, sometimes from another; their liaison officers viewed the situation as it suited them, not taking into consideration the opinions of those fighting on the spot, and the commander-in-chief appeared unable to form an opinion or to impose it on this medley of conflicting views held by his staff. How was I to act under the circumstances? Was I to observe the silence imposed by the regulations and to allow the catastrophe, which I saw coming, to take place? I was the commander of one-third of the army, and I considered that I not only had the right, but that it was also my duty, to enlighten the Supreme Command on the real situation, for if I did not do so, and the catastrophe occurred, I should deserve the hangman's rope. The Supreme Command, no doubt, had the right either to listen to me or to command silence, and it was my duty to obey whatever decision was taken. Anyhow, my action did not overstep the bounds of discipline, for I did not on my own initiative address any official document to the commander-in-chief containing my opinion and advice, and never attempted to lower his prestige or that of GHQ. On the contrary, the letter explaining my views was written at the request of the commander-in-chief himself.

That same morning (6 September) Colonel Botsaris returned from the HQ of the 1st Army Corps, where I had sent him as liaison officer, and he reported that the losses of that corps were terrible; the 1st Division had 3,000 bayonets out of action, and the IInd had only 3,000 effective bayonets available—that is to say, the corps was reduced to one-third of its full strength. The colonel was convinced, from discussions which he had had with the staff of the 1st Army Corps, that only by adopting the enveloping movement suggested by me would the continuation of the operations be made possible, and to my question whether Major-General Kondulis had been informed that the advance to Angora would be abandoned, he answered that he did not know, but that if this had been decided, he—the colonel—considered it would be equivalent to a defeat.

Captain Skylakakis, as already stated, arrived from GHQ and gave me the information that the Memorandum, of which Lieutenant-General Papulas spoke in his letter, had already been sent to the minister of war at Brussa, and that only in the event of the continuation of the expedition being decided on would the enveloping manoeuvre from the left be executed, otherwise the retreat beyond the Sakharia would be ordered. As regards the enveloping manoeuvre, GHQ had ended by deciding to execute this with the Vth and IXth Divisions, to which would be added one division of the 1st Army Corps, the XIIIth Division and the cavalry brigade remaining at Kalé Grotto.

The order for the 7th ordered an energetically organized defence:

Reserves will be reconstituted by placing as many guns as possible on the first line, and as few infantry as possible. Sections occupying advanced positions, isolated by chance, will be withdrawn, so as not to be exposed to useless losses.

6/8/21. 9 p.m.

Papulas.

In the course of the day, the following order was received:

General Headquarters,
September 7th, 1921. 11 a.m.

1st, 2nd, and 3rd Army Corps.

1. The Army Corps will at once proceed to consolidate the positions they already occupy. This does not mean that G.H.Q. have renounced the offensive and the advance. On the contrary, with a strongly organized defence of our front we will be able to economize forces for the enveloping movement during the offensive. A position properly entrenched is equivalent to reinforcements in men and material, and it is criminal to neglect such important factors, besides which it contains great advantages in case of an attack by the enemy.

The enemy, with energetic and appropriate use of an organized defence, has succeeded in extending his front further than ours, though using fewer troops than we do, and also in keeping larger reserves than ours.

2. Zones of Army Corps laid down as follows:

2nd Army Corps, Kalé Grotto (inclusive), heights S.W. Temkeui (exclusive).

1st Army Corps, heights S.W. Temkeui (inclusive), Mount Tchal (inclusive).

3rd Army Corps, Mount Tchal (exclusive), heights Sagtsilar Yaila (W. of Sakharia) (inclusive).

The Army Corps will maintain liaison with each other between the zones.

3. 1st and 3rd Army Corps will each form a reserve of one entire division posted in the rear in a suitable position Proportionate reserves to be constituted by 2nd Army Corps.

4. The Army Corps on the basis of the above and after local reconnaissances will issue their orders, drawing up plans of fortifications and a scheme of defence which must be submitted to me as soon as possible. The work to start at once, without waiting for the plans to be prepared and approved.

Every third day, from September 14th, the Army Corps will submit plans drawn up to show in detail work of organization executed the past three days.

The Commander-in-Chief of the Army of Asia Minor.

A. Papulas.

This order probably meant that we were to await the government's answer to the commander-in-chief's report, but the paragraph relative to the report to be sent every three days from 14 September was not calculated to soothe the overstrained nerves of the combatants. The entire army had been in the front line since 23 August, and even after the enemy had been pushed back from his first line local actions had not ceased; since 3 September the enemy had begun to make attacks which were occasionally of a serious nature. It was, therefore, natural to expect a decision either in favour of an advance or of a withdrawal, so long as there was still time to do so. The above-mentioned paragraph of the order gave rise to the suspicion that trench fighting of the same nature as in the European War was about to begin. In addition, GHQ next day ordered the corps (this order is not in my possession) to report the names of officers who had knowledge of trench warfare. With my approval, my chief of the staff wrote another letter to Lieutenant-General Papulas reminding him of his answer, and pointing out the necessity of transferring the 2nd Army Corps before it became impossible.

The morning of the 8th the chief of the staff of the cavalry brigade, Colonel Papagos, came to my HQ and reported that there was no more fodder in the district within a radius of 10 kilometres, that the horses were dying every day from starvation, and that no horseshoes had been received yet. Besides this, supplies of every kind in the corps were getting more scarce. Hardly any ammunition had been received, only a quarter of the bread ration had been issued for the last nine days, we were entirely lacking in firewood, and for three days there had been nothing with which to prepare breakfast. The cold at that height at night was very marked, and the men's clothing and boots were in a wretched condition: the transport convoys, bringing the few supplies from a great distance, suffered greatly from daily attacks, which obliged us to protect them with detachments formed from various units. I do not know if the other two corps suffered the same serious privations as we did, as they were closer to the lines of communications.

That same day the commander of the engineers of the corps, Colonel Botsaris, gave me his views on the work of fortification, which he had been ordered to study, and which had been begun in sections during the night. He explained that the fortification of the corps sector—which, according to the views of GHQ, was to be held by one division only, the other remaining in reserve—presented many difficulties, and would take a long time to execute for want of tools; there was no wood for shelters, dugouts, etc. After the completion of the earth works, the front (20 kilometres) was too long to be properly held by one weak division, and even if the right and rear were protected it was liable to be surrounded.

GHQ did not consider this aspect of the situation, and this, as well as many other similar cases, was a proof of their complete ignorance of the local conditions of the corps, besides which they would not take my reports into consideration. In any case, I made up my mind to explain to them for the last time my views on the situation, and the reasons for which it was urgent to strengthen the left wing of

Right: Prince Andrew of Greece and Denmark, *c.* 1900. (*Public domain*)

Below: Tatoi Palace, birthplace of Prince Andrew. (*Public domain*)

Prince Andrew (left), with his brothers, Crown Prince Constantine and Prince Nicholas, *c.* 1902. (*Public domain*)

Prince Andrew's wife, Princess Alice of Battenberg (Princess Andrew of Greece and Denmark), with two of their daughters, Princesses Margarita and Theodora of Greece and Denmark, *c.* 1912. (*Wikimedia Commons*)

Above: Prime Minister Eleftherios Venizelos of Greece. (*Library of Congress*)

Right: Anastasios Papoulas, Prince Andrew's commanding officer and Commander-in-Chief of the Greek Army in Asia Minor. (*Public domain*)

Greek troops posing for a photograph. (*Public domain*)

Smyrniots welcome the Greeks with garlands, flags and a picture of Premier Venizelos, May 1919. (*Levantine Heritage Foundation*)

Smyrna barracks, then occupied by the Greek Army, flying the Greek flag in May 1919. (*Levantine Heritage Foundation*)

Greek soldiers in Smyrna, 1920. (*Public domain*)

The aftermath of the Battle of Sakarya. (*Public domain*)

Evacuation of Greek soldiers. (*Public domain*)

Greek soldiers retreating, 1922. (*Public domain*)

HMS *Calypso*, the ship that took Prince Andrew and his family into exile. (*Wikimedia Commons*)

Left: Prince Andrew of Greece, January 1921. (*Wikimedia Commons*)

Below: Prince and Princess Andrew of Greece in London, 1922, shortly after his exile. (*Wikimedia Commons*)

the army by the immediate transfer of the whole of the army corps, and I ordered Colonel Botsaris to go to GHQ for that purpose.

The army was, at this time, from a military point of view, in a very exceptional and precarious situation. The commander-in-chief and his staff, confronted by an unforeseen military situation, had not the courage to take the responsibility of either continuing the expedition to Angora or of discontinuing it by retiring to the west of the Sakharia. Instead of this they stopped the advance and left the government to take the responsibility of giving a decision on a military problem, which could only be solved on the spot. In my personal opinion, the situation was most serious, but not desperate; we had not 'lost the game'—far from it. The advance to Angora was still possible, the morale of the troops was good, and the determination to enter Angora sufficiently strong. I have no hesitation in saying that GHQ would still have carried their scheme to a successful conclusion if they had appealed to the men's good will, instead of preferring to keep them idle for so many days, and at the same time trying to shift the responsibility for their further decisions on to the shoulders of the minister of war, who was far from the scene of operations and ignorant of the science of war. By strengthening the left wing of the army with the 2nd Army Corps, and attacking the enemy's right, which was weakly protected, from that flank, our entry into Angora was assured (as far as one can prophesy in war), and the enemy's retreat might even have degenerated into a serious defeat.

Such was the situation when, suddenly and without warning, the event which I had rightly feared, and tried time after time to point out to GHQ, occurred. At 5 a.m., the morning of 9 September, I received order No. 19531/6239/3 from GHQ, which can only be described as a cry of ill-concealed panic:

No. 19531 /6239 /3. A.

1st, 2nd, and 3rd Army Corps.

According to information, which can be considered reliable, enemy concentrated considerable forces against 3rd Army Corps. Will probably execute main offensive against it, with a feint against the rest of the front, to push back 3rd Army Corps and cut communications of army.

In face of such a serious situation, the following action is imperative. An energetic defence to the last by 3rd Army Corps, and an immediate violent attack by 1st and 2nd Army Corps in force ... towards the north.

Impossible to transfer forces from our right to our left; this would have definitely brought about ... yielding to the enemy, and these forces would have arrived very late whatever the result.

When the enemy attack against 3rd Army Corps declares itself, 1st Army Corps will immediately execute attack with objective Osmanié, heights Sarighiol and secondary objective ridge Kiutuk, and 2nd Army Corps to the N. in the direction Bolatli Tchair (Boyali?) covering 1st with mixed detachment. Corps to attack violently and desperately. 3rd Army Corps will resist energetically to the last, and will try to attack with XIIth Division towards N. and N.E. 3rd Army Corps, when positively convinced of facing a general attack, will report to me and inform 1st and 2nd Army Corps, who will begin the attack without further order. All Army Corps, on receiving present order, will issue their orders and keep commanders of divisions and of units informed of situation.

9.45 p.m.

Papulas.

On reading the order carefully the agitation of GHQ becomes apparent. Certainly the situation, as the order pointed out, was most serious, for if the lines of communication to the river were cut off the army ran the greatest risk of finding itself without any supplies in food and ammunition. But even though the situation was very serious, the solution suggested by the order was not the only possible one. An offensive by the 1st and 2nd Army Corps towards the north, however violent and desperate, would not have saved the 3rd Army Corps from the threatened attack. The enemy, strongly fortified opposite the 1st and 2nd Army Corps, would have left few, but nevertheless sufficient, troops to prevent these corps from advancing more than 3 or 4 kilometres in two days, during which time he would have pushed back the 3rd Army Corps by reason of his superiority in numbers, and succeeded in cutting the communications of the army. Further, the experience of the fighting of these last days had shown us that, from August 24th to 29th, the army corps had advanced about 15 kilometres, fighting day and night, after expending nearly all their ammunition, and utilizing the greater part of their troops. How could they now advance, with insufficient ammunition and their units weakened by heavy losses, sufficiently far to relieve the pressure on the 3rd Army Corps? The other solution consisted in transferring the troops on the right flank—i.e., the two divisions of the 2nd Army Corps—to the left (or rather to the centre); these could then, in conjunction with the 3rd Army Corps, push back the enemy and execute an attack on his right, portions of which only were entrenched.

An operation such as I have just mentioned had been considered by Lieutenant-General Papulas, but he had hesitated too long and had been forestalled by events. In his order he says that he does not order the transfer of the corps, as there was no time to do so, but in my opinion there was still time. If the corps had been got ready, down to the smallest detail, during the day, to start moving at nightfall so as to reach Sivri near the 3rd Army Corps by a forced night march at noon the next day, then, in the event of the enemy not yet having commenced his attack, the 2nd Corps would have been in a position either to support the 3rd Army Corps, if attacked, or to take part in an offensive against the enemy's right; if the enemy had already attacked, he would have been repulsed by the intervention of the 2nd Army Corps; or, again, if the 3rd Army Corps had given way, the 2nd could have attacked the left flank of the advancing enemy.

I immediately enquired of the 1st Army Corps, with whom we were connected by telephone, if there were any signs of an attack on the 3rd Army Corps, and I learnt that complete calm reigned. The chief of the staff of the 1st Army Corps, Colonel Stylianos Gonatas—the same who, about a year later, as president of the revolutionary government, accused me before the military tribunal for disobedience and abandoning my position before the enemy—communicating with my chief of the staff by telephone, declared that an attack by the 1st and 2nd Army Corps, however violent and desperate, would not succeed in averting the danger from the 3rd Army Corps. As to the plan of transferring the corps, he considered this to be the only solution, though he was uneasy in his mind about the right wing of the 1st Army Corps being properly protected after the departure of the 2nd, which had been on his right from the commencement of the operations.

After receiving the information that the attack on the 3rd Army Corps had not yet begun, and taking into consideration (1) Lieutenant-General Papulas' letter in which he wrote agreeing with the intervention of the 2nd Army Corps on the left wing of the army; (2) the last phrase in his order, saying that he had not ordered this action for lack of time; (3) the highly critical state of the situation in general, I decided to make preparations for the possible transfer of the corps. The transfer, if carried out, would be effected during the night—firstly, so as to give GHQ the necessary time, either to approve of or to forbid the operation before evening; and, secondly, because it was impossible to transfer the corps during the daytime without being observed by the enemy.

Having taken this decision, I immediately sent for the two divisional commanders, and when I had communicated my plans to them, I issued the necessary preparatory orders for the execution of the transfer, which was to start with the fighting troops at 7 p.m., at which time it begins to get dark at that time of year. Of these, an infantry regiment with a mountain battery would remain, while the corps was passing, on the right of the 1st Army Corps, so as to cover it, till further orders. The operation had to start at once with the movement of the transport convoys of the corps, because, as these moved every day by daylight, the suspicions of the enemy would not be aroused. I had to send them off long before the fighting sections, because they included hundreds of carts, moving very slowly, and herds of cattle for slaughter, and if they did not start early enough, they would impede the fighting units considerably, and would run the risk of falling into the enemy's hands. In case GHQ should not wish to approve the transfer, the transport, which would not have moved very far, could return, or rather some of it; as for the rest, such as the pontoon company, the sanitary detachments, and cattle, the safest place for them was the rear of the 1st Army

Corps, on account of the situation in which the 2nd Army Corps was placed. Besides this, three days before, reconnaissances had been executed by my orders and those of GHQ to decide on the safest route for the transport to the rear of the 1st Army Corps.

To this I must add that my order to prepare the transfer was only communicated to the commanders of the two divisions and the cavalry brigade and their chiefs of the staff; consequently the accusation that my decision had a damaging effect on the morale of the troops is false, for no one outside the staffs had any knowledge of this order.

It was also stated that it was my fault that the morale of GHQ fell, as the latter, entirely misunderstanding my object, thought that the 2nd Army Corps could no longer be regarded as a fighting force. This way of justifying themselves was invented later, and was used as a means of covering the responsibility of those who had already decided to order the suspension of the advance and the immediate passage of the army across the Sakharia. My action was not misunderstood by GHQ, nor was it ever possible to misunderstand it. If anyone reads my message on this subject, he can see that it is quite clear that my intention was to reinforce the 3rd Army Corps, and not to retire from the fighting line by crossing the river. Finally, I must reject the third accusation made against me that my decision was the result of many conferences and counsels.

No conferences or counsels ever took place while I was in command of the army corps; and when I called together the divisional commanders that morning, I did it to explain matters to them personally, so that there should not be the slightest doubt about my aims and intentions, and after I had explained the situation, I gave them my orders.

After this I sent the following report to GHQ:

HEADQUARTERS 2ND ARMY CORPS,
9/9/21. No. 1491. 8 a.m.
G.H.Q. IN ASIA MINOR.

Your order No. 19531 received. Attack by 2nd Corps in the direction indicated impossible, the enemy's left wing extending much more east. If enemy shows signs of attacking 3rd Corps, our frontal attack of no avail on account of nature of ground and strong fortifications; eventual progress insignificant and slow. On the contrary, transfer of corps to Sivri will permit of energetic and decisive intervention in the struggle. Our first sections can reach Sivri tomorrow noon. The reflections and spirit of your order in which the transfer was not ordered only because it was not considered possible to execute it in time, in combination with know ledge of your intention to reinforce left wing, led me to decide transfer corps tonight to Tambakli, continuing tomorrow march to Sivri. I consider it possible to execute this in time, as 3rd Army Corps has not

been attacked yet. My preliminary orders relative to this were issued 7 a.m., and movement of transport in above direction has commenced.
2nd Army Corps,
Andrew.

No doubt the above message was not in accordance with ordinary practice, but I think that, beyond that, it does not constitute an infraction of orders, nor does it show any lack of fighting spirit. There is, however, a breach of formality, and this lies in the fact that in the message the correct phrase 'subject to approval', was omitted, but the omission of this phrase cannot possibly form the basis of an accusation for disobedience and abandoning one's position. There is no infraction of orders, because the order of GHQ had fixed an attack by the 1st and 2nd Army Corps as soon as information was received from the 3rd Army Corps that they had been attacked; such information was not received. The plans and preparations for the transfer of the 2nd Army Corps do not constitute an infraction of orders. It would be an infraction if the transfer of the corps had been carried out without the approval of GHQ: it would have been an infraction of orders and a crime if even one company had been withdrawn from the firing line it would have been an infraction of orders if, information having been received from the 3rd Army Corps, a violent and desperate attack to the north had not immediately been ordered. None of these events occurred; the transfer was not carried out, because I waited for the approval of GHQ, which in the end was not forthcoming, and the corps remained in its position. That neither the 1st nor 2nd Army Corps made an attack on 9 September was not due to want of initiative on the corps commanders' part, but simply because the circumstances, necessitating the 3rd Army Corps asking for an attack to be made, did not arise. It is true that the transfer of the transport was begun, but this movement cannot be characterized as the commencement of the transfer of the corps. The commencement of the move of the transport was simply a preparatory move. The reasons, for which the transfer of the transport was decided, were not dictated only by the necessity of sending them ahead sufficiently early so as not to put obstacles in the way of the fighting units, but also to ensure a better supply service. For this latter reason the corps had already decided to move them two days before, and even if the answer of GHQ had forbidden the transfer of the corps, this move would have taken place and would have followed that route.

It was certainly not a question of moving the fighting units without approval; this had never been my intention; if so, I certainly ought to have been accused of direct infraction of orders and of disobedience. The fact that such an idea had not crossed my mind for an instant is proved by the telegraphic message that I sent early that morning to GHQ, and to which I was bound to receive an answer before dusk either by wireless or by motorcar. If I had intended to move at 7 p.m. without the previous approval of GHQ, I would not have reported my intention as early as 8 a.m. The minute the message was sent off, the wireless operators of the corps, as well as of the divisions, were cautioned that an order from GHQ was expected. In the morning, when I gave my orders personally to the divisional commanders about the proposed transfer that night, I particularly told them that the preparations for the transfer were being made on my personal initiative, and that, consequently, no movement or communication of orders was to take place before the approval of my action by GHQ. The divisional commanders, Colonel Digenis of the XIIIth; Colonel Trilivas* of the Vth; Colonel Nicolaïdes of the cavalry brigade; old and tried soldiers, who had gained their experience of war on the battlefields of Europe and Asia, together with the chief of the staff of the corps, Colonel Gavallias; the commander of the artillery, Colonel Papaïoannu; and the chiefs of the staffs of the divisions, Major Kalliangakis and Major Demestichas, were all in complete agreement with me, which would surely not have been the case if they had understood that an infraction of orders of GHQ had been contemplated. Moreover, the commander of the engineers of the corps, Colonel Botsaris—absent at the time of issuing my orders to the above—a personal friend of Colonel Saryannis, and sharing his political opinions, congratulated me afterwards on the decision I had taken, which he considered to be the only correct one to take and a salvation, in face of the panic which had seized GHQ and especially Colonel Saryannis.† I have already said that Colonel Gonatas had declared to my chief of staff that the views of the 1st Army Corps coincided with mine.

It has been contended against me, then and later, that it was on account of my action at that time and my lack of 'offensive spirit' that the plan to advance to Angora was frustrated. This accusation is the main excuse of Colonel Saryannis and of his friends at GHQ, who had so lightly conceived this advance to Angora. This accusation is in itself one of the legends created at that time, for there is proof that GHQ had taken the decision to retire on 2 September, whereas the proposal to transfer the 2nd Army Corps was not made till 9 September.

It is true that Lieutenant-General Papulas in his letter writes as if the plan to go to Angora was still being followed; but this is probably due to the fact that the commander-in-chief, either did not wish the decision to withdraw to be known yet, or that he was not kept informed of the plans and decisions of his staff. However that may be, we have the clear deposition of Major-General Stratigos, as well as the definite declaration made by Major-General Pallis at the trial of Gunaris and the others, to Captain Skylakakis, that the decision to retire from the

* Lieutenant-General Trilivas describes these events in exactly the same spirit in the review, '*Nea Epochi*' of 14 March 1926.

† Colonel Botsaris tried in vain to appear as a witness at my trial, but it was forbidden by the military tribunal.

Sakharia had been taken before my action of the 9th, and was, in consequence, quite independent of it.

I do not suppose that Colonel Saryannis' accusation, that 'my lack of offensive spirit which influenced the 2nd Army Corps was the cause of the suspension of the advance to Angora,' was founded on a better basis, for any impartial critic on reading my message (No. 1491) will see that it breathes a spirit of attack from beginning to end. This attempt on the part of Colonel Saryannis to justify the failure of his plans does not correspond with the facts, for if the 2nd Army Corps had really lost its fighting spirit, GHQ would not have said afterwards in their order of 10 September (No. 6349/3) that they were considering an attack and the use of the 2nd Army Corps by placing it between the 1st and the 3rd. Besides this, the further use of the corps clearly proves that GHQ had not at all lost confidence in its ability to attack.

After sending off my message, I awaited the development of the situation, until the order of GHQ, approving my decision, should arrive (about which I had not a moment's doubt) in readiness, in the meantime, to undertake the violent and desperate attack to the north on receiving an appeal from the 3rd Corps.

But the enemy did riot attack the 3rd Army Corps on 9 September as GHQ expected. On the contrary, this corps advanced a little, capturing some points. This event seemed to have sufficed for the staff of GHQ to swing round as usual from panic to optimism. Perhaps they thought that the information as to the enemy concentrations against the 3rd Corps was not true, as had been the case on 23 August. I suppose that all these reasons, and the indignation which GHQ felt at the insistence with which I had been trying for days to enlighten them on the real situation, affected the answer to my report, sent in the afternoon, which was as follows:

> No. 19556/6265.
>
> 3.35 p.m. 9/9/21. Tel.
>
> 2nd Army Corps.
>
> Astonished at plan of abandoning your positions, I order corps to remain in its position. Only person competent to judge and decide is myself as Commander-in-Chief. Cancel all orders of transfer movements.
>
> Papulas.

I think there can be no doubt that the expressions used in, and the phraseology of, this message are too strong for the case in question. Seeing that my action was in accordance with the commander-in-chief's views; seeing also that my action had not yet begun, and that there was time enough to cancel it, if necessary, I think that the expression about abandoning my position was too strong and unwarranted into the bargain; it was a complete lowering of my prestige as commander of an army corps and as a general officer. I again sent for the divisional commanders, cancelled the order for the transfer, and ordered them to be ready at any minute to attack violently and desperately to the north. The night passed in absolute calm, and the enemy remained inactive in his positions.

The morning of 10 September brought me a fresh surprise: an order from GHQ, received at 5 a.m., relieved my chief of the staff, Colonel Gavallias, of his duties, placing him at the disposal of the commander-in-chief, and appointing in his place Colonel P. Nicolaïdes, till then commander of the cavalry brigade. Cowardice was now added to the panic which dominated the actions of GHQ. GHQ, not wishing or not daring to touch me, turned against Colonel Gavallias and punished him for an act the responsibility for which was mine, and mine only. They did not wish to touch me, because—as Lieutenant-General Papulas and Colonel Saryannis deposed at my trial—they were afraid that perhaps, as I exercised a great influence on the troops as brother of King Constantine, my dismissal would have a dangerous moral effect. From this act it is evident how much the morale of the Supreme Command had declined, for what else did Colonel Gavallias' dismissal betoken but the displeasure of the commander-in-chief towards the commander of the 2nd Army Corps? Colonel Gavallias was not the commander of the corps—I was. I do not know how to express my opinion of a commander-in-chief who, having lost the confidence he has in the commander of a higher unit, does not immediately replace him in his command. To keep this commander in his place and to dismiss only his chief of the staff, an officer of recognized ability, simply because he executed the orders given him by his chief, betrays a lamentable lack of moral courage. It is inconceivable to think of the holder of the highest command in the army as lacking in moral courage. The situation was unbearable to me, for, besides the accusation of abandoning my positions, I appeared, in the eyes of the whole army, as devoid of military ability. My retention of the command of the army corps, after the dismissal of the old and the nomination of the new chief of staff (no matter whether he was Colonel P. Nicolaïdes, an excellent officer from every point of view, or another), was equal to a supervision of my subsequent conduct, and was a public and marked expression of the mistrust and lack of confidence which the commander-in-chief felt in me. I could not possibly accept such a situation, and answered immediately as follows:

Tel. 10/9/21. 6.30 a.m.

GENERAL HEADQUARTERS IN ASIA MINOR.

After the reflections on my conduct contained in your message, No. 19556/6265, and in general the fact that views of corps on questions supported by responsible opinions of divisional commanders and other competent officers are not taken into slightest consideration, it is absolutely impossible for me to continue in command of corps. Please order my immediate relief.

The 2nd Army Corps,

Andrew.

As soon as the dismissal of my chief of the staff was known, the commander of the artillery, Colonel Papaïannu, submitted to me a letter in which he requested to be relieved of his duties, as he considered himself as equally responsible with the chief of staff. Later the same request was verbally submitted by the commander of the engineers. Naturally I did not hand in these requests, but it is clear from them that there was no disunion or difference of thought in the staff of the 2nd Army Corps.

About 11 a.m. I received the following personal and confidential telegram:

Important reasons do not permit nor do I contemplate replacing you.

Papulas.

I must here note that the above telegram was personal and confidential, whereas the first was not so.

I answered that I insisted on resigning—unreasonably, perhaps—but my indignation had reached its height. Finally, the question of my relief was solved by the following wireless message from the commander-in-chief:

No. 58.

6 p.m. 10/9/21.

COMMANDER 2ND ARMY CORPS.

Neither your opinion nor that of divisional commanders was submitted to G.H.Q. I desire, and situation demands, you should remain in your place.

Papulas.

Shortly after receiving the order of GHQ dismissing my chief of the staff—that is to say, about 8 a.m.—the enemy began an attack against the right wing of the 1st Army Corps by the much-discussed gap between the left of the 2nd and the right of the 1st. In a short while, cavalry reconnaissances reported that an enemy column, taking three-quarters of an hour to pass, was advancing in the direction of Kerpidj towards the rear of the corps. These movements of the enemy gave me the impression that the attack against the 3rd Army Corps was imminent, and that the enemy was trying to immobilize our right wing. Besides the attack of the enemy by the gap on the left of the 2nd Army Corps and the appearance of a column in our rear, the enemy commenced a heavy artillery fire against the right, and soon after a severe bombardment started all along our front.

For the moment there was a tendency on the enemy's part to encircle us, and the situation appeared to be extremely critical for the 2nd Army Corps. As regards the front and the right wing, the action was left to the local units there. The cavalry brigade (Colonel N. Varthis), with a battalion of infantry and some artillery, was sent to make a fuller reconnaissance and oppose an initial resistance against the column appearing in the rear. To deal with the more important action—i.e., the enemy attack on the right flank of the 1st Army Corps—we had a force composed of two regiments of the Vth Division, which had been placed to the rear and left of the XIIIth Division on 3 September in view of just such an attack by the enemy.

The Vth Division, at the first symptoms of this serious offensive, attacked spontaneously, thanks to the spirit of initiative which distinguished its commander, Colonel Trilivas. I approved this action, and issued my order No. 1497. The enemy consisted of two divisions (the Vth and VIIth), and our attack was executed by the 33rd Infantry Regiment (Colonel Rokas) and one battalion of the 43rd, the whole of the mountain artillery of the division, the 2nd Field Artillery Regiment, and the brigade of Skoda under Major N. Papadimas through the gap between the two army corps, obliquely towards Kizil Koyundou. The enemy, attacked frontally at the same time by a detachment of the 1st Division, was easily held back.

After the above-described action, involving the whole corps, the following order was received from GHQ:

No. 19574/6301/3. B.

GENERAL HEADQUARTERS,
10/9/21. 9.45 a.m.

2ND ARMY CORPS.

At 5 a.m. today offensive commenced against 1st Army Corps; became general opposite its front; principal efforts directed against right. Give suitable support to right of the 1st Corps in conjunction with it.

Papulas.

As is evident, the action ordered by GHQ had already been taken before the receipt of the above order.

The impression I had gained from the morning's military situation, that an offensive against the 3rd Army Corps was imminent, was correct, because, about 1:30 p.m., that corps informed the 1st and 2nd Army Corps that the expected offensive had commenced, that they were holding back the enemy for the present, and that these corps were to be ready for action—that is to say, for the violent and desperate attack to the north. The situation was very critical from every point of view, but what disturbed me most was the fact that the offensive against the 3rd Army Corps had started just at the moment that the 2nd Army Corps was fixed to its place and the 1st Army Corps was being attacked on its right and, as I was subsequently informed, its centre.

In the meantime, the operations of the Vth Division were being excellently carried out, the enemy attacking the centre was easily held back, and thus the pressure against the right of the 1st Army Corps was considerably lightened. On the rest of the front, the enemy confined himself to a heavy bombardment.

At 4 p.m. I received the following totally unexpected order from GHQ:

No. 19580/6315/3. C. 10/9/21.

1st and 2nd Army Corps.

Left wing of VIIth Division (extreme left 3rd Army Corps) was pushed back by enemy. Therefore 2nd Army Corps will start on receiving this, and will proceed by forced marches to Karahamdjali–Tchanakdji.

1st Army Corps will take measures for safety of right. XIIth Division starting at once will make for Tchanakdji. Superfluous corps transport to be sent bridge Kavundji.

Papulas.

The 2nd Army Corps was ordered to move to the left of the line of battle, to the rear of the 3rd Army Corps—that is to say, that GHQ was now ordering that which they had forbidden the day before, and they ordered it at the moment when the left wing of the 3rd Army Corps had given way and the two other corps were unable to move. The preceding day, GHQ had decided that there was not sufficient time to make the transfer when there were no signs of an attack, and now they ordered this same transfer after the attack had declared itself in the middle of the battle. I think that comment is superfluous.

The move which GHQ now desired could not be executed at once, as was laid down in the order, because the corps was itself involved in a severe action, and its withdrawal was not easy. I was obliged to wait for nightfall, for if the enemy should realize that the corps was abandoning its position, no matter whether it was a transfer or a retreat, he would react with all his strength; and this reaction would take the form of a strong attack that would either bring the units, who were attempting to break off the action, to a definite standstill, or create confusion amongst them. As I had fortunately issued my orders for the transfer the preceding day, the details thereof were known, and it was now only necessary for me to give instructions that the order was to be executed the coming night, with some changes, of course, for the units involved in the fighting. There still remained a hope that the enemy, according to his usual custom, would cease his offensive and stop firing in the evening; but this hope was slight, because all the symptoms pointed to a decisive battle, which the Turkish Army was at last delivering after a campaign of many months.

During the course of the afternoon, the force, composed of two regiments of the Vth Division, penetrating into the gap, repulsed the enemy and pursued him to his fortified positions from which he had sallied forth, during which time almost the whole of my corps artillery was engaged. This action of the Vth Division, in conjunction with the activity of the 1st Army Corps, was so successful, that the enemy retreated in disorder, and for the first time since the beginning of the operations we saw even officers fleeing full tilt. I attribute this panic to the fact that the enemy had ventured rather far from his fortified line, and on being defeated lost his morale, which was excellent only as long as he was defending himself inside the fortified lines or making a counterattack.

Fortunately, towards evening, the firing ceased along the front and also the embarrassments of the right wing, as a result, I suppose, of the successful action of the Vth Division. The column which had appeared at the rear of the corps, according to information from the cavalry brigade, was composed of cavalry, which turned to the west in the direction of Inlar Katrandji. I therefore reported this to GHQ to enable them to take measures to protect the field hospitals there.

As I was later informed, this cavalry detachment was the one which crossed the Sakharia by the bridge of Fethioglou and occupied Sivri-Hissar.

The Vth Division was ordered to avoid being drawn into further pursuit; all the details of the move of the corps were arranged, and finally, with the greatest difficulty, I succeeded in concentrating the entire corps and commencing the march to Suzundjali about 11 p.m. This most difficult movement was executed to perfection without even leaving one sheep to the enemy, and without his having the slightest realization of what was happening, and it was only the following morning, about 8 a.m., that a hostile aeroplane discovered our march when near the village of Evli Fakeli (lower). Unfortunately, the march took place under the worst conditions, because, on account of the conflicting orders of GHQ, the fighting troops found themselves entangled with transport of every kind, which I had been obliged to recall in accordance with the order of GHQ of 9 September.

At 10 a.m. on the 11th, the corps reached the district of Suzundjali, where a halt for rest was made. In this village, I received the following order from GHQ:

No. 6349/3. D.

General Headquarters,
10/9/21. 10.15 p.m.

1st, 2nd, and 3rd Army Corps.

Enemy today made violent attack against 3rd and 1st Army Corps and was repulsed. He succeeded only in capturing twin hills W. Basrikeui. 2nd Army Corps has been ordered to proceed by night march district Sarihalil–Karahamdjali, where it is reckoned it will be tomorrow noon. Tomorrow 3rd Army Corps will defend itself energetically to the last to keep its positions and regain twin hills. The 1st Army Corps, to whom the cavalry brigade is attached, will defend the right of the army energetically, holding Mount Tchal at least, and will refuse its right flank towards the south. G.H.Q. consider possible undertake counterattack, placing day after tomorrow 2nd Army Corps between 1st and 3rd. Superfluous transport of corps to be sent to the west of the Sakharia and concentrated as follows: 3rd Army Corps by two bridges at Beilik and two at Kavundji to district Mulk. 2nd Army Corps via Kavundji to district Kaves. 1st Army Corps via Kavundji to district Merdjan.

The Commander-in-Chief of Army,
Asia Minor,
Papulas.

This order, issued late in the evening of the 10th, shows clearly that until that hour (10:15 p.m.) GHQ were apparently only thinking of continuing the action and of making use of the 2nd Army Corps for the attack of September 12th.

A study of the three orders issued by GHQ on September 10th leads to the following conclusions:

Until 9:45 a.m. of September 10th—that is, until after the issue of order marked B, No. 19574/6301/3—the circumstances necessitating the execution of the first order marked A, No. 19531/6239/3 of September 9th had not yet arisen—namely, the enemy had not yet made a decisive attack against the 3rd Army Corps. The circumstances necessitating the execution of order marked A, No 19531/6239/3, did not actually arise till 1:30 p.m. on the 10th—i.e., at the moment that the 3rd Army Corps informed the 1st and 2nd Army Corps that the attack against it had begun, but even then the 3rd Army Corps simply asked that they should be ready for action.

From these two orders issued by GHQ on 10 September, it is clear that they had the conviction, firstly, that the 2nd Army Corps was still in its positions after the non-approval of the proposed transfer on 9 September; and, secondly, that the corps possessed the necessary fighting strength to give a suitable support to the

1st Army Corps. The 2nd Army Corps had already carried out this support by sending the Vth Division before the receipt of order marked B, No. 19574/6301/3, and the successful outcome of their action was reported to GHQ; consequently, they had full knowledge of the local situation of the corps. It remains, therefore, to examine the event which had obliged GHQ to order the transfer of the corps (see order marked C, No. 19580/6315/3). Certainly, it was not a lack of confidence in its ability to attack, as Colonel Saryannis asserted. The fact that such a lack of confidence did not exist is made evident in this order: 'The left wing of the VIIth Division was pushed back by enemy. Stop. After that, 2nd Army Corps is to start on receiving …' etc. It is clear that the calculations of GHQ were fundamentally erroneous, because they reckoned that the attack to the north by 1st and 2nd Army Corps would oblige the enemy to lighten his pressure on the 3rd Army Corps, but this did not occur. On 10 September (see order marked D, No. 6349/3) the enemy attacked the 3rd and 1st Army Corps. The 3rd did not consider that the moment for the intervention of the 1st and 2nd Army Corps had arrived, and simply contented themselves by asking them to be ready. The 1st was kept to its position by the enemy's attack, and the 2nd by undertaking an attack of its own volition (before the receipt of order marked B, No. 19574/6301/3) brought about an important local success; but the efforts of these two army corps in nowise influenced the outcome of the fighting on the front of the 3rd Army Corps, whose left wing had been pushed back by the enemy long before 4 p.m. 'After that' GHQ, realizing that not a diversion from the right, but only a serious reinforcement of the left could save the extremely precarious situation, ordered the transfer of the 2nd Army Corps to take place.

It has been said that if the whole of the 2nd Army Corps had attacked on 10 September, and not only the Vth Division, it could have influenced the outcome of the attack on the 3rd Army Corps, but this is incorrect, as those who support this view forget that virtually the whole of the corps—that is, two divisions at reduced strength—were actually fighting that day. The Vth Division attacked the enemy and penetrated into the gap between the 2nd and 1st Army Corps, while the remaining troops on the front and on the right wing (XIIIth Division) were kept in their positions by the enemy's action. It must also be taken into consideration that the action of the Vth Division, which was crowned with such success, was not an attack against the enemy's northern fortified front, but against forces penetrating into the gap on their flank, and it was a battle on the open plain.

After this digression, I will resume the relation of the events.

Order marked D, No. 6349/3, clearly demonstrated the intention of GHQ to undertake the counterattack with the 2nd Army Corps between the 3rd and 1st Army Corps (in the probable direction of Korsakli-Baïbourt), on 12 September, and I was obliged to reach the district of Sarihalil–Karahamdjali by the evening of the 11th, so as to be ready for the attack next day. The men were exhausted by the battle of the preceding day (10th) and by marching all night, but this could not be helped, as we were marching towards a battle on which the fate of the whole army depended. Consequently, after a halt of a few hours at Suzundjali, I was obliged to order the march to continue to Sarihalil.

This march, which was very laborious, was executed rather slowly on account of the exhaustion of the men and beasts, and the last troops of the divisions were not in camp till midnight. The corps was certainly not in the best condition in which to undertake a serious offensive in the morning, but, in spite of everything, its fighting spirit was not diminished. Establishing my HQ between Sarihalil and Karahamdjali at about 8 p.m., I waited for the order of operations for the following day. This order, received at 10 p.m., is as follows:

No. 19709/6386/3.

GENERAL HEADQUARTERS,
September 11th, 1921.

1ST, 2ND, AND 3RD ARMY CORPS.

Enemy today executed repeated violent attacks against 3rd Army Corps and was repulsed with great losses, amongst them hundreds of prisoners. 1st Army Corps will abandon its position and will proceed during night, September 11th to 12th, to occupy general line heights Sarihalil–Ilidja. This line will be decisively defended against all enemy attacks. Under orders of 1st Army Corps will be placed mixed detachment at Inlar Katrandji and bridge-heads, with field artillery at confluence Gheouk, Sakharia. 3rd Army Corps will hold and defend decisively positions it is occupying. During the night of today, September 11th to 12th, it will withdraw a little its right wing towards heights Sarihalil. 2nd Army Corps during day, tomorrow, will study occupation in the night, September 12th to 13th, defensive positions on heights, western bank Sakharia, between Kavundji and Purshak, for defence of river, taking special care of existing bridges and probable crossings.

Supplies for tomorrow. 1st and 2nd Army Corps bridge Kavundji by motor transport. 3rd Army Corps rail-station Sagtsilar.

Army Corps to send within day, tomorrow, indispensable transports W. Sakharia to points named.

Commander-in-Chief of Army.
Papulas

This order was entirely unexpected, for I did not for a minute imagine that GHQ would decide to cross the Sakharia and thus break off the battle, when they had such forces at their disposal. I do not exactly know what fact influenced GHQ to take this decision—that is to say, the suspension of the

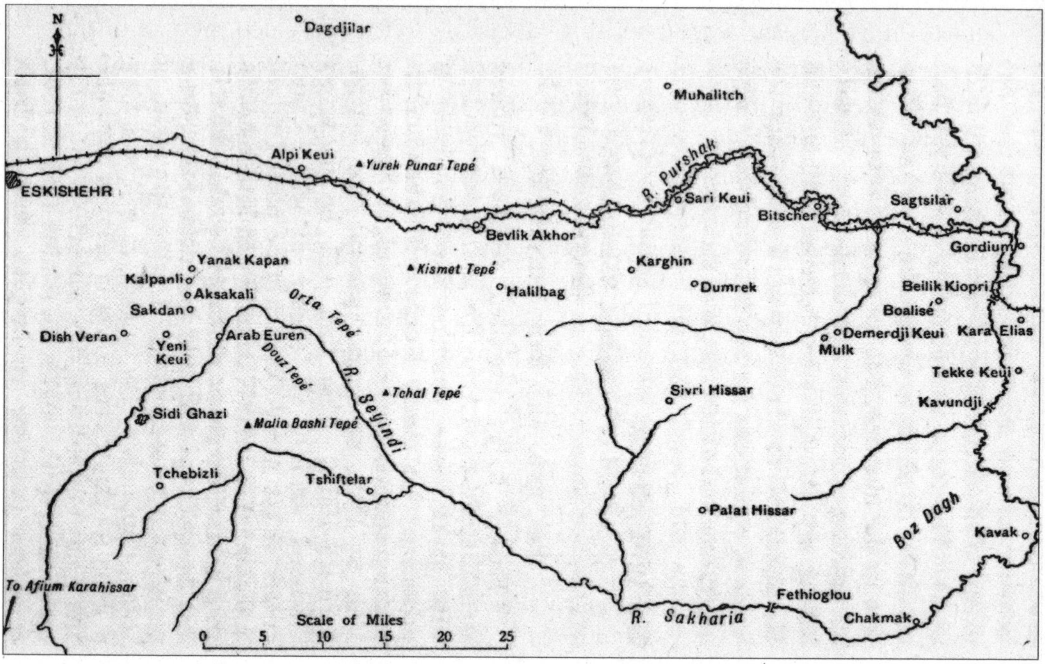

The movement of the 2nd Army Corps, 12 September to 23 September.

advance to Angora. I know for certain, however, that they did not take this course as a consequence of receiving an order from the government, because in a conversation with the minister of war, N. Theotoky, after the campaign, he explicitly declared to me that such an order was not given, and expressed himself with great severity against this initiative of the commander-in-chief. I am consequently obliged to infer that the members of GHQ in this case followed their usual habit of changing rapidly from enthusiasm to the deepest pessimism. The initiative shown by the enemy, and the strong blow against the 3rd Army Corps, apparently convinced the commander-in-chief, and those about him, that further insistence on the original plan would expose us to destruction. According to Major-General Stratigos' review of the campaign, the suspension of the advance and the crossing of the Sakharia had been decided on as long ago as 2 September; but everyone will agree with me that the moment chosen to interrupt the battle was unfortunate, because the retreat was ordered at the moment of strong hostile pressure, and thus gave the enemy the impression that this was the result of his attack. The military situation was undoubtedly serious, but not desperate; if it had been so, the order to cross the river would have been useless. The 3rd Army Corps was fighting very steadily, recapturing some of the lost positions, and if the VIIth Division gave way a little, to the rear of it were the Vth and XIIIth Divisions of the 2nd Army Corps, who were well able to restore the balance. The 1st Army Corps also was fighting with success, holding the enemy's attacks. There is no doubt, as it happens, that the decision to retire was taken prematurely.

After receiving the above order, I sent off the superfluous transport and appointed the officers who were to proceed on the morrow to study the ground west of the Sakharia between Kavundji and the Purshak. A little later a second order was received, issued at 9:15 p.m., which named the various bridges over the Sakharia by which the army corps had to cross. A paragraph referring to the 2nd Army Corps reads thus: 'The 2nd Army Corps by bridges Kavundji and Tekkekeui towards the positions appointed by reconnaissance for occupation'.

The following morning, 12 September, I sent my chief of staff, Colonel Nikolaïdes, to GHQ to obtain personal and detailed information of the commander-in-chief's final intentions. The unexpected day's rest was most acceptable to the over-exhausted men, who had marched for twenty-four consecutive hours the preceding day. About 2:30 p.m. I received an order from GHQ, according to which the whole army was to cross the river that night and establish itself on the further bank.

I cannot understand why such a hurried crossing of the river was decided on, seeing that the enemy, once repulsed, did not resume his attack against the left wing. I do not know the reason for this decision, but at all events it was a serious one to make, for such a hurried action might have created great confusion during the passage, which was a very difficult operation to carry out, especially for the 3rd Army Corps, then in immediate contact with the enemy. In any case, the necessary orders were given, and at the appointed hour the divisions were on the move towards the Sakharia.

I marched ahead with my staff, and established my HQ at Tekkekeui close to the bridges. In this village I met my chief of staff, who had returned from GHQ, and he reported that the commander-in-chief's intention was to establish the army in defensive positions west of the Sakharia. The reason for the acceleration of the crossing was that news of fresh enemy concentrations had been received, and if the enemy were given an opportunity to make fresh attacks against the 3rd Army Corps, the latter would probably be held and unable to move, which would render the safe passage of the army doubtful.

Colonel Nikolaïdes further told me that he was charged by Lieutenant-General Papulas to ask me not to misunderstand his telegram, in which he described my action 'as abandoning my position', and to assure me of his absolute devotion to the dynasty. It does not seem to me that this kind of devotion can have anything to do with a simple question of discipline.

The passage of the 2nd Army Corps by pontoon bridges at Tekkekeui was accomplished in very orderly fashion, and the XIIIth Division, after crossing, occupied the sector from Kavundji to Beilik Kiopri, and the Vth from Beilik Kiopri to the Purshak. But the word 'occupied' in nowise describes exactly what occurred that night after the passage, because from want of sufficient time to study the appointed lines, as well as on account of the darkness and the disorder amongst the transport trains of the army corps, the troops soon lost their way. The divisions crossing the river found themselves in chaos and darkness; roads and even cart tracks were non-existent, and they occupied hills and ravines at haphazard.

I tried to find the direction of the village of Boalisé, situated to the rear of the centre of my line, and I rode along the river to the north in the hope of locating the road marked on the map, but I instantly found myself in the middle of a broad and disintegrated disorderly moving mass of all parts of the corps, of every kind of transport, and over everything a thick cloud of dust. The presence and the disorder of the transport trains was owing to their inability to get across before the fighting troops forestalled them. The transport of the 3rd Army Corps, having to cross by the same bridge, as well as that of Kara Elias further north, added to the general confusion.

It was lucky that the crossing of the Sakharia was ignored by the enemy, for if he had realized this and brought down, not artillery, but a few machine-guns to his own side of the river, our departure would have been turned into a flight, if not a panic, and the destruction would have been utter and complete. The temperament of the Greek soldier is very sensitive; so long as he advances, so long as he attacks, in spite of all unpleasant conditions such as toil and hunger, he considers himself the victor, and his morale is perfect. But the moment that he retreats, even when victorious, as was the case of the 2nd Army Corps on 10 September, his morale collapses and the slightest occurrence upsets him. For that reason, if the enemy had pursued us that night with a few shots, our retreat could easily have been turned into flight. In these circumstances, when the fate of the whole army depended on three or four wretched bridges, not one officer from GHQ was present to guide or control the passage. I undoubtedly consider that if that night did not end in a catastrophe, it must be attributed to the capacity and self-sacrifice of the officers of the line of every grade, considering that the whole night through the divisions were wandering about on utterly unknown ground. Added to all this, the 3rd Army Corps was ordered to traverse the lines of the 2nd Army Corps, which operation in the dark and in ignorance of the enemy's movements was a very dangerous undertaking.

As I was wandering about all night trying to restore order, I found myself finally, at about 6 a.m. on 13 September, in the village Demerdjikeui, appointed as HQ of the 2nd Army Corps and as a camping place for the IXth Division; but as a result of the general confusion I found the village occupied by units of the VIIth Division, who, after many attempts, had been concentrated and directed to the station of Sagtsilar, where they supposed the division to be.

I again must stress the fact that it was a blessing that the enemy did not realize that we were crossing the Sakharia, for, after the river was crossed, it was impossible for the divisions to occupy, as they should, the sectors marked down for them, on account of the steepness of the ground, the lack of roads, and the utter blackness of the night.

The 2nd Army Corps had been charged with the occupation of the heights west of the Sakharia from Kavundji to the Purshak, and also with the most important mission of supporting the 3rd Army Corps, if it should be pressed by the enemy while crossing the river. But in the darkness and the frightful disorder caused by the transport marching towards the front (for there was only one road they could use, parallel to the river to the north), it would have been easy for the enemy to cross the river, without our realizing his presence at all, on the western bank. But even if the enemy's presence over the river had been known to us, our activity would have been paralyzed for the above-mentioned reasons. I do not know why the enemy did not profit by circumstances so favourable to him; this may have been due to his ignorance of the movement we had undertaken, or the fighting on the preceding days may have exhausted him and forced him to remain inert. My personal opinion is that it was more a question of the former than the latter, for the enemy could not have imagined that we would have had the audacity to cross the Sakharia under the conditions in which we did; otherwise, however exhausted he was, it would have been impossible for him not to try to make some profit out of a circumstance which would literally have brought about the destruction of the Greek Army. In any case, the situation appeared to me to be most critical during the whole night, because I knew nothing about the position of the enemy or whether he intended to attack. I shall not discuss under what conditions the passage of the other corps took place.

When day dawned on 13 September the situation was certainly altered; the divisions had been able to occupy their sectors rapidly and in good order. But in the meantime the enemy, having at last realized the departure of the army, proceeded to make desperate attempts to cross the river in small parties, but his attempts were easily frustrated, and he confined himself to bringing his guns nearer to the eastern bank, from whence he hampered our movements. This action of our adversary was undertaken principally with a view to verifying our positions, and, with the exception of a rather more serious attempt at the ford of Gordium, which was finally repulsed, the day passed quietly. The situation, however, was anything but rosy, because we were in absolute ignorance of the fate of the other two corps, as well as of the position of GHQ, for, in spite of all the efforts of our wireless, we received no reply.

On 14 September I met Colonel Kalinsky, commander of the IXth Division, who reported that the situation of the division was not good, that the spirits of the troops had begun to fall from the moment of the retreat, and that the lack of various supplies was exercising a bad influence on discipline. He also related the manner in which the passage of the Sakharia was affected by the IXth Division. In accordance with the order of GHQ the division was to start at 7:30 p.m., but this order only came into the hands of Colonel Kalinsky quite by chance at 8:30 p.m.

One can imagine what commotion ensued, more especially as the division was at the time in contact with the enemy.

Here I was in total ignorance of the general situation, and only knowing that the commander-in-chief's intention was to maintain a defensive on the heights immediately west of the Sakharia. It must be understood that the river flowing before our front was not an important tactical obstacle, for though the Sakharia is deep, its want of breadth makes it easy to cross all along that part which immediately concerned us. Thus, in the early hours of 14 September, the enemy succeeded in uniting both shores of the river at Tekkekeui with two ropes, on which were placed doors from the houses of the upper village, and by this means he was able to move over some small forces. Certainly, the disposition of the army was more favourable than on the eastern shore of the Sakharia, for in any case its lines of communications were assured, and the supplies were more easily delivered on account of the proximity of the railway line; but, in spite of that, the right wing was exposed to a wide enveloping movement, against which the southern branch of the river gave no protection. A glance at the map suffices to enable one to realize that the direction of Tshiftelar–Sidi-Ghazi towards Eski-Shehr lies entirely outside of the Sakharia, and consequently open to an enemy having the initiative and courage of the Turkish Army. The fact that the river was not a serious obstacle was at once demonstrated, for in the course of that morning (14 September) I received a report that enemy cavalry had entered Sivri-Hissar, where various army formations and a field hospital had been left; and before the arrival at Mulk of a battalion and the artillery of the IXth Division a disaster had occurred, and the enemy had departed unhindered, taking a number of prisoners with him. The definite establishment of the army west of the Sakharia (for this appeared to be the intention) presupposed the taking of a whole series of measures, amongst which was the building of roads, for after the severe winter of the high table-lands of Asia Minor none of the existing country roads could be used for heavy-wheeled traffic. It was also necessary to construct suitable fortifications, buildings for the men, and sheds for the beasts. All this required much time and labour and, above all, that a decision should be made as soon as possible, so that work could be started before the commencement of the rainy season.

Towards noon I at last received an order from GHQ, which, however, brought no substantial change to the situation, and my ignorance of the final intentions of HQ remained the same. An event which caused me the liveliest uneasiness was a telephone message from GHQ late in the afternoon, in which I was asked to inform them if I knew anything about the 3rd Army Corps. It was already the second day after the army had crossed the Sakharia, and GHQ were in ignorance of the fate of one of their corps—that is to say, of one-third of their forces. This fact proved to me that the operation of the night of 12–13 September had been carried out under much more adverse conditions than I had imagined, showing that GHQ had lost contact with the army corps, and that after two days this contact had not been entirely re-established. I was not uneasy about the 3rd Army Corps, because I knew that it lay to the north of the Vth Division at Sagtsilar, but I was uneasy about the command of the army. When things were going well the movements of the corps were followed and reported on by liaison officers, but in difficult moments all contact was lost, and the staff of the commander-in-chief merely criticized the conduct and the actions of those fighting at the front.

The morning of 15 September, Captain of Artillery Presetakos, a staff officer of the XIIth Division, arrived at my HQ and made me acquainted with the disposition of the division extending from Boz Dag (west of Kayak) to Palat-Hissar (south of Sivri-Hissar) and beyond. It had been entrusted with the defence of the whole of the southern arm of the Sakharia, and also with the task of destroying the bridge of Fethioglou. This latter operation seemed to me to be unnecessary, especially with a division of the quality of the XIIth, as the river was not a serious obstacle, and the troops carrying it out might easily meet a superior enemy force. Captain Presetakos had already reported that the situation in general of the XIIth was not good, from the point of view of discipline and morale.

For an exact understanding of the bad state of discipline in the army, I think it will not be out of place to mention here a characteristic episode which took place that morning at my HQ at Demerdjikeui. A superior officer (whose name I will suppress) came to me and began to speak of the latest events, expressing himself in severe terms against GHQ in general and the commander-in-chief in particular, and blaming him and his ignorance of the art of war for the whole of our failures. Finally, encouraged by my silence (for unfortunately I had not silenced him), he began to unfold a scheme, by which he proposed that General Papulas should be forcibly seized and dismissed, and that the officers should appoint Lieutenant-General Prince Nicholas to be commander-in-chief, and, if he refused, then myself. Amazed by such a proposition, and rendered almost speechless by the magnitude of the effrontery of such a scheme, in the middle of the war, I hastened to impose silence, and to tell him, without any chance of mistake, that a repetition of such a proposal would instantly result in his being arrested and sent to GHQ. Perhaps it will be of interest if I add that a year later this officer was discovered in the revolutionary ranks.

Not being able to understand the real aim of GHQ, and considering this secrecy to be detrimental to the future scheme of operations, I decided to go myself to Sarikeui to see the commander-in-chief. I left by motor about 1 p.m., but I must not omit to mention here that shortly before my departure I was informed that the whole of GHQ had passed through Demerdjikeui, a little while before, on their way to fresh quarters. The commander-in-chief and his staff did not consider it worth while to stop and inform themselves about the details of the crossing of the river, the disposition of the troops, or the situation in general; though they on the previous day had no knowledge of the whereabouts of the 3rd Army Corps. I must confess that I was astonished. After the campaign was over, I was informed by the minister of war, N. Theotoky, to whom I had related this episode, that Lieutenant-General Papulas had purposely refrained from stopping at my HQ, fearing reproaches and an outburst on my part on account of the episode of 9 September. I do not think that a commander-in-chief could have expressed his disfavour towards a commander of an army corps more clearly, in spite of all his sentiments of devotion for the dynasty.

At 3:30 p.m. I at last encountered the escort of GHQ at Bitscher at the HQ of the 3rd Army Corps. I presented myself at once to the commander-in-chief, who received me with the warmest demonstration of friendship and esteem. Lieutenant-General Papulas began the conversation by assuring me that he had been obliged to send me that famous telegram, compelled thereto by the necessity of maintaining his authority which had been violated by my action, and that in any case he had signed the document brought to him by Colonel Saryannis without having previously read its contents. It sufficed for me to answer that there was not the slightest necessity for the commander-in-chief to justify his action; but once the question had been touched upon, I considered that my action had been described in somewhat strong terms, and that this attitude continued in spite of all the assurances of his friendship, esteem, and devotion towards me; that in any case I had not followed him to Bitscher to discuss this episode; but because it was necessary for me to learn what his intentions were and how he intended to continue the campaign. After this Lieutenant-General Papulas, who appeared to be very dejected and depressed, took out of his pocket the famous Memorandum, which had been composed at GHQ after the Council of Kiutahia, and tried to justify his whole action by wishing to convince me that he had executed the retreat of his own free will and in agreement with the Memorandum. The commander-in-chief was in a pitiable frame of mind, and told me that he had been drawn into this by his staff, by Major-General Stratigos, and by Colonel Saryannis, who had also convinced the government of the possibility of the expedition to Angora.

I replied to the commander-in-chief that there was nothing to be gained by showing this document about now and complaining of the members of the staff. The attempt to reach Angora had been made with the results we know, so what was the use of these tears and lamentations? The government's task was to present the events in the best light, and ours was to bring the campaign to as favourable a conclusion as possible. I added that I did not consider the present disposition of the army to be conducive to this. I was then sent in to Major-General Polymenakos and Colonel Pallis, and from them I learnt that our stay here would last seven or eight days for the purpose of rest, revictualling, and re-formation, in order not to create the impression that we had retreated, and afterwards the march would be continued towards our old lines east of Eski-Shehr. Colonel Pallis subsequently explained that, if the enemy should happen to cross the Sakharia at any point, he would find five divisions—the ones not on the front—ready for action. Having at last been informed of the intentions of GHQ, I returned to my HQ at about 6 p.m., where I learnt that an enemy force of about a thousand men had succeeded in crossing the river in the sector of the XIIIth Division, and that this force had been thrown back over the Sakharia after a lively action. This had not only a local significance, but was a significant proof of our opponent's energy and of his spirit of attack, which were not to be despised.

That evening I informed the divisional commanders by telephone of the aim and intentions of GHQ.

The afternoon of the following day, 16 September, hostile forces, supported by heavy artillery, attacked the sector of the Vth Division at Gordium, and attempted to cross the river.

The fighting was severe, the enemy succeeding in establishing himself temporarily on the western bank, but at 4 p.m. the Vth Division reported that the enemy had been thrown back across the river. As the days passed, the enemy's activities were increasing in energy, as he evidently wished to maintain the supremacy which he had acquired after our retreat.

About midnight a fresh order was received from GHQ, ordering the retirement to be recommenced during the following night to the line Tchebizli–Maliabashi Tepé–Douz Tepé–Orta Tepé; Yurek–Punar Tepé; heights Dagdjilar. The retirement was to be effected by occupying successive defensive positions.

Thus the decisions of the previous day were reversed. I cannot say that I was displeased with the acceleration, because I considered that once the decision to retire had been taken it was necessary for us to establish ourselves as soon as possible on the definitely selected line east of Eski-Shehr. By halting at different intervening lines, the enemy were continually given opportunities of making encircling manoeuvres and attacks, the impression was strengthened that this retreat was imposed on us by him, and that we had definitely relinquished the initiative. A rapid retreat and an establishment on a definite line would have the advantage of a definite check to the enemy, and the possibility of throwing him back from our front. In spite of the above reflections, I cannot but regret this fresh example of the ever-changing attitude of GHQ by which the troops were made to suffer from the results of the changes in the orders of the commander-in-chief. Only on the day before I had informed the divisional commanders of the decision communicated to me to remain seven or eight days more on the Sakharia.

After issuing the necessary orders to the divisions, I left Demerdjikeui at 1 p.m. with my staff, and went in the direction of Karghin via Dumrek. In this village at about 5 p.m. I met Major-General Kondulis, who was beside himself on account of the eternally changing attitude of GHQ. From him I learnt that our immediate departure was due to the appearance of hostile forces near Muhalitch north of the Purshak, as well as to information by air that an enemy column had been discovered south of, and parallel with, the Sakharia, marching westward;

and, lastly, that enemy forces of 3,000 to 4,000 men had been reported east of Tshiftelar. The commander of the 1st Army Corps and his chief of staff, Colonel Gonatas, expressed themselves with great irony about the manner in which the army was commanded by GHQ, who, in their nervousness at the appearance of insignificant hostile forces and large numbers of cavalry on our flanks, ordered entire divisions to be moved, entailing great fatigue on the troops. The general also complained that whereas he was supposed to be in the centre of his corps, divisions were so far away that it was almost impossible to visit them. The general considered the whole situation to be most serious, because the failure of the expedition to Angora had depressed the elan and morale of the troops, and discipline was not at a high level. With the army in that state and winter approaching, we had to occupy a line of defence—not yet constructed—from Eski-Shehr to Afium-Karahissar, not counting the sections to the north and south of the main line. The troops, instead of being demobilized, found the war dragging on, and gradually being transformed into trench warfare; but the worst of all, according to the general, was that the authority of the Supreme Command had been seriously shaken and confidence in its judgment had disappeared. Major-General Kondulis cast the whole responsibility of the last events on Colonel Saryannis, and with reason, because the conception, preparation, and execution of the expedition to Angora was entirely his work, and being contrary to logic and prudence, it naturally came to an unhappy end.

I arrived at Karghin at 9 p.m. at about the same time as the IXth Division, and from that hour till 3 a.m. I was given ample opportunity to realize the state of indiscipline in the division, and the complete indifference to the state of affairs of some of its superior officers.

On 18 September I formed a committee, composed of the commander of the artillery, Colonel Papaioannu, the commander of the engineers, Colonel Botsaris, and the commander of the infantry of the IXth Division, Colonel Tsiroyannis, for the purpose of studying the front to be fortified east of Eski-Shehr. In the afternoon Major-General Kondulis passed on his way to his new HQ, and from him I learnt that the morning aeroplane reconnaissance reported that there was no enemy at Muhalitch, and that the column marching to the south of the Sakharia was composed of oxen, and only the column of 3,000 to 4,000 men reported near Tshiftelar was a fact. It was difficult for anyone to form a picture of the situation, if one had to depend on the information of the air service alone.

In the night, a composite force of nearly three divisions under the 1st Army Corps was ordered to attack the hostile force near Tshiftelar, which shows that this was more important than was at first supposed.

At 4 a.m., on 19 September, a further order was received, in which it is stated that this force consisted of from 10,000 to 20,000 men, and that it had passed through Tshiftelar, moving towards the north-west. The composite force was given the mission of 'crushing and cutting off the enemy'.

The enemy's intention was plain, his objective was our base at Eski-Shehr, against which he was preparing a raid; one can imagine the confusion and commotion which would ensue on the dislocation if not destruction of this base. This operation shows what vitality and initiative of movement the enemy still possessed, even after our operation against Angora.

Though the material means of conducting a war have undergone radical changes through the development of industry and the progress of chemistry, the philosophy of war and the lessons gained by experience remain unchanged. Those who decided to undertake an expedition to Angora did not take sufficiently into consideration the wise sayings of the great philosopher of war, Klausewitz, who writes: 'It is impossible to achieve the conquest of a great State. For the defence, the probabilities of a final success are not always diminished in proportion to the battles and the ground lost. It often happens that the defender, being the stronger, when in the heart of his subjugated country, is able in his turn to undertake a strong offensive at the moment that his opponent is over-extended and his keenness is at an end'. Unfortunately, the above is only too true as regards the whole of the campaign in Asia Minor from beginning to end. The expedition to Sidi-Ghazi resulted in the enemy's entering it, where he caused no little damage to the base of the 2nd Army Corps, by destroying materiel and especially the ovens for baking bread, and by causing irreparable damage to the records of the army corps. The action of Major-General Kondulis was correct from every point of view, only the enemy's great mobility permitted him to retire in time to the south, and thus it became impossible to carry out to the letter the sonorous phrase of the order: 'to crush and to cut off'.

Before my departure from Karghin, fixed for 11 a.m., I received a visit from Karvounis, journalist and war correspondent of the *Politia*, who had just returned that morning from Brussa. During the campaign Karvounis had at the beginning followed the XIIth Division and afterwards the 2nd Army Corps. He related to me all the happenings in Brussa, where the exact situation at the front was not known, in consequence of which a certain nervousness was felt there. Amongst the curiosities of the campaign of 1921, it must be recorded that GHQ did not consider themselves obliged to keep either the king, the minister of war, or the chief of the HQ staff informed of the situation. The king, minister, and chief of the HQ staff were only 'receivers' of the various orders of GHQ and the bulletins of operations, but no care was taken that these documents should be sent off in time. After the king's removal to Brussa from Eski-Shehr, on account of illness, it happened several times that he received the news from the front two or three days late. This was on account of the anxiety of Lieutenant-General Papulas and the various members of his staff to prevent it being said that their enterprising plans had been forbidden or influenced in any way by the king or the HQ staff; and yet, these same men, when questioned at the trial a year later, did not hesitate to depose that the real leader of the army was the king, and when Colonel Saryannis was asked how he explained the situation after the king's removal to Brussa, he had the impudence to reply that he considered him to be deserting his post in time of war. In Brussa everyone was in ignorance of the reasons for the suspension of the advance to Angora and the sudden retreat to this side of the Sakharia. They learnt all this from Colonel Gavallias, who was going to Athens, as well as from Karvounis.

Karvounis returned from Eski-Shehr by rail to Sarikeui, where he found the commander-in-chief and GHQ in a state of extreme nervous tension and anxiety, because just as they were preparing to take up their quarters at Bevlik Akhor, they were informed of the raid against Alpikeui, and returned in haste to Sarikeui; he received the impression that GHQ were being influenced by their immediate local surroundings to an astounding degree.

Karvounis had a conversation with Colonel Saryannis, and there for the first time he heard the accusation launched against me, that it was on account of my hesitation and indecision that the advance to Angora had failed!

The movement of 19 September took place according to the order, and passed off entirely unmolested, and in the evening I established my HQ near the village of Halilbag.

On 20 September, there was a day of absolute calm. At 4:30 p.m. an order was received from GHQ detailing the various sectors to be occupied by the three corps on the main defensive positions, and specifying the routes to be followed from the present positions to those sectors.

From this order it appeared that GHQ no longer foresaw any interference on the part of the enemy for the present—a correct prevision, for after the failure of his raid to Eski-Shehr, it was not likely that he would renew his attempts so soon. This pause was of great advantage to us, as it permitted us to establish ourselves unmolested in our appointed lines.

The march of the 2nd Army Corps, fixed for 21 September, was well carried out, and in the evening the divisions occupied the line Kismet Tepé–Tshal Tepé, my HQ being established in the village of Sherifié. In this village, which was also the HQ of the XIIIth Division, the rumour about Colonel Saryannis' statements again reached me. In the evening the commander of the artillery of this division, Colonel D. Vultzos, who was much disturbed, came to me and reported that a few days before he had met Major Philippu of the staff of the 1st Army Corps, and heard from him of the conversation which he had with Colonel Saryannis. During this conversation Major Philippu asked Colonel Saryannis what fact had been the cause of GHQ ordering such a hurried crossing of the Sakharia, and the sub-chief of staff answered that this was due to the unwillingness of the 2nd Army Corps to attack.

On 22 September, the 2nd Army Corps continued its march, and in the evening it was concentrated with the Vth Division in the district of Yanak Kapan and Kalpanli; the IXth at Arab Euren, and the XIIIth at Aksakali and Sakdan, HQ at Aksakali. Thus we once more found ourselves occupying the lines in which we were established for the first time just two months before, after the battle of 21 July. But with what a difference in our feelings! On the first occasion after the victory, and now after the heroic, but useless and harmful, expedition to Angora.

The fact that the Angora expedition did not end in a catastrophe was owing solely to the courage and self-sacrifice of the Greek soldier. The Supreme Command was never equal to the occasion. During the first days, so long as the army was advancing and plunging into the desert, and the enemy's advanced troops were retreating without giving battle, GHQ regarded the situation with optimism and confidence. As soon as the enemy stopped in a position chosen by himself, so as to deliver the decisive battle, the Supreme Command began to waver, coolness deserted them. When they saw the enemy attacking first our right flank and then our left, their spirits sank to the depths, only to rise to the heights again on hearing of some local success of one of the divisions. Seeing this pitiable exhibition, faced by the violent opposition of the enemy, knowing the lack of ammunition and, finally, enduring unimaginable privations, who can blame the troops for losing confidence in the Supreme Command, and for letting discouragement take the place of the enthusiasm of the first days?

A feeling of bitterness possessed us all at the thought that a commander-in-chief, succumbing to the advice and influence of such men in spite of his originally expressed opinion, should have led the army into the desert and there buried the wonderful élan of the troops and their faith in a great ideal.

The same evening Colonel Botsaris arrived at my HQ to receive orders for the fortification of the line and, amongst other things, he told me that the legend of the 2nd Army Corps' reluctance to fight was being spread far and wide, and that the source of these declarations was Colonel Saryannis. Colonel Botsaris was beside himself with rage, and advised me, although he was a friend of Colonel Saryannis, to do all in my power to refute these rumours, which touched the honour of the corps. It was no longer possible for me to overlook these rumours which reached me from all sides, and I decided to write next day to the commander-in-chief and expose to him the campaign of perfidy waged against me by his sub-chief of staff; and if I did not receive the necessary satisfaction, I could still take steps to denounce him. My letter to the commander-in-chief is given below:

Dish Veran,

September 23rd, 1921.

Sir,

May I be allowed to draw your attention to the following facts, which I think ought to come to your knowledge. I have recently heard, from sources which I am able to name, that there has been considerable talk about the conduct of the 2nd Army Corps in general. The fact that such a question is being discussed has certainly no special significance. But what is of serious moment is the fact that the sub-chief of staff, Colonel Saryannis, has expressed to certain individuals his opinion that the abandonment of the expedition to Angora, and the hurried crossing of the Sakharia, were exclusively due to the 2nd Army Corps, because of its supposed unwillingness to attack. As I have the honour to command this corps, I think it is my duty to bring the above facts to your knowledge, and to add that this reproach made against the 2nd Army Corps is most serious, for the corps has always and everywhere carried out its duty faithfully this is undoubtedly attested by its heavy losses. As regards myself, I am always ready to give an account of my command, when this is required by my immediate superior authority.

I know, Sir, that the theme of this letter is unpleasant, but I consider it to be my duty to make you acquainted with the above facts.

I remain, etc.,
Andrew.

To this letter I received the following answer:

Eski-Shehr,
September 24th, 1921.

Sir,

I have received your letter of September 23rd, and cannot imagine that the sub-chief of my staff should forget himself and express an opinion on the conduct of your corps.

But before verifying this, I consider it my duty, as the only one having the right to express a responsible opinion, to assure you that I have made no distinction until now as regards the conduct of the various Army Corps under my command. All the corps have carried out their duties with exemplary heroism, and in my *ordre du jour*, which was the same for all the corps, I enumerated the principal battlefields on which they distinguished themselves. The suspension of the advance to Angora, and the return to the position before Eski-Shehr were not in the slightest degree the consequence of any action or of any fault, but an action which G.H.Q. had foreseen before the commencement of operations, and the execution of which had been accepted as the only suitable one.

The 2nd Army Corps has so many heroic exploits to its credit, that its officers need not be disturbed at the propagation of senseless criticism of the corps' action.

I have the honour to be, etc.,
A. Papulas

In spite of Lieutenant-General Papulas' assurances, there ensued no contradiction of the rumour. I only know that when I saw the commander-in-chief on 30 September and spoke to him about this affair, he replied that, when he questioned Colonel Saryannis on the matter, the latter gave him his word of honour that he had never expressed himself in such terms, either about me or about the 2nd Army Corps. At that time I had confidence in Lieutenant-General Papulas' good faith, and his letter had the effect of stopping the denunciation I was prepared to make.

On 23 September, by my orders, the IXth Division was kept in the first line to guard the sector from Malia Bashi Tepé–Douz Tepé to the River Seyindi. HQ at Arab Euren. The Vth Division was ordered to replace the IInd from the heights west of Tchebizli to Malia Bashi Tepé (exclusive). HQ at Sidi-Ghazi. Lastly, I posted the XIIIth on the second line in the district of Sakdan, Yenikeui, and Dish Veran, with its HQ at Yenikeui. I established my HQ at noon at the village of Dish Veran.

It was necessary to solve the question of the organization for the defence of our front—a very serious question. The directions of GHQ implied an immense task—shelters, buildings for the men, and closed sheds for the beasts. According to Colonel Botsaris' calculations, 35 kilometres of barbed wire alone were required—an amount which did not exist in the whole of Greece. For this task thousands of hands were needed, and because our soldiers could not possibly suffice for this, we were obliged to use the Turkish peasants of the district—a fact which presented many disadvantages, more especially the possibility of their deserting to the enemy and the consequent exact information that the latter would obtain about our activities.

After that, seeing that our sojourn in these lines was likely to be of long duration, serious thought had to be given to the supplies for the army, in food, boots, and clothing, as well as to everything that was indispensable for the wellbeing of the men. This was extremely important if we wished to keep them contented and disciplined, for there was now no question of demobilizing them; on the contrary, they would have to be kept under arms for an indefinite period. Besides that, the season was well advanced, and in less than a month winter would be upon us, and consequently all these above-mentioned preparations were most urgent.

At that time, I never imagined that the army's sojourn on this chosen front would definitely last—except for a few local changes—for a whole year. I thought that our stay would be long, perhaps for the winter, so as not to give the impression that a further retreat had been forced on us after our ill-success on the Sakharia. I also considered that it was anyhow safe to remain there, for I did not judge the enemy capable of undertaking any serious action before the spring at the earliest. My views were strengthened by a study on the map of the front selected, because only a temporary occupation could possibly justify the disposition taken up by the army: three army corps at Eski-Shehr, and two divisions (southern group) in the district of Afium-Karahissar, with a wide space between the two army masses entirely unoccupied. One of the principal reasons for keeping the army in a position so far from its base on the sea was to occupy and guard the Baghdad railway; and how was it possible to guard this, with the army separated into two parts at the two railway junctions, with the intervening space open and exposed to every attack from the enemy? This disposition of the troops could certainly only be temporary, for it would be necessary to extend it in a continuous line from Eski-Shehr to Afium-Karahissar; the length of this line, however, was to my mind out of proportion to the strength of the army. All this tended to convince me that before the spring came the question would be decided in favour of a front for the army more suitable from a military point of view, unless the enemy in the meantime accepted terms of peace, which was most improbable. I also reflected that the enemy would become stronger and better organized the longer we remained there, whereas we, on the contrary, would not be able to mobilize any more classes. Finally, the fatal moment would arrive when the enemy, being the stronger, would attack our long front (which was quite out of proportion to our strength), and break through at a given point, which blow would be followed by the collapse of the whole front with incalculable consequences.

All my calculations were soon proved to be false, for in the meantime GHQ had definitely decided to establish the army, consisting of 30,000 bayonets, on the line Eski-Shehr–Afium-Karahissar. The front to be defended, if we add to the main line all the windings to the north and south, was about 300 kilometres! It strikes one as amazing stupidity that GHQ did not take into consideration the immediate extension of the front to the south. They allowed the 1st Army Corps to start, concentrating first at Eski-Shehr, and afterwards sent its divisions to Afium-Karahissar, thus giving the troops a colossal amount of extra marching to do. Also, after the task of establishing the 2nd Army Corps had commenced and much work carried out, this corps was ordered to proceed to the south as a kind of connecting link between the two bodies of the army. These movements were decided and ordered after the enemy had shown his power of initiative, during the last offensive in the general direction of Kiutahia, towards the end of September.

There is no doubt that the establishment of the army on that front was inspired by political considerations, but woe to the military commander who yields to political considerations. Lieutenant-General Papulas himself realized these dangers, and confessed to me that he personally was strongly opposed to this decision. But his opposition was of no avail, for in the end he gave in, just as he did in the case of the expedition to Angora; and in the same way as he was responsible for that expedition, so was he also responsible for the definite establishment of the army on the line Eski-Shehr–Afium-Karahissar. Consequently he must bear the whole responsibility for the catastrophe of September 1922.

The operations being now completed, I had time to think of my own position in the army and to weigh matters correctly. In diverse forms the echoes reached me of the base campaign directed against me by various noted members of GHQ. Their cry was that the failure of the advance to Angora was due to me. The polemics of GHQ began to take on a political aspect, and it is on this question that the first blows were struck at the party in power. As I have already recorded, these things had been made known to the commander-in-chief both verbally and in writing, but, in spite of his assurances, nothing had been done to stop these rumours and the campaign against me. The commander-in-chief was occupied in trying to gain ground—for his own advantage—with the party which had fared so ill at the elections of 14 November 1920. The influence of this party at GHQ was so great, that it was hardly possible for me to hope that Lieutenant-General Papulas would risk this popularity to do justice to the slandered honour of a general officer, who was a stranger to this party. The best solution doubtless would have been at the time to denounce Colonel Saryannis and his friends who had spread the rumours, but I did not do this for two reasons. Firstly, because I did not want to be the first to give the example of discordant denunciations between colleagues or to bring to light a picture of the internal dissensions in the army. Secondly, because I was certain that if I did so, I should not get justice done, as Lieutenant-General Papulas' own conduct being personally implicated, it was clear to me that many important points would be suppressed, and he would exert his influence for the enquiry to be held only as a matter of form, from which all would emerge with their honour intact. And even if I were to accept for one moment that the enquiry would be held conscientiously and by a thorough and careful examination into details, I could not possibly expect that GHQ would accept the conclusion as a basis for dispensing elementary justice.

On the other hand, I had absolutely lost confidence in the capability of the man who held the Supreme Command, and I had a deep-rooted conviction that any further action of his would lead the army to destruction—a fact which made it impossible for me to continue in command of an important but nevertheless subordinate unit. After the events which took place on the other side of the Sakharia, any opinion of mine, in whatever form submitted, would inevitably be misunderstood, and it would certainly end in a rupture between GHQ and myself. My command was too important for me to find myself continually at variance with the Supreme Command, and even if not outwardly apparent, my lack of confidence therein would not be conducive to the future good conduct of operations. Besides this, the Supreme Command, after all that had been given out against me, had themselves lost confidence in me, even though they never had the courage to tell me so straight out.

In face of such a situation there remained nothing else for me to do, but of my own accord to request to be removed from the army, in spite of the regret I felt at leaving it before the definite solution of the campaign. I also could not overlook the fact that many, who could not know the true facts, would and did accuse me of deserting my post; for I afterwards heard that many people said that it was unseemly for members of the royal family to keep away from the army when it was fighting. But even this I preferred to the suffocating atmosphere of Asia Minor. I could not conscientiously remain in the army any longer, because it is not possible for anyone to hold a position therein without mutual confidence and faith between the senior officers and GHQ.

As I could not ask to be appointed to any service away from the front, I could only ask for three months' leave, which Lieutenant-General Papulas willingly granted me, and I left Eski-Shehr on 30 September.

Epilogue

After an absence of two months I returned to Smyrna, where the council of Lieutenant-Generals, of which I had been made a member, was to sit. This council, called the Supreme Army Council, presided over by Lieutenant-General Papulas, was composed of the following lieutenant-generals: Bairas, of the 5th Army Corps (Epirus); Montferrato, commander-in-chief of the army in Thrace; Kondulis, of the 1st Army Corps; Polymenakos, of the 3rd Army Corps; and myself, of the 2nd Army Corps. I do not propose to enter into the discussions and decisions which took place at this meeting. I will only content myself with the observation that in any case a spirit of impartiality predominated in spite of the extreme severity with which it occasionally judged those officers who had been reinstated in 1920 and the proportionate mildness of the judgment passed on the others. There was also a discussion on the deserters in Constantinople, whom Lieutenant-General Papulas, in accordance with the policy he was pursuing, insisted on judging rather leniently, on account of their professional abilities; but on this point he encountered great opposition on the part of some of the members of the council, so that he was obliged to dismiss this question and send it up to the minister of war to be judged. A discussion also arose about some of the officers of the 'Amyna' (defence), who had especially worked for the recruiting of the revolutionary army of Salonica by going round Macedonia, Chalcidice, and the islands, using every means to secure men by force. On this point also Lieutenant-General Papulas gave in, realizing that these things had gone beyond the limits of what was permissible.

My four months' stay in Smyrna gave me an opportunity to understand the situation, and to appraise the state of affairs from near at hand. After the army had been definitely established on the line Eski-Shehr–Afium-Karahissar, the work of undermining the established order of things had commenced openly. This propaganda flourished in broad daylight; Colonel Plastiras visited all the army corps in turn, instructing and proselytizing, and came as far as Smyrna even, with the object of coming to an understanding with the representatives of the 'Amyna' at Constantinople. Minutes were circulated and signed collectively; parleys for an understanding with the deserters in Constantinople, whose movement was directed by the well known Kondylis, took place openly and without the slightest shame; and, most astonishing of all, the commander-in-chief himself was fully aware of all these machinations, and looked on at them in silence. This attitude of Lieutenant-General Papulas and his relations with the members of the 'Amyna'—by getting into direct contact with them through Colonel Saryannis—and his unconfessed and secret aims will one day be judged by history. I have contented myself with recording those events which came to my knowledge, as commander of an army corps at the front. My work in the Supreme Army Council kept me in Smyrna during that winter, and my substitute in the army corps was Major-General Digenis. The plottings at the front came regularly to my knowledge, and the course that things were taking was such that I drew Lieutenant-General Papulas' attention to it, recommending his (to my mind) absolutely indispensable intervention in order to take the necessary precautions. Such precautions were still easy to take at that time, for it would have sufficed to arrest Colonel Plastiras and send him into the interior. The latter, in spite of the fictitious reputation woven round his name, was not held in such high honour by the troops for his removal to create a dangerous rift in the corps of officers. As I have now the opportunity to speak of this renowned hero, the so-called 'black rider', I must confess that I cannot conscientiously say that his conduct during the campaign, as I was able to judge from personal observation, differed in any way from the conduct of any other regimental commander—as, for example, Colonel Rokkas, Colonel Ziras, or Colonel Panayotakos. His personal courage under fire was good, but nothing extraordinary; it was of the same quality as that of the others, and certainly less than that of Colonel Ziras, who was indeed possessed by a complete insensibility to danger in face of the enemy. Colonel Plastiras' fame was artificial, and was trumpeted abroad for the sake of the intrigues he was connected with, for it was believed by those who had charged him with the task of disrupting the army that the commander-in-chief and the government would never dare to touch such a hero; and this hope proved correct. It was also said about him that he had such influence over his men and they such adoration for him, that his removal from the regiment would provoke a mutiny. There is no doubt that he commanded his regiment well, and in his solicitude for his men had always made great efforts to provide them with food, boots, and clothing, and this is to his credit. But must it thereby be concluded that the other commanding officers were lacking in this respect? Assuredly not, and the argument that it was impossible to remove him for this reason was puerile. The truth is that his reputation had been created with such art and assiduity that the War Office really believed that without him the whole front would collapse, and the commander-in-chief encouraged this belief for his own ends.

The dismissal of Colonel Plastiras alone would not have sufficed to restore order, it would have been necessary to remove some of the others as well; but when once the head had been cut off, discipline and order could easily and rapidly have been restored. I reported Colonel Plastiras' activities to the commander-in-chief, because I was in a measure responsible for his conduct, as he commanded the 5th Evzones (highland regiment) of the XIIIth Division of the 2nd Army Corps. I proposed to make a personal visit to the front for the purpose of a closer examination and verification of the colonel's activities (as Major-General Digenis had not ventured to touch him), and if I found the charges correct to dismiss him from his command. My proposal was not accepted, as Lieutenant-General Papulas not only was unconvinced, but he considered that my intervention would have been prejudicial to an officer who was badly needed at the front, and who was falsely reported to have been involved in such practices. I then formally declared that it was impossible for me to take upon myself the responsibility of commanding the army corps under conditions which permitted discipline to be undermined and encouraged the officers to mutiny. Lieutenant-General Bairas was leaving the army at the time, and I asked for, and received, the command of the 5th Army Corps in Yanina (Epirus).

It is certainly not surprising that this situation should cause a reaction of a purely military character to take place, and I will here subjoin an extract from a letter of mine written in December 1921, to a friend in Athens:

> ... G.H.Q. guarantees the safety of the front until January. The serious part is that G.H.Q. fear a possible Turkish offensive, not at once, but unavoidably about February or March. A systematic defence of the present front is difficult, if not impossible, seeing its great length and our insufficient numbers. In consequence of which we may very possibly have to retreat, either of our own accord or under pressure of the enemy. One would think that under such conditions they would already have begun to study and prepare a second line, more compact and easier to hold, with the means at their disposal. The state of the troops does not inspire me with confidence; their elan is spent; and if they now remain quietly in their lines, they only do so because they think that they will soon have peace. But if the negotiations drag on too long, and if Gunaris returns from his mission abroad without any success, and we are consequently faced with a continuation of the war, then what? I do not think that the army is in a state to offer the enemy any serious resistance, and a failure at one point of the front will draw all the rest with it, and then where will we stop? With one stroke of the pen we lose the whole game.
>
> Something must be done as soon as possible.... I do not know what must be done, but we must stop bluffing and face the situation as it really is. For, after

> all, which is better—to fall into the sea or to go away of our own free will before this happens?...

However surprising all this sounds, it was unfortunately only too true. Major-General Hadjanestis related to me, after the final catastrophe, that his first care on taking over the command of the army, after Lieutenant-General Papulas' recall, had been to order the immediate study of a second line and to transform his predecessor's method of concentration into a front organized in a more advantageous manner, but unfortunately it was too late. Lieutenant-General Papulas was always so much occupied with his political schemes that he had abandoned all thought of even the most elementary kind for the safety of the troops under him.

But to return to the canker that was eating away the heart of the army, and owing to which the work of the mutineers was ultimately crowned with success. There were hosts of honourable and trustworthy officers in the army, but when they saw the inaction, and even sympathy, with which the Supreme Command contemplated these occurrences, they became convinced after a time that the state was aware of these things, and that it was deliberately urging the troops to rebel against their recall from Asia Minor. So true is this, that even I, after two months' stay in Smyrna, began to ask myself if this was not so in reality, and I only convinced myself of the contrary when, finding myself in Athens for a few days, I asked the king for information on this subject. He was most indignant and grieved at my doubts, and told me that he was not in the habit of working thus in the dark and acting insincerely.

It must also not be forgotten, that the greater number of those officers who had remained in service during the three years' interval, although they were legitimists, were, for the most part, very discontented with the return of the dismissed officers, and the consequent loss of privileges which they had acquired in the meantime. The latter, finally disgusted with the coldness shown to them, became gradually indifferent, and the greater number of them only considered how they could continue to keep their places, which they had regained with so much trouble. I do not speak of the 'Amynists'. Their subversive schemes were known; they proceeded with their work with the support of the commander-in-chief on the one hand, and the complete inaction of the state on the other.

Such was the situation, and far worse than I can possibly describe in a few words, when the state at last recovered its senses and dismissed Lieutenant-General Papulas, appointing Lieutenant-General Hadjanestis in his place. It was too late, and the new commander-in-chief himself, as he told me afterwards, before the catastrophe, no longer believed it possible to hold things together, for the decomposition in the army had reached its very marrow, and it would not be able to hold its own if the enemy should undertake an offensive.

Lastly, I might recapitulate the situation as follows:

The operations undertaken during the summer of 1921 did not improve the position of the army, nor did it bring any peace to the officers tyrannized over by political passions; on the contrary, they furthered the separation of the parties. The underhand and assiduous activities of the opponents of the ruling regime were considerably strengthened after the failure of the expedition to Angora, which had been so lightly planned and attempted. Certainly, at first view, the responsibility for this expedition appears to fall on the party in power at the time and on the commander-in-chief appointed by them; yet one must bear in mind that the GHQ staff in Asia Minor was the same, with few exceptions, as that which Lieutenant-General Papulas found there when he took over the command. One must also bear in mind the commander-in-chief's character and his military training. I do not hesitate to attribute the responsibility for that expedition, and the manner in which it was conducted, to those individuals at GHQ whose interest it was to profit by the mistakes of the leaders; and although I do not go so far as to think that they intentionally gave bad advice, I remain unshaken in my belief, proved by subsequent happenings, that they took advantage of these events to throw the responsibility of the failure on to the commanders—that is to say, on the reinstated officers and, as a natural consequence, on the party then in power. Unfortunately, the idea that those who were serving at the front possessed the greatest experience of war, and that their military knowledge was of value, was so deeply rooted, that their advice was often taken seriously into consideration, in spite of elementary logic and the lessons of the war. It was also seriously believed that the adherents of the fallen party had thrown off the old Adam, and had genuinely and honestly embraced the new state of affairs.

Events ended fatally in the catastrophe in September 1922; whereas from a purely military point of view there was no valid reason for the army to give in at once as it did. It required treachery for the enemy to enter a purposely abandoned sector, and to strike in the rear of the IVth Division. History will be the best judge. But I cannot bring this sad account to a close without emphasizing the monstrosity of this crime. For the first time after many centuries, since the time of the Byzantine rulers, a Greek king and a Greek Army trod the immense plains of Asia Minor. Full of eagerness, faith, and self-sacrifice, the Greek soldier threw himself into the age-old struggle of his race—the struggle of civilization against Asiatic barbarism. The glitter of Greek bayonets was seen once more on the fields of Kiutahia and Eski-Shehr, on the Twin Mountains, on the shores of the Sakharia and in the Axylos desert. Gordium, Justianopolis, once more heard the shouts of Greek victory, the echoes reaching as far as Angora. These achievements were realized at the cost of much pure and honourable blood, shed by the Greek soldier with heroic abnegation, because he knew that his sacrifice was made for the grandeur of Hellas, which he alone had doubled, and because this sacrifice had been demanded by him who incorporated the idea of Hellenism—King Constantine.

Alas! the Greek soldier, who had strewn his bones during an entire decade in Macedonia and Epirus, in Thrace and in Russia, did not know that all his sacrifices were in vain; he did not know that there was a traitor in his ranks, who, jealous of the fame of his predecessor at Thermopylae, surpassed him in his efforts, and brought the Greek Army to the catastrophe of 1922.

Is it in vain, this last sacrifice in Asia Minor? No! For the seed sown by the Greek soldier will one day burst forth into a great and flourishing tree.

Meanwhile our glorious dead lie by the side of their ancestors, the Hoplites of Alexander the Great and the Stratiotes of Heracles and Nicephorus Phocas, and the murmur of the waves of the Aegean bears to the Greek shores the re-echoing sounds of their message:

> O stranger, go, tell the Lacedemonians that here we lie, faithful to their orders.

END